"An incredible, entertaining and insightful story of one of the most important—and also underappreciated—promoters in wrestling history. A must-read for any wrestling fan, promoter, executive or any of the boys looking to laugh and learn."

—**Alfred Boima Konuwa III**, *Forbes*

"Sean Oliver has consistently found ways to add intrigue and light to the business of professional wrestling. A masterful storyteller, he and Tod Gordon have crafted a must-read story here detailing the colorful history of ECW."

—**Justin Barrasso**, *Sports Illustrated*

"*Tod is God* is the true, raw and unvarnished journey of an extreme influencer who changed the entire trajectory of the professional wrestling industry. The letters ECW never cease to fascinate fans and Tod Gordon finally reveals all the inner workings and machinations that came with the creation, rise and fall of the most influential wrestling company of the 1990s. Tod's deep diving, introspective autobiography brings you inside the greatest achievements and frustrations that come hand in hand with an unparalleled, chaotic ride into the upside down of pro wrestling and beyond."

—**Mike Johnson**, *PWInsider*

"ECW was figuratively (and occasionally literally) the match and accelerant that took the wrestling business from being a niche product to a staple of broadcast and cable television. Without Tod Gordon, there never would have been a WWF Attitude Era. He ended up changing an entire industry."

—**Dave Scherer**, *PWInsider*

"If there was ever such a thing as an honest promoter, it was Tod."

—**Bill Alfonso**, referee/manager

"Tod *is* God...He always had the boys' backs, even if he didn't always agree with us."

—**Pitbull Gary Wolf**

"If Tod hadn't sacrificed his own personal wealth to start a promotion, God knows how many careers might've been lost or might not have been discovered."

—**Blue Meanie**

"That man put his life on the line in the beginning of ECW, let alone his money, his job, and his family, and set that thing off. I don't think a lot of people realize what he did to get that rolling."

—**John Finnegan**, referee

"There wouldn't be a Sandman if there wasn't a Tod."

—**Sandman**

# TOD IS GOD

# TOD IS GOD

## THE AUTHORIZED STORY OF HOW I CREATED
## EXTREME CHAMPIONSHIP WRESTLING

### TOD GORDON
### & SEAN OLIVER

#### FOREWORD BY TERRY FUNK

PERMUTED
PRESS

PERMUTED
PRESS

**Permuted Press, LLC**
New York • Nashville
posthillpress.com

Published in the United States of America
1 2 3 4 5 6 7 8 9 10

*For Adrienne—my forever partner*

# CONTENTS

# FOREWORD

**ECW** certainly made its mark. It was a necessary thing for the athletes in the business at that time. They needed a place to establish themselves, create themselves. And that's what ECW was. It was a very creative place.

I was attracted to ECW because of the challenge. I was bound and determined that we would not fail as a group of individuals. It was a challenge for us, and for Tod Gordon too. It was a rough row to hoe, but I stuck with them and would like to think I gave them a rub, as it was my intention to do so while also putting a little scratch on Vince McMahon's arm. I did whatever I could to agitate that asshole up north.

I was very proud of all the people in ECW. They wanted to do something, to be a part of something, and Vince damn sure wasn't going to let them in WWE. They had only one choice, so I gave myself one choice also—to help make ECW. Eventually, Vince got a whiff of ECW, and he didn't like it at all. We went in other directions, and he had no choice but to accept us as a pain in the ass.

I look back at my time in ECW fondly. It was a marvelous time, and Tod was the one who stepped out onto that diving board and jumped right into the deep end—the one guy who could compete with Vince McMahon.

—*Terry Funk*
*Nine-time Hall of Famer and*
*Multi-time World Heavyweight Champion*
*July 2022*

# INTRODUCTION

I was warned.

It happened at the Philadelphia Airport Marriott in 1993, just before the explosive grassroots surge in popularity of my independent wrestling company.

I had no idea I would be meeting the world heavyweight champion when I woke up that day. In the early '90s, Ric Flair was the most recognizable name in wrestling, maybe second only to fellow bleached-blond megastar Hulk Hogan. Flair had held world titles more than ten times by then, having worked in a pro wrestling ring with just about every living legend of the sport. He'd toured the globe as the NWA world champion, facing top talent in every promotion under the sun, and was a top draw himself. This was at a time when world titles were reserved for the few elite wrestlers who could represent the business well and do huge box office. In all ways, Ric Flair represented the legitimate pro wrestling world.

I, in sharp contrast to Ric Flair in every way, was barely in the business.

I did own a wrestling federation, though that by itself was not sufficient grounds to share space with Flair—independent wrestling companies had popped up all over the country, each run with varying degrees of competency and professionalism. That's putting it mildly; most were a shit show.

Eastern Championship Wrestling, the company I'd recently started, was, at its heart, a regional independent promotion. But we began to pull away from the pack, garnering television coverage on SportsChannel Philadelphia and eventually SportsChannel America and popping up on all strange ends of the TV dial, literally. Remember UHF? It was for stuff like this and Bulgarian cooking shows. If you made it through Anastasiya baking strudel at midnight, you could catch Johnny Hotbody battling Jimmy Snuka at one in the morning.

Having TV distribution, any TV at all, is the single most important ingredient in keeping a wrestling federation afloat. The boys—wrestling parlance for the talent, also called "workers"—were far more willing to stay loyal to a company giving them televised exposure. It added an element of cachet to both the product and the individual workers in the ring.

From the promoter's standpoint, it allowed wrestling storylines to continue on a weekly basis. You could draw out more intricate feuds over time, advancing the intrigue weekly as opposed to having to tie everything up with a neat bow on top by the end of each monthly show. Television was what distinguished a wrestling promotion from a gaggle of day workers flipping each other in VFW halls before the locals. As limited as our broadcasts may have been, we had TV, baby. You could count the number of promotions that could say that in 1993 on one hand.

On this particular day, I was invited to lunch with Kevin Sullivan and his wife, Nancy. They were both ring veterans who'd come to do some shots for my company, Eastern Championship Wrestling. I knew Kevin couldn't stay—he was heading back to World Championship Wrestling (WCW), one of the two remaining major national federations at the time, and would eventually be given a spot on their booking team. Bookers are the writers and decision makers for wrestling shows; they're a crucial part of any wrestling company's office, as they make decisions like who wins, loses, and becomes champion. But they're even more important for big-time televised companies because they control everything that airs on the shows. In addition to fan reactions, TV ratings are their real barometer. It's a big job.

Besides being known as a booker, the short and stocky Sullivan was also a high-profile wrestler. He'd perfected an evil in-ring persona, conjuring references to the occult and black magic, with the statuesque and stunning Nancy at his side playing a character known simply as Woman. They'd done some work for me and, before heading back to WCW, Kevin asked me to have a bite with them at the Marriott. I was only too happy to oblige. Despite my owning ECW, there was still a wrestling fan living inside me.

I was open to picking Sullivan's brain, as the future direction of my company was a tad unclear. I'd recently lost my booker Eddie Gilbert for reasons I'll go into later, and I'd just asked his friend Paul Heyman to stay on board and help me with the creative decisions. Heyman, known to all as "Paul E" in reference to his WCW persona as manager Paul E. Dangerously, was a talented young man. He was great on the microphone, with a wit so sharp and an inherent knowledge of the business and how it all worked. The talent seemed to like him and, more importantly, I was finding we had a lot in common.

For starters, Paul was a fellow Jew. His mother, Sulamita, was a Holocaust survivor at Auschwitz—a fact that endeared her to my own mother when she came to know her. We had identical senses of humor, likely fostered by similar ethnic, big-city upbringings—me in Philly and Paul in New York. Well, Scarsdale, but close enough. I didn't know him that well at the time, but he'd offered to help me out in Eddie's absence and was doing a great job at his primary duty—keeping talent away from me so I could run the company.

Paul and I started sharing creative ideas, and soon enough we were seen as the one-two punch in Philly's fledgling, independent alternative to the sleepy WWE and moribund WCW. We were soon making waves, building a reputation among veteran, world-famous talent and getting some ink in the wrestling news-letters, known in locker rooms as the "dirt sheets."

Kevin Sullivan no doubt saw the potential in ECW, and I suspected that's what this lunch was about. Wrestlers are oppor-tunists—creatures wired to position themselves for survival in an unfriendly and perilous habitat. I knew my company was different from the others, and I knew Kevin knew it too.

I entered the Marriott at the appointed time and sat with Kevin and Nancy for lunch. After a few minutes of conversation, I saw "Nature Boy" Ric Flair step off the lobby elevator and head toward our table. This was historic. Prior to my starting Eastern Championship Wrestling, I would've only been able to meet Flair as a fan. But now I was here to dine with Kevin Sullivan, a major creative player for the very federation Flair sat atop. I'd hopefully be introduced as a company owner, and there was a chance Flair had even heard of us. Maybe he'd even seen the product after closing the bars last night and turning on the hotel TV at 4:00 a.m. Perhaps he was flipping around the deep channels hoping for free porn and instead found Don Muraco winning our heavy-weight title.

Flair's blond locks bounced as he strutted across the lobby, enrapturing all in his sphere. Ric Flair had that effect on a room. Hell, an arena.

"Hey, Devil," Flair called as he approached our table. It was the first and only time I'd heard Kevin referred to as such. The world champion got to our table, and the first thing Kevin did was make the introduction.

"Ric, this is Tod Gordon," he said. "I told you about ECW."

Before I could extend my hand and begin talks about why Ric needed to add the Eastern Championship Wrestling heavyweight title to his list of belts, he looked down at me.

"Brother," Ric started, "your piece-of-shit partner Paul is a fucking pathological liar."

# INTRODUCTION

I was too flabbergasted to protest that Paul wasn't really a partner. It was my company, and he was helping me book. I wasn't even paying him; he just showed up with his friend Eddie Gilbert one night and kept coming down to shows, even after Eddie was gone. I didn't know what had happened between Ric and Paul. They obviously knew each other while working at WCW together, but the source of this heat was unknown to me.

This was Ric Fucking Flair, royalty in the business, and he'd just officially given the thumbs-down vote on my new choice of booker.

Eh. What the hell did he know?

# CHAPTER 1

# BUSINESS

"Don't cheat anybody. Don't lie."

This was the only explicit business advice my father, Charles Gordon, ever gave me. It was a serious business we were in, taking responsibility for someone's jewelry and lending them money against it, and if you were not ethical and word got out, your whole business was shot. It was all about integrity. That's probably true of any industry, but pawnbroking in particular is a business of relationships. You had to foster strong ties with your community of potential customers, especially if you were running one of Philadelphia's institutions, which we were.

Carver W. Reed was a company started in 1860 by Carver Reed himself. My grandfather established a retail jewelry store on Philadelphia's Jewelers' Row in 1902 called Harry Gordon and Sons that he ran with his three sons—my dad and two uncles. He bought Carver W. Reed in 1949, increasing his portfolio to two locations. When he died in 1968, the two stores were split between the sons, with my uncles getting Harry Gordon and Sons and my dad getting Carver W. Reed. The Philly institution landed in my family's control, where it remains to this day.

By 1970, I was working there through my summers, beside my dad. My sisters, Nancy Beth and Leslie, had no interest in working at the store, so it was always Dad and me running the place along with around ten workers. My father was a master craftsman, a gifted jeweler with a killer work ethic and a reputation for honesty. He was the classic gentleman of a bygone era—he wore a suit and tie until the moment he got home, wherein he'd slip into his smoking jacket and the damn tie would stay knotted beneath until he was ready for bed. He might've slept in it, for all I knew.

I was a teenager without a care or a damn plan in the world. The shop was a place for me to kill time and hang out during the summers without any real responsibility. I could call in sick when I wanted without repercussion. It didn't matter to me—I saw no future there. There were almost a dozen employees making their entire living through the shop. But for me it was mainly a place to make a hundred bucks a week for pot money.

Carver W. Reed's legacy was very important to my father. That was something he drilled into my head not so subtly as decades passed, and I eventually told him I was starting a wrestling company. He saw my involvement in pro wrestling as nothing more than a pastime, which, quite frankly, I did too when I started. He would constantly remind me Carver W. Reed was my "bread and butter." It must've resonated because throughout my tenure running ECW, I never stopped working full time at the store.

There was a part of me that hoped my father would see ECW as a success story, my starting a business from nothing and growing it into a powerhouse. He didn't understand any of it—ECW, the business, or wrestling in general. He would say it was like roller derby, and truth be told, it kind of was. I loved it, but I understood it was an acquired taste. Pop was a serious guy, a hardened businessman, so watching Wild Samoan Afa ball-shot Dominic DeNucci was understandably beyond his purview.

"That's not real salt they're throwing," he would say to me as Mr. Fuji blinded some poor schmuck in the ring. I tried to argue but he wasn't hearing it. He'd shake his head and ask me when I was going to outgrow "that wrestling crap." It was a question he started asking me when I was nine years old and continued for quite some time afterward, to be exact, all throughout ECW.

No one in my family ever saw ECW, even though it was on TV weekly. But, later on, when ECW was at its height, my dad began to tell people about it. "My son," he'd brag, "he has a wrestling business!" The federation's success and press coverage suddenly justified the pursuit. But did Charles Gordon ever watch the thing? Never. Did he ever turn on the damn TV and watch one match? One promo? Not even once. Maybe it was better that way—ball shots were the *least* of what we did in ECW. My father definitely would've thought my lying bloodied in the ring or arranging catfights between scantily clad valets violated his singular commandment: "Don't you let that wrestling crap kill Carver W. Reed's legacy."

In all fairness, though, Mr. Reed never saw Francine's tits. I think he would've loved EC f'n W.

\* \* \*

I was a wild kid. Not a bad kid, per se; I didn't start fires or strangle field mice. I was just undisciplined. I no doubt had ADHD, but nobody had heard of that in 1962. My teachers would excuse me from class when I got too disruptive and make me run laps in the courtyard until I couldn't breathe. I'll repeat that for anyone who isn't now wondering what exactly the state of Pennsylvania required of one applying for licensure as an educator, beyond a pulse.

*My teachers would send a misbehaving, uncontrollable six-year-old outside, alone, in the cold, to run in circles until his tongue was wagging out of his mouth.*

I guess I'm being too critical—it actually worked. When I returned and sat down to thaw, I was too tired to act up.

In truth, my behavioral issues really amounted to an early display of leadership skills. That's how I saw it, anyway. I was kicked out of the car pool in first grade when I convinced all the other kids to punch Bonnie Wright in the stomach. True to society's mistreatment of leaders, I was the one punished, and I hadn't even touched the girl. My mom was less than thrilled, as she now had to drop me off and pick me up every day. But if you want to call that a behavioral problem, so be it. I tried to convince my mom it was leadership.

I lasted until third grade and then I was off to private school. Everyone had lost patience with me, and my parents hoped this would be a remedy. I can't say that I actually heard Drexel Hill Elementary School administrators celebrating when I was walked out the door for the last time, but I swear I heard champagne corks pop behind me.

My sisters seemed to escape such corporal punishment, but that didn't make them any holier. Leslie, the younger of the two and my senior by four years, was usually my partner in crime. She remained so throughout adulthood, as evidenced by the rearrangement of seating plans at family functions. Even into our sixties, everyone knew if Tod and Leslie were seated beside each other, it was only a matter of time before the giggles would begin, soon devolving into outright cackles and guffaws. We had the same irreverent sense of humor that was often appreciated by us alone. God bless her, Leslie was my evil twin.

Nancy Beth and Leslie couldn't have been more opposite. Nancy Beth was a reader, more of a loner like Dad. On your average day, if Nancy Beth was sitting at the table with a book, Leslie and I were choking ourselves with laughter while trying to make milk come out of our noses. Sophisticated humor was our specialty.

Around this time, I saw pro wrestling on TV for the first time. We got the WWWF product in Philly. This was the era of wrestling territories, and cable TV had not yet entered our lives. In fact, having never even seen a wrestling magazine, I didn't know wrestling existed outside Philadelphia. It would be many years before TBS would carry Jim Crockett's Mid-Atlantic shows and ESPN would send Verne Gagne's American Wrestling Association into our homes. Back then in Philadelphia, it was all Bruno Sammartino, all the time, baby. Throw in a little Bulldog Brower, Killer Kowalski, and the Graham Brothers and you have the recipe that got me hooked.

Look at those three names I mentioned—Brower, Kowalski, and the Grahams. What characters. That's the very thing I was most attracted to in wrestling—characters, guys who would grab the mic and cut a captivating promo. The guys I hung out with years later in ECW were unique personalities, like Sandman and Johnny Grunge; they were extreme characters, no pun intended. They were so different from me, and I was fascinated by that lifestyle on the edge, that shirking of responsibilities life thrusts on most people. I was jealous of guys that could disappear for days at a time without consequence. I couldn't understand how they lived that way—it was a stark contrast to my regimented life running Carver W. Reed and my responsibilities at home. I always wanted to know what that felt like. I got one vacation a year; these guys were on vacation all year long.

I realized early on that wrestling was built on characters. Without it, storylines didn't mean anything, fans wouldn't care, and talent would forever be interchangeable. Paul E and I would meet new talent and try to find the authentic character living inside them. That's exactly the reason I fought Paul to allow Sandman to come to the ring with a cigarette and a beer, but more on that later.

I was alone with my love of pro wrestling in my childhood home. The only family member who enjoyed watching wrestling was my grandfather on my mother's side. I showed it to him, and he got such a kick out of it he would leave the TV tuned to UHF channel 17, where it aired on Saturdays. He was afraid he wouldn't be able to find it again, and he'd bark at my grandmother in his charming Romanian/Yiddish mix if she tried to change the channel. To him, every blow in the ring was real.

My prankster expertise no doubt developed due to him. At some point in the 1970s, when he was about seventy-five years old, my grandfather was headed to a doctor's appointment without a ride, so he hitchhiked on City Avenue and snagged a ride from some dude in a sports car. Upon being dropped off at the doctor's, he turned to his ride and said in his thick accent, "Thank you. I'll be out in about an hour."

The guy was dumbfounded and began to protest when my grandfather began yelling at him until he sped away. My grandfather would throw his head back and howl in his guttural guffaw. He was always up to some shenanigans, even at home when that old rascal would chase my grandmother around the dining room table, grabbing at her boobs in front of me and my friends. We thought it was funny as hell, and that was all the encouragement he needed. That was my guy, Grandpop. He'd slide me pickles under the table throughout family dinners after my father barked I was ruining my appetite eating too many of them. He was great. I laughed all the time around him.

My father was not outwardly funny, but he would occasionally do something more low-key, like changing the table numbers on his friends' seating cards when he was checking in at a wedding. I eventually used that one myself. I love to see the reactions on people's faces. Even now, I do shit like that. I was in the doctor's office recently for an epidural in my back when the nurse told me, "Lie on your stomach." I lay down and said, "I was really tall in high school...I married a movie star...I had blond hair." I kept going until the doctor figured out what I was doing and laughed. That crass nurse didn't crack a smile and is still probably trying to figure it out as I write this. I'm definitely a cross section of Grandpop and my dad.

\* \* \*

I graduated without incident and went to Pitt, where I majored in psychology, business, and drug use, pushing myself further from a pursuit in something creative. Word on the street said psychology was the easiest degree to get. It was really just knowing people, and I had an innate sense of that.

My only experimentation with illicit substances to that point had been some pot in high school, which, for the '70s, might as well have been chocolate milk. College was different—there was shit available to me all over the campus. They say the '70s were all sex, drugs, and rock 'n' roll, and I can confirm it was indeed the best era to be a teenager. Women were experimenting with a newfound freedom, and much of it was sexual. There was no AIDS, but plenty of burning bras.

I tried my hand at acting, doing some shows at the college theater in an effort to scratch that itch. One semester, I loaded my schedule with acting and creative writing classes. I got a 4.0— my highest GPA ever, by at least a three-point margin. Doing those shows and taking the acting classes satiated my hunger for a creative outlet, but as soon as they were over, it was back to the doldrums. Then, quite by accident, I got a unique opportunity to exercise some creative muscle. One night, while out at a local watering hole, my friend Pete Theodorous and I started yukking it up with some older guys who were starting a comedy magazine called *Rag*. They pitched the idea as a *National Lampoon* magazine for sports. They planned to write parody articles about real-world pro athletes and sports teams, like a fictional, sarcastic *Sports Illustrated*.

I was all in. This fit me perfectly—I loved sports as much as I loved sarcasm. We jumped in and got working on issue number one, featuring the cover story, "Women in Sports." Our tasteful first cover was a woman sitting on a bench in a locker room wearing a baseball uniform, beside a bloody tampon.

Yeah. It lasted one edition.

Though Pete Theodorous had no comedy writing work on the horizon for me, he did throw a job offer my way. His father had a pipe painting business in Cleveland, and it seemed he was looking for workers to put on the payroll at $500 a week. That was nothing to sneeze at for a twenty-two-year-old in 1977, added to the fact that I still had absolutely no plans after graduation. It sounded like a million dollars to me. Pipe painting—sounded fun.

I ran it by my father, who wisely shot holes in it. He was thinking long term, whereas I was thinking about the next paycheck. He made the tired old pitch again—work at Carver W. Reed. He went through the litany of old person things that reinforced responsibility, a future, and a way to put food on my table. It was like nails on a chalkboard. Worse—it was like Shane Douglas's nails on a chalkboard while dressed in his Dean Douglas gimmick. Oof.

Dad reminded me that I had free parking at the shop. I'd have health insurance provided for me, and nothing offered quite as much job security as a family business. He asked me to try out Carver Reed again and, without an argument left in me, I capitulated.

Unwittingly, I'd just moved myself into owning the first of two businesses in my life.

\* \* \*

When I decided that Carver Reed was to be my future, I grabbed it with both hands and never let go. I was now a college graduate—full of piss and vinegar, and convinced I knew more than anyone in the world. Never mind that I'd be proven wrong again and again, as I learned from my dad by being at his side. I brought personality to the job and, in time, I was building rapport with customers. They could go anywhere and pawn that diamond ring, but I made sure they knew they could trust us being responsible with their valuables. It also helps to be able to tell a customer you've been in business a hundred twenty years, now a hundred sixty. Customers had a friend in Carver W. Reed.

The most poignant thing that came from my decision to commit to Carver Reed was the strengthening of my bond with my dad. He became my best friend in the most organic way possible—working with each other and relying on each other. He taught me all aspects of the business.

Then, in 1985, my father underwent a quintuple bypass surgery, largely putting him out of action from that point forward. I took the business on my shoulders and ran with it. He'd prepared me perfectly in the ten years prior, and the transition felt seamless. His old-time business connections already knew and liked me; it was easy to pick up and move ahead with the company. I was comfortable accepting his contemporaries as my own.

I also found myself to be a natural manager, as first displayed in the car pool offensive against Bonnie Wright—a skill that would come in rather handy when in a few years I would be dealing with a crop of workers slightly more challenging than pawnbrokers. I was equally comfortable talking with people from any walk of life, whether having martinis with heads of businesses or smoking a doobie with a wrestler at a backstage door. In short time, I was made president of the Pennsylvania Pawnbrokers Association, and I'd go on to become president of the international charity the Variety Club. I soon felt I couldn't join anything without becoming president.

I was firing on all cylinders and managed to make Carver W. Reed more successful than I had ever imagined possible. My personal life was in order too, and I was able to provide long-lasting stability and security for my family while preserving the long legacy my father and grandfather had established. I was, by all accounts, a success.

But one fact remained—Carver Reed was killing my creative side. Someone reading this might intone that I should've shut up and been happy. It's a hard thing to understand unless you have that creative bent inside you. The impulse to create isn't attached to a switch or a schedule. It's an inherent part of you. It's not something you do; it's something you *are*.

I suppressed the creative urge as much as possible and plowed ahead, working at the business nonstop. I took a nighttime improv class taught by a local comic, and that worked as a temporary pacifier. But there was a hankering to do something more, on a much greater scale, but how the hell was that going to happen?

One Saturday morning, I was listening to Philadelphia Sports Radio WIP 610 AM, and I had a little idea that just happened to change my entire life. It would build and destroy so much of me over the next decade.

# CHAPTER 2
# GOODHART

**A** Saturday morning wrestling program on Philly sports radio caught my ear, mostly because that business hadn't been considered mainstream before. I'd loved the sport since I was nine years old, so naturally I listened to the program with interest, but I also thought I could run some ads on the show. That would be a great opportunity to stick my toe in the business. It was impressive, pro wrestling getting an entire hour on the same radio network that dealt in the Flyers, Sixers, and Eagles all week. What I didn't realize was that the show's host was buying the hour from Sports Radio WIP.

That host was Joel Goodhart, a local independent wrestling promoter using the purchased airtime to advertise his live events. His cards ran Eastern Pennsylvania, Delaware, and South Jersey, thus the federation's name, Tri-State Wrestling Alliance, or TWA.

Goodhart was offering talent for personal appearances as well. I tested these waters in addition to running the radio spots, as it would be my first opportunity to meet a pro wrestler. I figured getting a wrestling star fresh off national TV would be a good draw for Carver Reed. I asked Goodhart whom he had access to for such an event, and he had more former WWE and WCW stars than I could shake a Singapore cane at. I thought it would be great

11

to have a ripped, real-life superhero and former world champion hanging at my store some Saturday afternoon, greeting the fans.

So, after careful consideration, I went with the obvious—the blonde, buxom announcer Missy Hyatt. Made sense to me.

Okay, in all honesty I wanted to see her—all of her—in person. I'm a man, sue me. But the choice wasn't without merit—*every* male wrestling fan in Philly would want to see her in person too, and that was the real purpose here, as I explained to my wife.

Missy was great. She knew her place in the business and exactly what assets she brought to the table. At Carver Reed, she actually laid those assets *on* the table as she hopped up and lay across the long counter. Fans lined up and had their pictures taken, making the outing a success from a foot traffic standpoint. Money well spent, though if my father walked in the store that day, he would've marched up to me and growled, "Legacy."

Legacy schmegacy—Mr. Reed never saw Missy's tits.

I got to know Joel Goodhart over the next few months and even headed out to some of his live cards to see his operation in person. Here's a crash course on the business of assembling a local wrestling show. You are working on a limited budget as a local promoter, so your expenditures have to be chosen wisely. Your income will be derived almost entirely from the gate, meaning ticket purchases. There's a limit to how much you can charge for a wrestling ticket. Wrestling fans weren't coming to shows between trips to the opera. Charge too much and no one is coming back next month. The goal is exactly that: keep 'em coming back.

At Goodhart's TWA shows, I saw local guys like Johnny Hotbody, Larry Winters, and DC Drake working hard for little money. But I also saw former WWE stars like "Cowboy" Bob Orton and "Magnificent" Muraco. Those guys drew the fans while the undercard guys kept them entertained most of the night. The margins were slim, but you could make it work if you really wanted an extremely time-consuming and low-yielding hobby.

Around that time, I'd become involved in the aforementioned charity the Variety Club. It's an amazing organization dedicated to raising money for local children with a host of disabilities. The Variety Club bought wheelchairs, walkers, prosthetics, and almost anything those children would need to integrate into society. We ran events and summer camps for them—it quickly became a passion of mine, and little else has come close to impacting me as much. Getting to know the kids and their families made me realize how blessed I was. I had three healthy children at home, and I was inspired to give back. I also wanted my kids to see how blessed *they* were. There are children I met when I became president of the Philadelphia chapter that I'm still in touch with today, like Steven Cope, who visited me as recently as last summer at a wrestling convention.

The Variety Club operated exclusively as a result of our fundraising efforts—medical equipment and summer camps were not cheap, so we worked hard at raising a ton of cash. Many members were leaders of business, and our board of directors was an absolute who's who, featuring executives from Bell Telephone, Philadelphia Electric, the police and fire commissioners, bank owners, and more. Throughout my tenure and presidency, I came to know power players like Mayor Ed Rendell, who would go on to become governor.

I was working hard to contribute and make a splash in this charitable organization. This was back at the turn of the '90s, before I became president, and I saw an opportunity in my new relationship with Goodhart and TWA. Through him, I arranged for a charity wrestling card at the Civic Center. That charity show was also an opportunity for me to get in the ring. In a moment of what some would consider delusional ambition, I suggested Goodhart use me as a vehicle to get heat on one of his heels. That's wrestling jargon for "making fans hate your bad guy." Goodhart got it. He knew the business at that local level and appreciated any edge, like having a heel throw some local businessman looking to help handicapped kids across the arena.

At the Civic Center show, I suggested the chosen heel, Johnny Hotbody, take our charity check and tear it up. Then, as I protested, he would toss me across the concrete floor. I figured fans would go white hot seeing the children's money torn up by some scumbag. Further, I would get physically manhandled when I tried to intervene. Everyone bought it, and I was a performer again. The difference between this performance and my college stage portrayal of Slim in *Of Mice and Men* was that I didn't break a rib in the play. I landed on my side when Hotbody tossed me, right on my belt-clipped beeper. I lay on the concrete in great pain, but also flying high from having pulled off what amounted to my first booked angle. Goodhart would no doubt be happy, and Hotbody got all that heat—the crowd wanted to kill him. That's success for a heel.

Gary Juster, an NWA representative present at the Goodhart show, ran over to me, concerned as I lay against the steel barricade.

"Was that a shoot?" he whispered. I had no idea that "shoot" meant "real" in a wrestling locker room. He might as well have asked, "Was that a porcupine?"

I just stared at him as I lay there with broken ribs.

"That bump," he said. "Was it a shoot?"

"Bump? Uh, sure. A shoot."

"Goddamn it!" He stormed off and grabbed hold of Johnny Hotbody and began chewing his ass out for hurting a mark, telling him how much trouble Goodhart could be in right now. Hotbody was protesting that it was "a work" and not "a shoot." I had no idea what the hell anyone was talking about, but I felt bad as I watched Hotbody getting ripped for doing something I'd suggested. It all got worked out, and Goodhart was happy as a clam. A big bearded one.

\* \* \*

I began spending more time around Goodhart and TWA. As our relationship grew stronger, he confided in me that his company was having financial troubles. I threw him a thousand bucks to get through that month's show, but then he came back the following month in the same bind. He said his payroll would again be short by another thousand dollars.

"Joel, I can't do it again," I said. "I have a business and a family."

"Could you do it for fifteen percent?"

I thought about it. What would 15 percent of a wrestling show be? I didn't think I would come close to making my thousand dollars back. As far as investments go, this made buying the Ben Franklin Bridge look like getting a thousand shares of Apple.

"Fifteen percent of one show?" I asked.

"No. Fifteen percent of my company."

Oh, *that* was different—15 percent of an entire failing *business*. That made sense. It's the old adage, throwing good money after bad, and I knew better. It didn't take long for me to figure out that's exactly what I would've been doing if I'd spent any more money to keep TWA afloat.

It was early 1992 and Goodhart was just a week away from the show for which he wouldn't be able to make payroll, but he was still telling fans on his radio show, "See you all next Saturday night!" Unless the listeners worked at a bank, I didn't think anyone was seeing Joel the following week. He'd booked the Civic Center, and I knew they charged four grand just to turn on the power in the building. Goodhart needed to cut and run and forget the "see you Saturday" shit.

Worse than his resistance to canceling was his stacking the card with more stars, i.e., more expenses. He couldn't afford to pay everyone he'd announced already, let alone all these new names he was promoting—Austin Idol, Abdullah the Butcher,

Cactus Jack, the Freebirds, the Sheepherders. It was one thing to seek a loan to bring Hulk Hogan out to your show, but Austin Idol? How the hell was that going to help? I asked him, "Why are you advertising all these names for a show you can't put on?" All these wrestlers were fly-ins, plane tickets needed for all—there was no way TWA would live to see another day. Naturally it didn't, and that was the end of Joel and me. The show was canceled, and the poor ticket-buying fans lost their money.

A few weeks after TWA imploded, I got a call from the company's ring announcer, Bob Artese. He, along with TWA sound guy Steve Truitt and Larry Winters, a local talent who worked all the TWA cards, wanted to come talk to me. Goodhart wasn't returning anyone's phone calls, mine included, so the guys reached out to me. I hosted them in my office at Carver Reed—an office that would see double duty from that point on.

"We want to keep this going," Artese began, "but we need your help." He went on to explain that they couldn't get a promoter's license without a bond for which they couldn't put up enough collateral. That's where I came in, they explained. If I secured the promoter's license, they'd do all the work. Artese said he'd announce for free, Truitt would do sound for free, and Winters just wanted to wrestle. With TWA gone, they'd likely never again get a shot to work in the business they loved, whether or not they ever made a dime from it.

That kind of passion was infectious and common to the indie wrestling scene. There were no grandiose dreams; they just wanted a place to do what they loved for people. It's an expensive hobby and impossible to do unless someone sets up a ring and gets people to sit in the bleachers. They wanted me to be that guy for them, and I agreed, never knowing in five years we'd be on pay-per-view.

## CHAPTER 3

# EASTERN

It was TWA's style, with its touches of hard-core action, that initially attracted me to it. But I had no intention of my new federation being associated with TWA, given the questionable business practices that precipitated the end of the company. I needed a new name. Eastern Championship Wrestling seemed to flow, and in the stroke of attorney Mike Goss's pen, ECW was born.

I eyeballed a date in late February for the first show I intended to run at Phillies legend Mike Schmidt's sports bar on Market Street in the heart of Philly. It was a recurring venue for TWA, so fans would likely return, but with the understanding it was a new federation on more secure footing. They could come back to Schmidt's bar without the fear of being screwed out of their ticket purchases like had happened at the end of TWA. Never mind that when the ring was set up in the center of the bar, wrestlers couldn't stand on the top rope without their head going through the ceiling.

Joel Goodhart had proven a cautionary tale for me, so I managed a slender list of expenses. The venue was free for a Tuesday night—the place would make a killing off the bar tab, so Tuesday night it was. Our sound guy was free, as I'd taken Steve Truitt up on his offer. The ring was free too, as it belonged to wrestler Max Thrasher, who certainly knew the way to get booked on independent wrestling cards. Bob Artese would don the tux and announce our matches at no cost, leaving the wrestlers and advertising as my only expenses. This is where I could get into trouble, so I kept a lean card, offering six matches with almost all local talent. They all got between twenty-five and fifty dollars each, and my ads were basic flyers. I was counting on the local fans that came out every month for Goodhart's show. There was no need to buy an hour on sports radio.

As word spread that the local shows were coming back, I began getting incessant phone calls from Mr. Sandman, a local wrestler who did a surfer character in the ring, surfboard and all. Sandman, or Hack as he would come to be known by all in the business, was looking to get booked on the show. I'd seen him work for Goodhart so I had no problem with that, except for one detail. Seemed during a previous show at Mike Schmidt's bar, Hack had spit on a waitress and was barred from entering the establishment. I told him I'd call the venue back, tell them he'd found Jesus, and see what I could do. I got them to agree to a two-month ban, provided he apologize to the young lady in person.

"Fuck that," he said. "I ain't apologizing to some bitch for something I don't even remember doing."

"That's fine," I said. "I just can't book you now."

"All right, what's her name?"

Looking back now, it seems I've spent half my adult life getting Hack to apologize to people. One time he got himself suspended by the Pennsylvania State Athletic Commission, so I convinced their executive director, Greg Sirb, to come by my office so he could meet Hack and hear his heartfelt apology. I explained that he was playing a character and it was nothing like the real man, Jim Fullington. I then told Hack exactly what to say to Sirb and went over it with him ten times. Within five minutes of the meeting starting, Hack had snatched Sirb, who stands about five foot four, out of his seat and literally had him pinned against my office wall. Pictures and plaques are falling all over the place and I'm trying to cover, acting like Hack is playing a role.

"Okay, Jim," I said, invoking his real name for effect. "No more jokes. Mr. Sirb isn't going to think this is funny for much longer." My fake-ass laugh was the only one in the room. I could've killed Hack. Many times over.

Sandman apologized to the waitress and was eventually allowed to return for our April show. I booked his wife Lori, ring name Peaches, to come out to the ring in the months before his return and portray a manager taking notes at the events, looking for her next protégé. Once Hack returned, I saw how gifted he really was. Sure, he was a pain in the ass sometimes, but he was so incredibly smart about the wrestling business. He wasn't particularly big and had no physique. He resembled a hard-living roofer more so than a wrestler. But we hit it off immediately and our bond would continue for years, even as he became considerably more intoxicated and unpredictable.

I was getting ready for ECW's first show in February, and I still didn't have any star power. One of the wrestlers told me that former WWWF champion Ivan Koloff, the Russian Bear himself, was living in Maryland and worked independent shows for $300. I was excited by the prospect—this was the ferocious, bald Russki that had stripped Bruno Sammartino of his world title and stunned the world.

He hadn't gone back to Moscow? He chose Maryland? Was I just supposed to call him up? Did he even speak English? Did I need an interpreter?

Go figure, Ivan was actually a French Canadian and, yes, he was living in Maryland and speaking perfect English to his neighbors. I called him and got the booking done for $300 with no airfare or hotel, as it was just a two-hour drive. I would have a former world champion getting his hand raised in the middle of my ring. Max Thrasher's ring, technically. And yes, he was on the card too.

Ivan also taught me another of the million wrestling lessons I'd learn over the years. "Who am I putting over?" he asked me. That means "Who is beating me?" in wrestler-speak.

"I have you working Tony Stetson, but I was going to have you win," I said, doing my best to honor a legend. I thought, *Have Stetson beat you? You're Ivan fucking Koloff!* He then explained why it made no sense to have him win the match.

"It does you no good," he said. "That guy I beat will be there for every show you run. You need to have him beat me. That will build him up for you to use week after week. That's how you make money." I was enraptured. It was brilliant, selfless, and true.

The first wrestling card I ever promoted came together, and on Tuesday night, February 26, 1992, a passionate crowd of a hundred or so fans saw Ivan Koloff lose to local worker Tony Stetson. The opening bout featured a twenty-minute time limit draw between Jimmy Jannetty and a new young talent named Stevie Richards, who would later make his mark in ECW, making his appearance in the first match of the first show a popular trivia question today. Future fan favorite JT Smith was in our tag team main event, and, when the show ended, we'd broken even at the door and sent the crowd home happy.

The show was unforgettable for one fan in particular—my friend Mark Goldman, who'd come to support me. I asked him how he liked it, and he was absolutely beaming. The show was good, but he looked like he'd seen something he never had before.

Turned out he did.

"Oh my god," Mark said. "Some wrestlers were changing in the men's room, and Ivan Koloff just washed his dick in the sink next to me!"

* * *

The first ECW show was booked by Larry Winters. That's another little piece of trivia for the hardcore fan. Here's another one: the first ECW show was the *last* ECW show booked by Larry Winters.

The booker is arguably the most important role in a wrestling organization, and it made sense that I ask Larry to take that job. Of the three men who stood in my office pledging to work without pay if I resurrected the Philly federation, he was the only wrestler. When Bob Artese said they'd handle everything for me, they earnestly intended to do so. Bob had ring announcing covered, Steve ran sound, and Larry would handle booking the matches. In essence, that's a wrestling show.

So I was more than a little disappointed when Larry tried to screw me over on our first card.

Larry came to me with an idea about the tag team main event, which featured him tagging with Johnny Hotbody against JT Smith and DC Drake. They wanted to paint JT, the only black guy in the match, white. I wasn't comfortable with the idea to start with. Though I hate prejudice of any kind, largely fostered by having pennies rolled toward me by other kids on the school bus, I thought it was just stupid. The black and white thing was the dumbest way to get crowd heat, but I didn't veto it out of hand.

"If you're going to do that," I said to Larry, "then *you* have to get painted black." In some way it made sense to me. The black guy gets painted white, and a white guy is painted black—some moral balance in the universe. It was an arbitrary solution I came up with on the spot, but he agreed and they headed out for their match. I didn't realize it at the time, but they didn't even bother to bring the black paint up from the basement. JT got painted white, and that was it. We had just done an angle where a black man was racially humiliated without the counterpoint I suggested, which would've made it a little less racially charged.

I was pissed. It was a diss to the boss on our first show, some stupid power play they might've gotten away with on some money mark. I grabbed them as soon as the match was over.

"That's it," I began. "You guys fucked up. We could've done something here, but you just blew it."

"We're sorry," Winters said. "We forgot the paint can when we went out."

"No, you didn't. So now, I'm taking over the booking, starting next month. And if one thing happens in that ring I didn't call for, that person is gone. I don't give a shit if I have an empty locker room by the end of the show. I don't play that shit."

They needed to know from the jump that the inmates were not running the asylum. I got right in their faces; I didn't care how big they were. My authority was not to be fucked with. JT didn't say anything about being painted white in the angle, but he wouldn't have; he was a quiet type that just went with the flow. I'd imagine he wasn't thrilled, though.

Our door was around eighty people, which meant an $800 gate. Ivan Koloff was my biggest expense at $300, which left me $500 for the other thirteen workers. Do you see why flying in three Freebirds would've been certain death?

Working with Koloff was great, so I parlayed his and Tony Stetson's match into a return bout the following month in a Russian Chain Match. Ivan was cheap, plus he drove in and saved me airfare, so that was a no-brainer. I wanted to spread my wings and bring in some more name talent, while also being careful. I wasn't about to start dropping hundreds on airline tickets and follow the Goodhart path off a cliff.

No federation is complete without a heavyweight champion, so I had to crown one. "Superfly" Jimmy Snuka was a huge babyface name in the '80s, and he'd just completed a second though much less successful run on WWE television. I knew people would come out to see Jimmy, so if I could get him at a reasonable price, that would be my guy. The name was big enough to hold our first belt, if even for just twenty-four hours.

I was put in touch with Jimmy, or should I say Jimmy's wife at the time, Sharon. She handled all of Jimmy's affairs but, more importantly, I was told that she worked for an airline. Boom. Free flight from Utah for Jimmy. And apparently for Sharon as well. Seemed she was acting as his manager and needed to come out and see our setup before Jimmy could work. That would obviously include accommodations and dinner at a nice restaurant for the happy couple.

She worked me, but whatever. Free flight for my first world champion. I made the deal.

I preceded them to Bookbinder's restaurant and sat waiting in my customary suit and tie. It wasn't a gimmick—I was doing everything for ECW after closing Carver Reed, so I was always in business attire. The boys thought I was working, but I wasn't—I was *working*. (If you get it, you get it.)

In short time, I noticed Jimmy and Sharon had arrived. Actually, everyone at the upscale restaurant noticed Jimmy had arrived in his flip-flops, beaded headband, and flowing Fijian ring robe. I hoped Sharon wasn't ribbing him that we were holding a card in the kitchen.

The three of us sat and ordered some appetizers. Jimmy was particularly fond of the shrimp cocktail, so much so that he kept ordering them at twenty-one bucks a pop. He even asked the waiter to bring more between the salad and main course.

"Brudda, bring me more of those shrimp gimmicks." He gestured to me and Sharon. "And bring for the table, brudda."

I waved him off like he'd ordered me a colonoscopy. "No, no, table is good, Jimmy. Table's good."

We ate and talked business, and I must've been saying the right things because Jimmy leaned over to me when we were alone. "From now on," he began, "you do business with me. No Sharon.

We are good now, brudda." And that was it. I never saw her again. I used Jimmy a ton of times, put my belt on him, and he was soon engaged in the first feud I ever booked against his archnemesis from his WWE days, "Magnificent" Don Muraco. Jimmy and I became tight. We were "boys," as you say in the business, meaning we hung out outside the arena, bullshitting and smoking doobies together. I could've left the business right then and felt satisfied.

Jimmy smoked so much weed it was remarkable. I'd been smoking since I was fifteen, but there was no keeping up with Jimmy. The guy lived to wrestle and smoke. Maybe that explains his "out there" promos that seemed to go on forever with no real direction. They sounded mystical, and maybe fans wondered if it was some existential musing going over their heads. Nope. Jimmy was just stoned.

As Snuka and I got closer, I eventually had to stop riding with him. The amount of smoke he blew in the car made it impossible to drive. Or stay awake. Or move. One night Jimmy came over to me as usual and said, "I ride with you, brudda." I told him I couldn't and got in another car. I had to draw the line.

One time Jimmy was riding with me to a show in Trenton, New Jersey, and I got lost. I'm notoriously terrible with directions. I can make a wrong turn and get lost in my bathroom. It's awful. On this occasion I was so lost we were in danger of being late, and I couldn't be late for my own show. I was freaking out and getting pissed. I stopped and asked five people for directions, and they each sent me a different way. I must've been getting close to a panic attack when Jimmy reached over and grabbed me to shake me out of it.

"Brudda, brudda, brudda," he growled in his Fijian accent. "There's only one thing you can do in situation like this."

He'd broken me out of the panic and had my full attention. He was ready with some veteran, road-tested wisdom, no doubt.

"What?" I asked.

"You gotta smoke a little bit. Make you calm down." He was as serious as a heart attack.

Muraco was another easy get thanks to ring announcer Bob Artese. Muraco had done shots for Goodhart's TWA so he knew Bob and, remarkably, Muraco's wife also worked for an airline so his flight from Hawaii would be free. I was excited by the prospect of booking the two in a resurgence of their famous feud when Muraco had spit on Snuka at a 1983 WWE TV taping in Allentown. I wisely elected not to use the new "Husbands of Flight Attendants" angle I'd discovered.

The Muraco booking was doubly attractive, as not only would I be spared a plane ticket but also a hotel since Bob Artese had offered Muraco a bed in his house. We were leaving the show that night when Muraco came running out of the venue and dove into my back seat before I pulled out. Jimmy was smoking a joint the size of a small blimp when Muraco reached over and snatched it.

"I need some before I go home with Bob," he said. He took a drag that must've lasted thirty seconds. The smoke billowed out of every hole in his head and he passed it back to Jimmy, then leaned back into his seat. "You can't put me at Bob's anymore."

"What's wrong?" I asked. "The bed not comfortable?"

"I have to sneak out into the backyard to smoke my ganja. Bob and his wife are real straight, and I don't want to disrespect them, but I feel like a little kid sneaking around. I love the guy, but I need to smoke."

Around this time, Sandman and I started to get close as well. As you can see, I look for friendships in the most stable of places, so Hack was a natural selection. He started calling me every day. We would talk wrestling, different angles, or play Phillies trivia while we rode to shows. He wasn't yet as difficult as he'd become. Back then he was a different guy, other than spitting on a waitress in public, of course. But I'm sure that's happened to you.

* * *

Running bar shows was a reliable and easy route for us in the early days of ECW. Most bars charged us nothing considering we were delivering drinking patrons, so our expenses stayed low, reduced to basically talent and advertising. The Chestnut Cabaret was a nightclub on Thirty-eighth and Chestnut Streets in the university district of Philly that hosted live music over the years, so I approached them about hosting an ECW card. We booked the venue for a day they were closed in July of 1992.

Despite strong advance ticket sales, the show was a disaster. A week before the show, I got a call from the venue's manager telling me we couldn't have anyone under twenty-one years old attend the show. I was incredulous. Fine time to tell me—a great number of wrestling fans were kids or teens. I'd already presold over four hundred tickets and was expanding the card based on that income. My lineup was nine bouts, which amounted to twenty wrestlers. I'd added a couple of recognizable names, including former WWE tag team champion Nikolai Volkoff and enhancement talent favorite Salvatore Bellomo, in addition to Jimmy Snuka. Now this shit from the venue.

It didn't add up to me—the nightclub was closed. They sold beer at Eagles games and there were kids all over Veterans Stadium. What the fuck? I argued my case, but the manager said clubs were different and it was tantamount to letting minors in a nightclub. Whatever. It was his joint.

We had the show, and I ended up refunding hundreds of tickets. In the end, there were fewer than a hundred people in the crowd, and I stood there paying off the talent after the show feeling like I was in a sinking dinghy. One by one, workers took their pay and thanked me. Wasn't their fault—they did a great job. I didn't. Maybe painting pipes with Pete Theodorous at $500 a week wasn't such a bad idea.

I found JT Smith packing up and handed him his check.

"No way," he said as he continued packing his gear. "I know you got killed tonight."

I tried to shove the forty-dollar check in his hand, but he wouldn't take it. Finally, at my insistence, he took it, but ripped it up. "I can't do that to you," he said.

Only one wrestler, the man who'd been painted white in some shitty angle not even worthy of a backyard wrestling show, refused the payday because he knew the venue had fucked me. I didn't expect him or any of the workers to do that, and he shouldn't have. But he did. I asked what he did for a living, and he said he was ushering at a movie theater.

I hired him as a Carver Reed employee the next day.

I was back at the store every morning despite rain, snow, or a Chestnut Cabaret wrestling show the night before. I had a normal and predictable homelife with my first wife, Amy, and our three kids. She didn't mind my doing the shows, not yet at least. It competed for some time at home, sure, but I was with them when I could be, and I kept my business going. Amy knew I needed a creative outlet and was happy I was enthused about something.

One of the first ribs—practical jokes—I witnessed in the wrestling business happened at the Chestnut Cabaret and involved Jimmy Snuka. He was slated to wrestle Metal Maniac, a worker Jimmy was mentoring and taking on the road to work matches with. They were sitting in the locker room taping up before their match when Snuka turned to Ivan Koloff, who was dressing beside him.

"Brudda, you got a blade I can use?" he asked. For the uninitiated reader, a wrestler bleeds by slicing their forehead with a concealed sliver of razor blade. The resultant flow, mixed with sweat, creates a crimson mask and electrifies the crowd. Maniac heard Jimmy ask Koloff for the blade and perked up. Apparently, he didn't know that blood would be flowing in his match that night.

Koloff, somehow sensing a rib was at hand, replied without missing a beat. "I got one, but it's rusty." Now Maniac's heart was surely palpitating.

"That's okay, brudda," Snuka replied. "Let me have it anyway." Maniac's eyes bugged. Ivan handed Jimmy something and Superfly started taping it up, as one would do a regular blade.

"Hey, Jimmy," Maniac stammered, "what are we doing out there tonight?"

"Just let me lead, brudda."

"Yeah, okay, but are we getting color out there?"

Jimmy ignored the wrestler-speak for "Are we going to bleed?" and concealed the supposed rusty blade under his top lip, then gave Maniac a wink. He continued the rib all the way into the ring and for the match. The time came in the ring when Snuka gave Maniac the signal that he was about to cut him. He reluctantly gave Snuka his head, awaiting a potential case of tetanus. Jimmy pretended to palm the blade and instead raked his fingernail across Maniac's forehead, as if it were the rusty blade. Maniac assumed he was zipped real good and turned to the crowd to show the carnage, though in actuality showed them nothing but a sweaty head.

"Squeeze," Jimmy quietly instructed, telling Maniac to scrunch his face in such a way that would make the blood spurt more aggressively. Maniac was standing there in the ring, turning purple trying to get blood to flow from a nonexistent cut. Jimmy raked his fingernail again and Maniac assumed he was opened up. "Squeeze more, brudda. Nothing coming." I thought Maniac would pass out puffing his cheeks and wrinkling his face. Jimmy and I rode home together after the matches laughing our asses off.

One night during a Chestnut Cabaret show, I had the dubious fortune to be a recipient of the famous Superfly splash, the star's finishing move wherein he leaps from the top turnbuckle and crashes down on his prone opponent, torso on torso. I was in the ring as part of an angle that was designed to turn Snuka into a heel. He quietly called the spots to come—headbutt, scoop, slam, splash—and before I could process the word "scoop," I was deadlifted into the air and slammed to the mat. In a flash, I lay in the center of the ring as Snuka posed on the top turnbuckle. He was then airborne and I closed my eyes for the impact, of which I felt none. I sure as hell heard it, the smash of the mat around me as Jimmy landed. But he'd used his knees and forearms to take the brunt of the blow, and I truthfully didn't even realize he was on me. He was such a pro.

I'd been booking the bar shows since I took that duty from Larry Winters back in February. I was becoming more adept at it and started taking more chances, with my increasing comfort breeding creativity. We did a great spot in a match between Tony Stetson and Johnny Hotbody in October '92. The two brawled out of the ring and all the way to the locker room for a count-out finish. Bob Artese went into the ring, announced the result, and moved on to the participants of the next match. They came out, and the next match began.

Then, Hotbody and Stetson crashed through the curtain and continued pounding each other back down the aisle, through the fans, and eventually back to the ring. Hotbody had a toilet seat around his neck and the crowd loved it. All eighty of them.

Terry Taylor was the marquee name we added to that card. He'd been a standout young wrestler years earlier in Florida, the Carolinas, and with WCW. He had an odd run in the WWE as something called the Red Rooster in 1988, so he'd only recently been off TV. He was a good addition to our card. Taylor would later go on to be a member of the office staff at WCW, TNA, and WWE. He turned to me as the Stetson and Hotbody brawl spilled back out into the crowd.

"That's brilliant," he said, smiling ear to ear.

"Thanks, Terry." I was glowing. A bona fide compliment on my booking from a wrestler who'd done the whole circuit. To think just a year ago I couldn't book lunch.

Two months later, in January 1993, I was watching WWE Raw, the flagship TV broadcast of the world's largest federation. There was a great match going on between Ric Flair and Mr. Perfect, a battle that turned into a vicious brawl that carried them out of the ring, down the aisle, and into the locker room area.

Then, back out into the arena as the next match was ready to begin.

What a frigging coincidence! Had to be, right? There was no other way anyone at WWE could have seen our angle at the bar show in Philly. I was fairly sure no one on our ECW roster had been called up to the WWE. Had the Raw ring broken and Max Thrasher been contacted? It was a real head-scratcher.

It didn't remain mysterious for long. That same week I saw Terry Taylor wrestling on another WWE TV show. Seems he was called back to the WWE in November, about two weeks after he'd worked for me and complimented my booking of the brawl.

That's supposed to be a compliment in this business, but I was hot at the time. Then I realized it was a validation of what I'd been doing by the seat of my pants, having taken over the booking with no experience or any real plan. It also showed me that my foray into the more outside-the-box booking was the right direction to take.

It was right around this time that a local guy named Matt Radico would get thousands more eyes on that outside-the-box booking than I ever thought possible.

\* \* \*

Matt Radico was recording our bar shows and helping us sell the VHS tapes, a testament to his willingness to tackle impossible challenges. I don't think he sold one copy. But he came to me with an interesting proposition. Matt knew a guy named Sam Schroeder, who was an executive at Prism, a local cable network. His boss there was Ed Snider, owner of the Philadelphia Flyers and the Spectrum sports arena, and he was starting a new network called SportsChannel Philadelphia. He'd handpicked Schroeder to get the new channel up and running and was pretty desperate for sports programming to air around their hockey coverage. Radico would bring Schroeder a tape of a pilot show if we could put one together. I sure as shit wasn't sending him the bar shows, so I set out to shoot a more professional-looking product.

I booked the Tabor Youth Center in northeast Philly for the pilot show. I called my contact there, Frank Talent, and asked him to grab a bunch of the kids at the youth center and pack the house with them for free. It was a guaranteed way to get an audience in the seats for our TV cameras. The pilot was in no way indicative of what our future ECW shows would look and sound like, which is the exact opposite of what a pilot show is supposed to do for a network's decision makers. Your pilot show—of wrestling, sitcoms, or dramas—should be an example of what's to come every week, should the executives decide to air your show. It's a taste test.

Well, the kids at that pilot show were enthusiastically giving babyface pops all day, booing the bad guys, and acting like proper citizens. It was the exact opposite of what ECW was, but it was the best we could do, short of sending SportsChannel some hand-held-shot bar show where an African American is painted white. Cheering kids it is!

We sent the tape over, and SportsChannel soon called asking if we could do one show every week to air at 6:00 p.m. on Tuesdays.

"We sure could," I responded, while telling myself there was no way possible.

Now we needed content, and a lot of it. I was used to the pace of booking one card a month, roughly eight matches, with very few ongoing storylines. Now, I needed four weeks of content every month, with lots of ongoing storylines. My workload had just quadrupled. Of course, wrestling shows aren't *shot* every week—multiple weeks of programming are shot at a single event. This allows you to bring out talent and fans once but get a few weeks of TV out of them.

I scheduled Cabrini College for March 1993 as the location of our first TV shoot. We would shoot two shows Saturday night, then one show Sunday afternoon, and close the weekend with three weeks' worth of programing. The venue would look great— it was a real gymnasium used by Cabrini's NCAA basketball team. We just needed to outfit it with fans, which I didn't think would be a problem once we posted flyers advertising a TV wrestling show to college kids.

I was cognizant that as booker my duties had multiplied with the addition of four weekly TV shows per month, plus our local shows. I really needed a booker to handle all this while I managed the logistics and Carver Reed, which, as my dad had brainwashed me to remember, was my bread and butter and was supporting me, my family, and my mom and dad. As fate would have it, I was handed a solution to that problem at an independent show in Jersey.

Around this time, I got a call from Dennis Coralluzzo, who was a local indie promoter out of South Jersey. He was running a big card as part of a wrestling convention at a hotel in Philadelphia, which violated our gentlemen's agreement to stay out of each other's territories—I'd stay in Philly and Dennis would keep to Jersey. But since he was part of this convention here in Philly, he offered me a percentage of the take and also allowed ECW to have a match in which we could feature some of our talent. We booked his champion, Spider, against our guy Sandman.

Dennis had WCW heel Kevin Sullivan in town for both his convention and the card that night. At some point before the card,

Sullivan inexplicably said the cops were after him and he had to bail. He was gone and Dennis now needed a replacement for him. Fortunately, there were a handful of stars still hanging around at the convention. I wanted to help Dennis out on his trip into the City of Brotherly Love, so I approached Kerry Von Erich, the talented though troubled star of Dallas's World Class Championship Wrestling and a member of the equally troubled Von Erich wrestling dynasty. He agreed to fill in for Sullivan.

A word about Kerry: He was a super Adonis type—looked great and moved equally as well in the ring. He could grapple, he could also fly high. He was great...when he was sober. This was near the end for Kerry, and there were reports of him falling asleep face-first in plates of food at restaurants, in full view of fans. From what I'd heard, Kerry was always a little slow on the uptake anyway. Add to that any chemicals he might've been taking and you've got a recipe for a scene worthy of the Marx Brothers.

I told Kerry we were going to make his appearance in the ring a surprise, so I wanted him to come out in a mask, known as a "hood" to a wrestler.

"Okay," he said. Then, "Wait...why am I wearing a hood?"

"It's a surprise, Kerry. Nancy will bring you to the ring instead of Kevin, pull off your hood, and the crowd will pop."

"Oh." He wandered off, wearing a blank stare while struggling to digest the concept.

The show was ready to start, and Kerry was there at the appointed time. So far, so good.

"Hey, man," Kerry said as he approached me backstage. "Why am I wearing a hood?"

Maybe he'd forgotten. It was an hour or so since I'd explained it, after all. So I told him that he was the surprise guest that night, and he'd come out in the mask, keeping the fans guessing until he ripped it off and revealed himself.

"Oh." And off he went.

The show began and I got the mask he'd be using for his match. I brought it to him, went over the match with him, and told him I'd see him out there. He stopped me.

"Why do you want me in the hood?"

I explained it again. I walked away wondering if I should just put on the damn mask myself and work the match, but this body isn't made for television unless it's on Cartoon Network. I just crossed my fingers.

The time arrived for Kerry's match and I watched my masked mystery wrestler step through the curtain...wearing a ring jacket with a glittery Kerry emblazoned on the back. I dropped my head into my hands. Maybe he'd realize it before he got to the ring and slip out of the jacket—only the fans seated on the aisle would've seen it. I picked up my head in time to see him prancing around in the center of the ring wearing a fucking mask with his name stitched onto his jacket. That was that. I didn't even bother to explain to him what he'd done wrong. He wouldn't have gotten it—he was too far gone. Sadly, he committed suicide a few days later.

Coralluzzo came up to me after the show and thanked me for helping out, which I was more than happy to do. Any show that does well in our area was a big rub for business. Besides, I did have a piece of this show due to his promoting it in my territory. I'd be nuts to have wanted it to fail.

"Just one thing," Coralluzzo said. "If my partner Larry Sharpe calls you, tell him we had thirty-five hundred people here tonight." Dennis was messing up his zeroes with that figure, and I didn't understand his motivation for lying to his own business partner. But there he was, asking me to lie for him on our first deal together. Talk about a red flag. I told him that was between him and Larry, and I wanted nothing to do with it.

It is said the universe has some balance to it. At the same event that featured the Kerry Von Erich escapade, I'd met Eddie Gilbert.

Eddie was universally regarded as a great hand in the ring, a great talker on the microphone, and he was a former booker for the Louisiana-based Universal Wrestling Federation and Alabama's Continental Wrestling Federation. I introduced myself.

"You book TV?" Subtle, wasn't I?

"You got TV?"

"I will."

Eddie agreed to meet with me the following morning before flying back home. We spoke about what it would entail to have him as a full-time booker—I couldn't have someone half-assing this. He said he was willing to move up here if I could guarantee him a thousand bucks a week. I made the deal with him, and I found him a corporate housing development outside Philly in time for our first taping at Cabrini College.

I had Steve Truitt—the sound guy who'd worked for free after coming to my office with Larry Winters and Bob Artese—doing commentary with Jay Sulli. Steve's on-screen persona was Stevie Wonderful, and I also had him working as a manager. I also flew in NWA legend Terry Funk to join Stevie and Jay on commentary. We had a multicamera setup run by Matt Radico and a friend of his. Eddie Gilbert showed up with three weeks of bookings and his friend Paul Heyman, whom I knew as Paul E. Dangerously from WCW television. Paul E was there to be a manager on the show and also to support his friend Eddie, with whom he had booked in Alabama. He was cool, and I liked his manager gimmick in WCW. Everything was set, but an absolute comedy of errors ensued.

First off, we got thirty-five inches of snow on the day of the shoot. If that wasn't enough of an impediment, we'd booked our live wrestling shoot on the college campus...during spring break. We walked onto a snow-covered campus with its entire student body back home sleeping. Our audience for the televised shoot was around forty people. We'd have to aim the cameras in such a way that the cavernous, empty venue wasn't shown. Unfortunately, the only way to do that would've been to point the cameras at the floor. Wouldn't have seen any wrestling, but you'd sure hear the slams on the mat in between Jay Sulli's awful play-by-play.

We solved the problem of the anemic crowd by asking them all to move. They were scattered around the ring in the first couple of rows, so we figured if we stacked them all on one side of the arena opposite the hard camera, that might give the illusion of a fuller house in our master shot. We explained our request to the crowd and they willingly obliged. That's a very Philly thing, that sense of community. People could've objected to moving from their first-row seat to a fourth-row seat just because we couldn't sell a show. But they just did it to help us out.

Unfortunately, that did little to help the bad, full-wash lighting of the gymnasium's overheads, lackluster in-ring action, and the indescribable announcing of Jay Sulli. Did I mention that yet? At least our Sunday audience was bigger than the Saturday night crowd. The snow had begun to melt and went from thirty-five inches down to about twenty-seven.

Despite all that, I was pretty elated after the shoots. We'd pulled it off in the face of some steep odds. I was walking away from that weekend in March '93 with enough footage for three weeks of pro wrestling TV featuring names the fans knew, like Snuka, Muraco, Gilbert, and Funk. I was proud of what we'd done.

I joined the broadcast team for the show's sign-off. I stood with Sulli and Funk and said how proud I was of our exciting show and told the fans they could expect more of that every week. That's when Terry Funk, one of my wrestling idols, picked up his mic and told fans, "And don't worry, it'll get better."

*Did he really just say that?*

I forced a smile, though it took the air out of me like a pricked balloon. The voice of God was pretty audible on the drive home, reminding me that I should get the hell back to work; diamonds are where it's at.

Or maybe that was my dad's voice.

Either way, I'd successfully gotten three weeks' worth of TV in the can, and I felt some momentum, however slight. I'd also met a very creative guy named Paul Heyman.

# CHAPTER 4

# ENTER PAUL

Eddie Gilbert was great for me. He was a hardworking booker with such a deep understanding of the business for a young guy. He was just thirty years old when he started working for me, and he was fearless. He was also in great shape and had a marketable look, with his feathered locks and manicured beard. He was well built without being a steroid freak.

Eddie had worked with Jerry "the King" Lawler in Memphis, and it was clear he idolized him. Eddie soon became "King" Eddie Gilbert on ECW TV, wearing a crown and cape and carrying a scepter. Eddie wouldn't only wear that to the ring—he would drag me and Matt Radico and his camera outside and wander around South Philly to shoot vignettes in his garb. We went into nightclubs without having given the establishment any prior notice and started shooting. Matt would turn on the camera's mounted light and wander onto the dance floor with King Eddie as he bumped and grinded in sunglasses, cape, and crown. The club goers around him were like, "Okay, whatever."

We took the camera to Jim's South St., a place that touted itself the "King of the Cheesesteaks." Obviously that didn't sit well with King Eddie. He pushed his way through the throng of South Street partiers to the window and let Jim's employees know it.

"You think you're the King of Cheesesteaks?!" Eddie yelled at the perplexed worker who was no doubt wondering why a grown man was wearing the remnants of a kid's meal at Burger King. "There's only room for *one* king in Philly, and that's King Eddie!" No one knew what the hell was going on, but Radico was taping it all. Eddie didn't give a shit what anyone on the crowded street was thinking. He walked around in gimmick like he owned South Street. He was trying to become our Jerry "the King" Lawler. The vignettes were hilarious. Eddie was a great performer.

Eddie's risk-taking was also coming out in his booking. I didn't realize just how similar to Memphis we were becoming, but it didn't matter to me. I hired him because I wanted that violence in the Lawler-booked product. The mainstream wrestling product on national TV was lacking that danger in the early '90s. The clips I saw from Memphis always looked like a crime scene. There was blood everywhere, and Moondog Spot was busting people open with chairs every week for like eighty-five weeks in a row. They did it on Memphis TV all the time, and I wanted that shit. If you watch our first couple of TV shows, you'll see Sal Bellomo running around smashing garbage cans over everyone's heads. Eddie was bringing Memphis up here, and I was happy. He just wasn't able to take it to the next level, but in its larval stages I liked what he was doing.

Paul Heyman was still accompanying Eddie to the shows. He was doing his Paul E. Dangerously gimmick, managing Eddie, Snuka, and Muraco. We started talking and hit it off. We had exactly the same sense of humor and our influences seemed to be similar, even down to the recitation of Bugs Bunny lines from the old Looney Tunes shows. I liked having him around.

There was one name I could never utter around Eddie when I suggested bringing in new talent. Anytime I mentioned Kevin Sullivan, Eddie wouldn't let me finish my sentence before cutting me off with a no. I never knew the source of that heat; I could only surmise. Maybe it was something over Eddie's ex-wife Missy Hyatt, who'd worked closely with Sullivan in WCW. Maybe Eddie and Kevin had more in common than just both being great minds, great bookers, and similarly built. Or maybe there was only room for one short, stocky genius in any wrestling federation. Who knew?

Eddie was a great person. All the workers liked him and he worked hard as hell. The only drawback was he couldn't get out of that Lawler worship. He even brought Lawler's kid Kevin to referee for us. He was always at Eddie's hip as his gofer, or "youngboy," as they call them in Japan. Everything he wanted to do in ECW revolved around Lawler and things he'd tried in Memphis. Eddie's girlfriend even looked like Lawler's wife. It was bizarre. But this is wrestling.

Eddie didn't shy away from risqué stuff either. We had a match booked between female worker Tigra and Sandman's wife Peaches where the loser was to have her top ripped off. I hated strip matches because they never delivered, and I didn't want to screw the fans. In what would become a staple of ECW's success, my booking was guided by my fandom. I loathed stipulations that weren't carried out, whether it was a promised unmasking that didn't happen or the breakup of a tag team that doesn't last. You might've seen those two specific situations handled properly in ECW's later years, with the masked Super Destroyers and Ian and Axl Rotten, respectively.

I told that to Eddie, and he said not to worry—someone *would* have their top taken off.

"You can't do that in the middle of the ring," I said to him.

"You can do *anything* in the ring." I guess he wasn't wrong, because I never forgot that. In many ways it was defining our style and would force me to reconsider some of the risk-averse booking decisions.

We obviously checked in advance with Tigra, a stripper, and Peaches, always down to help the show. They both said they'd do it if called upon. Until the night of the event, that is. Peaches looked outside and said there were kids in the audience, she was out. Exotic dancer Tigra changed her tune upon hearing Peaches wouldn't do it, despite having lap-danced two hundred men that week. So there we were, forced to either fuck the fans out of a promised finish or come up with some bait-and-switch consolation that would piss them off and make them distrustful of our next advertised attraction. It's generally bad for business, though unfortunately, it happens all the time in wrestling. I prepared to become one of the schlockmeister carnies promoting wrestling because I couldn't get a woman wrestler to pull out her tits in the ring.

That's when female wrestler Angel Amoroso spoke up from behind us.

"I'll do it." She said she was willing to get involved in the match and have her top pulled off for the fans that came to see that match instead of visiting the library. She saved the day. I was so thankful and told her she had a job with us for as long as she wanted. Sure enough, during a fracas in the ring, her top came off and the face of some kid in the front row, frozen in shock with his mouth agape, is the greatest frame in ECW history.

I felt Eastern Championship Wrestling was making moves, but it still didn't feel like we had a place in the national landscape. I confessed as much to Eddie.

"Where do you want to go with this?" Eddie asked.

"Can't we get national coverage? Jim Cornette has a small promotion in Knoxville, and he's in the newsletters."

"You want to get in the sheets?"

I did. We needed to start selling our VHS tapes outside the local market. For the first time since doing the bar shows, I thought we were ready for the next step. We were using more name talent like Funk, Davey Boy Smith, Road Warrior Hawk, and Ivan Koloff, who joined our recognizable regulars like Snuka and Muraco. I thought we deserved a spot in the national eye.

I don't know who Eddie called or how he made it happen, but ECW shows started showing up in the dirt sheets. That one thing, as insignificant as it may seem, meant the world to me. I was a bar show guy no more. I'd taken ECW from a granular idea to one that was airing on Philly cable television and now being written about in the national wrestling publications. Our talent list was growing, our television product was looking better, and now every pro wrestler in the universe that read the sheets knew our name. We were fast-tracking in the right direction.

I added another detail in an effort to move us up the food chain—NWA affiliation. The National Wrestling Alliance was the most recognizable wrestling organization for decades. The NWA was the umbrella alliance under which smaller territories throughout the nation fell, following their governance but also getting the weight of their recognition. The NWA world heavyweight champion would come through their local territory and face their top stars, drawing huge houses for the territory. In the kayfabe days of the business, being in the NWA was huge.

Though, in 1993, not so much. The NWA still existed in name, but national expansion and cable coverage allowed Vince McMahon's WWE to swallow the nation. The NWA fractured, and the national WCW emerged as the remnants of the territories that once existed. But Eddie was pretty insistent that it would add some validation and separate us from the pack of endless indies running all over the country. It couldn't have hurt us, and I suppose I was caught up in the nostalgia of the NWA's onetime grandeur, so I ponied up the crippling sum of $500 and joined. All it did was give us the right to use the NWA brand, and we became NWA Eastern Championship Wrestling.

There was never an NWA meeting and never any obligations at all, beyond paying. It was all bullshit by that point, to everyone except their executive board consisting of president Bob Trobich, Jim Cornette, Jim Crockett, Steve Rickard in New Zealand, Dennis

Coralluzzo in Jersey, Gary Juster, Howard Brody, and a couple of others. Maybe it was just a bullshit scam to them too. I'm sure they split my $500 evenly and put it to good use furthering the invisible NWA's business.

SportsChannel Philadelphia was the local cable branch of the larger, national SportsChannel America cable network. Whereas your local team's games would air on your local SportsChannel affiliate, SportsChannel America's programming was carried nationally. We sent them a tape of our shows and got a slot on SportsChannel America. There, before our very eyes, we had national television coverage. Airtimes were weird from place to place, and SportsChannel wasn't exactly the USA Network, but I'll repeat that—our local Philly company, just a little more than a year old, had a slot on national cable TV. It seemed like just yesterday I was telling Sandman that spitting on waitresses in our venues was a no-no.

I should've been dancing on clouds, but instead I was noticing some cracks in the foundation, specifically with Eddie. He'd begun missing editing sessions, and I had to step in and work with Matt to get the shows done. He'd give me an excuse here and there, saying he was sick or something came up. He only needed to come to the studio one day a week to cut that week's show, but he couldn't even manage that.

His behavior began to change also. One week I asked why he missed the editing session.

"I was sick," he said. "You don't fucking believe me?"

Jeez, I'd never said that. I'd actually not said anything but, "Where were you?" He hadn't spoken to me like that in the five or six months he'd been booking for me, so it was disconcerting.

I asked Paul E if he knew anything about his buddy's absences, but he said he didn't. Paul and I had actually been talking a lot more. We'd call each other a few times a week and bullshit about everything *other than* the booking. I know where your mind was going, but truthfully Paul and I were just becoming good friends. Nothing deep, just bonding over the things that we had in common, which, as I said, was a lot. We were *lonsmen*, which is a term used between Jews that doesn't really have an accurate translation. "Partners" would be closest; it suggests more than a friendship, more along the lines of kinship, a bond of common experiences.

Slowly and almost imperceptibly, the pieces on the chessboard were shifting.

\* \* \*

Paul E let me know early on that his work with ECW would be short term. He said Jim Crockett, the wrestling promoter whose product ran on Ted Turner's TBS for years, was starting an all-wrestling TV network called World Wrestling Network, not to be confused with the current streaming service of the same name. Paul said Crockett had tapped him to run the network, so Paul wanted to use ECW as a testing ground of sorts, bringing in talent to work with and prepare them for Crockett's TV.

"Don't pay me," he'd tell me. "I'm going to be gone soon. Just let me bring in talent and see how they do, and then I can take them with me to Crockett." That was fine with me, and that guy wasn't kidding when he said not to pay him. He was at all the TV tapings, helping out his friend Eddie, managing the wrestlers at ringside, and cutting promos for our shows, and I couldn't shove a dime into his hand.

Eddie, on the other hand, had used Jim Crockett's name as negotiation leverage. After booking ECW for a few months, he came to me and said Crockett had offered him $1,500 a week to work for the new network. I told him that was a great deal and I wasn't going to match it. He knew my budget and what an additional $500 expense would've done to us, so I knew he wasn't really expecting the 50 percent raise. But the truth was, he'd been doing great work, both in the ring and as booker. I offered to meet him in the middle at $1,250 and he took it. It seems small, but it added more weight to our growing expenses.

Along with his salary, Eddie's paranoia began growing as well. It might've always been there, though I hadn't seen it to that point. I always thought it was chemically induced, but later on I saw that same quality in Paul. I thought maybe they'd been friends too long, working the same territories too long. But it's a trait I'd come to learn was extremely prevalent in the wrestling business; it wasn't unique to Eddie and Paul, though their levels were off the charts.

Eddie was the first to show me that bug-eyed paranoia. At that point, Paul was just busy managing for us and cracking me up on the phone all the time. But Eddie would storm into the locker room waving the latest issue of one of the dirt sheets and start flying off the handle about something strange. One time he read me a news item that stated he was not going to be working in Alabama because he was booking for ECW in Philadelphia.

"You believe that shit?" he barked.

I didn't get it. "But it's true, Eddie. You're working here now."

"They ain't saying that. They're saying I fucked the promoter in Alabama and no-showed them."

He must've been leaving something out. I took the article from him and read it myself. He hadn't. He'd read exactly what was printed.

"Eddie, I don't get that when I read it."

"Look at the way he says that shit...'Eddie won't be in Alabama because he's booking in Philly.' That means I fucked over that territory."

I just handed him back the newsletter and shrugged.

A short while later he approached me about my friendship with Paul.

"What are you doing with Paul?"

"Nothing. Just what you have him doing on TV."

"But why are you two talking so much?" he asked like a jealous high school cheerleader.

I didn't really have an answer. I told him to give me a break and go write some TV.

We were heading toward our biggest show yet at Viking Hall, the space at which we'd begun shooting TV after the Cabrini College debacle and would later be known as ECW Arena. The lineup was heavy. We were bringing in Stan Hansen, who wasn't being used outside Japan at the time, to team up with Terry Funk against Eddie and Abdullah the Butcher, who was always a big draw. We also had the Headhunters, Shane Douglas, and Sherri Martel. The card was nine matches long and would feature a battle royal, a strap match, a baseball bat match, and a bunkhouse tag team match. We were going all out for this event, dubbed UltraClash.

Paul came to me while I was planning the big show and said Jim Crockett wanted to speak with me. Damn. He'd been one of the biggest promoters on the planet, and I'd seen him and his product on Ted Turner's TBS network a million times. Of course I'd take that meeting. I wasn't sure what he'd want from me, but it likely had something to do with the new wrestling network he was starting. Hopefully Paul had put a good word in about me and there was an opportunity for ECW to do something with him.

I called Eddie to pick his brain about this prospective meeting. He knew the business; he might have some insight.

"What are you doing with Crockett?" he asked.

"Nothing yet."

"You're with Crockett now?"

"What does that even mean? I own ECW."

"Why you meeting with him?"

"Eddie, I don't know! I'm coming to you because you're my booker."

We hung up. I'd always been up front with Eddie, telling him about every phone call and opportunity that came our way. Now he was acting like a wife who smelled perfume on my clothes. This was beyond normal paranoia and a definite shift in his personality. I began to suspect there was an addiction issue at hand, which our wrestlers would later confirm was true. Eddie had fallen into the grips of pain pills, and in no time it was turning him into an entirely different person.

We were just a couple of weeks away from the UltraClash show. We'd been shooting angles and promos leading up to the big night and assembling them into our weekly SportsChannel shows. Everything was in place; however, Eddie was late with that week's show. We had to get it to SportsChannel ASAP if it was going to air, so I drove out to the studio, where I found Eddie and his brother Doug, who'd been wrestling for us as the masked Dark Patriot.

"What's going on?" I asked.

"What's going on with *you*?"

"Where is this week's show, Eddie? I have to turn it in."

"Well, maybe I don't got it," he barked and glared at me. Then he called out to his brother. "Hey, Doug, let's go."

He got up, collected his brother, and they headed for the door.

"Are you serious?" I said.

"We quit. You wanna go work with Crockett, now you can."

I started after them. "I don't want to work with anyone. I'm telling you so you know what's going on."

"Go meet your Jew friend Crockett." And with that they were gone. I didn't even get a chance to explain that Jim Crockett was closer to being Amish than Jewish.

I was standing in the studio with a half-edited show, due at SportsChannel yesterday. Adding to what I thought might be a growing ulcer was the fact that I was again without a booker. I'd have to suck it up and just go forward. I was booking for all those months before I'd hired Eddie; I would just do it again.

My first order of business was to replace Eddie in the tag team main event. I wanted my selection to fill two purposes—first, to replace Eddie as booker, then to piss him off. I guess I was starting to learn the business.

I called Kevin Sullivan.

* * *

A rumor made the rounds that I'd fired Eddie over something he'd said about my wife at the time. It wasn't true. For all his growing troubles, he was never disrespectful to me. He might've said it, but I was never told about it and, therefore, couldn't fire him for it. It was a pretty innocuous comment for a wrestler, saying that she looked "good in jeans." That was it. Workers began to repeat that story, and I heard it for years afterward. Paul even came to me about it as we were getting friendlier.

"Hey, you upset about the jeans thing?" he asked.

"What jeans thing?" That was the first I'd heard about it, and guys ran with it ever since. I've seen it reported in the dirt sheets and mentioned in shoot videos. None of that shit happened. Eddie was getting fucked up and quit on me.

Word spreads quickly when you have national coverage. We were now appearing regularly in the newsletters, and our product was on SportsChannel America. Any booker has to deal with out-of-work wrestlers lobbying for a spot on the card, and now that Eddie was gone my phone began blowing up at Carver Reed. I was trying to conduct negotiations over jewelry when every five minutes one of my employees was poking their head in and telling me some guy was on the phone asking for me.

One afternoon, I was interrupted and told there was a Bob Merrian on the phone. I picked up the call and a deep, accented voice inquired about future bookings for ECW. I asked if he had ring experience.

"I been wrestling since 1980," he said.

"Have you been on television?"

There was a pause. "Yes. This is Bob Merrian, I said."

"Yeah, I got that." I just had no idea who the hell Bob Merrian was. "Is that your ring name?"

"Of course. Bob Merrian."

"Okay, Bob, can you just mail me a tape of your work please."

"I'm Bob Merrian. Don't need no tape."

This guy had brass balls. I was ready to hang up, but his moxie had me transfixed.

"Where would I have seen you?"

"All over," he said. "Been in WCW and WWE. Tagged with Warlord."

Warlord? The only tag team in WWE to feature Warlord was the Powers of Pain, where he tagged with Barbarian.

This wasn't Bob Merrian at all—it was *Barbarian*. His Tongan accent added a five-minute Abbott and Costello sketch to the call.

I was soon getting audition tapes delivered to Carver Reed by the sack. I had tapes from guys both with experience and also greener than Snuka's ganja. It was a good sign—I'd wanted national exposure, and dammit we had it.

Eddie called to apologize a few days after having quit. He said he was ready to get back to work.

"You quit, Eddie," I said.

"I know. But I'm ready to get back to work."

"That's not how business works. When you quit on someone, they have to assume you're not coming back. When you quit on me, you left me less than a week to replace you."

"And?"

"I replaced you."

"With who?"

I told him it was Sullivan, his archenemy for unknown reasons. There was a pregnant silence.

"Good luck," he finally said. I don't know if he meant it. He did ask for the opportunity to come back and just thank the fans at the show. We'd worked together perfectly for six months. He was a great asset at a crucial time in ECW's ascension. We were friends; of course he could come and say goodbye to the crowd.

Paul and I still spoke all the time, but we hadn't yet discussed any creative decisions for the company. He didn't seem to even care about our booking decisions—he was there to audition talent for the Crockett network. He was probably busy enough with that to worry about what was going on in ECW.

Paul had already brought a few guys down that seemed to have real promise. There was an impressive tag team called Public Enemy, comprised of Johnny Grunge and Rocco Rock, and also a good hand named Jason Knight. I knew they would eventually follow Paul over to Crockett's network, but I was happy to use them until then. They were professionals, and their ring work elevated the product.

UltraClash arrived on Saturday night, September 18, 1993. The show had already been booked by Eddie and myself, so I didn't need to worry about that. But there were a million managerial duties I had to handle throughout the night. Since Eddie had been booking as we grew, I didn't realize something—wrestlers on a big card will hound the booker all fucking night long. I couldn't believe it. Everyone was bugging the shit out of me with this idea or that concern. I couldn't even pretend to care about half the nonissues the workers were obsessing over. This wasn't WWE, with ten agents backstage handling all that. It was just me, after my ten-hour day at work.

The one match Eddie hadn't booked a finish for was the tag team main event now featuring Kevin Sullivan and Abdullah the Butcher against Stan Hansen and Terry Funk. Sullivan told me I couldn't have a clean finish, meaning a definitive winner and loser. All the names in that ring were big draws in Japan, and tape of this show would surely find its way back there. If it showed any of them jobbing—"losing"—it would kill their demand overseas.

"Let them just rip everything up and do their thing," Sullivan said. That meant all four guys would beat each other to bloody pulps out of the ring, through the crowd, and into the locker room. Double countout. Done.

After that, it was back to beating wrestlers off of me for the rest of the night. Paul E caught me looking as browbeaten and exasperated as I felt.

"What's wrong, buddy?"

I told him I couldn't fully tend to one issue without being swarmed by the talent. It was wearing on me.

"Let me help you."

With that, Paul Heyman became the most important person in the venue that night. He left me and proceeded to run interference all night long. He had me tell the locker room that he was handling any issues that arose and, man, did he. It allowed me to book the talent's finishes and oversee the timing of the card. I was free to book. Paul was a hero that night.

I've seen it incorrectly reported that this was the first show Paul booked for ECW. It wasn't. Eddie and I had booked Ultra-Clash and five shows beyond that. What Paul did that night was shoulder the minutiae that wrestlers cook up during a show and keep them away from me. I was so grateful, but the actual show was already booked.

Truth be told, though, I watched Paul work behind the scenes that night and thought I should offer him the booker spot, but I didn't broach the subject with him for weeks. I was hesitant because I knew he was leaving for Crockett's network. Was it worth getting all that momentum going with someone who had one foot out the door?

Paul was also still refusing any offer of payment from me. He was working on camera, managing, and doing promos like he did for any other federation, but he wouldn't let me pay him. "Just let me keep trying out talent here for Crockett," he'd say whenever I brought it up. He kept saying he only had a few months left before he'd have to go.

Paul was pretty pissed when Eddie Gilbert did his farewell segment in the ring that night, and he made a big scene in the locker room. He was yelling that Eddie was trying to undermine the show and make it all about him. It wasn't the most outlandish observation, but the level to which Paul was carrying on seemed excessive. It looked to me like he was putting on a show in front of the other workers, including Eddie's brother Doug, who was still doing the Dark Patriot character for us despite Eddie's quitting. Doug got angry at Paul for calling out his brother in front of the locker room and proceeded to smash up the room with a baseball bat. As angry as he might've been, that wasn't the way to handle it. That was Doug's last night with the company, and as far as Eddie and Paul's friendship, the sun had just set on that too.

In retrospect, Paul's grandstanding in front of the boys on the same night he'd told them he'd be dealing with the talent rather than me is poignant. Though he had no real authority and wasn't contributing creatively, the locker room would now see him differently, with an assigned authority. At the time, it was all just a series of unrelated events. Yet within a couple of weeks, the newsletters were reporting his apparent elevation in my company.

The following ECW Arena show is where Kevin Sullivan asked me to join him and Nancy the following day for lunch at the Marriott. Kevin is a crafty guy—the perceived shift in the locker room was obviously not lost on him. He also must've seen the rumblings in the dirt sheets that Paul had been elevated backstage in ECW. After my brief and telling introduction to Ric Flair and his comments on Paul, Sullivan began to offer me some advice, advertised as no strings attached.

Of course.

"Have you thought about where you wanna go now that Eddie is gone?" he asked.

He offered to help out "as a friend" and come along for the ride as just an informal consultant. "I just want you to know I'm not making a play for any official position here." He ended every sentence with "...not that I want the book."

Of course not.

I'd quietly had Paul in mind as my next booker and told Kevin I intended to make that move.

"Bright kid," Kevin said. "Not much experience, but a bright kid." He was feeling me out on how committed I was to that decision. He said it was a good idea and he hoped this discussion would stay between us.

Of course.

If I'd hired Sullivan as booker instead of Paul, things would've gone very differently for ECW. He would've added the blood and guts that was as prevalent in Florida, where Sullivan booked, as it was in Memphis. But Paul brought an element of cool that Sullivan would've missed. That hip-hop and grunge wouldn't have been in the stew, and that would become a big part of ECW's appeal. Under Sullivan, we wouldn't have been as young and in touch with edgy popular culture.

But I also consider how things that became problematic under Paul might've been better under Sullivan, and you'll be considering them too as you read on. But the one thing I really wonder about is Nancy. How might her course have been diverted if she and Kevin had stayed in ECW rather than heading back to WCW?

I eventually asked Paul how much money he'd want to manage on camera and also book the federation. He still said he wanted nothing. He reiterated that if he took the job, he'd only be doing it as a way to build the talent he wanted to take with him to Crockett's network. He was up front about it, and I appreciated that. I felt terrible allowing him to work for free, but I'm not exaggerating when I tell you he refused taking a penny from me. He explained it as my doing him a favor by letting him prep talent for Crockett's network while in my territory. And that's how it went, though I fought a sneaking hunch that he might be refusing money to mitigate any guilt he'd feel about raiding my locker room. He might take not only the guys he was building but also the ones I had made.

I brushed that aside and made it official in late 1993 when I told the boys Paul was our new booker.

\* \* \*

"Good luck."

That was the message from Eddie on Paul's answering machine. I thought it was pretty gracious given how their relationship had imploded. Paul, in predictably paranoid worker fashion, saw it differently.

"It's a jinx," he insisted, fuming that Eddie would dare to leave such a message.

"Maybe it just means 'good luck,'" I said. "Ever think of that?"

"No way. That message was meant to throw me off. You don't understand how those guys are."

Oh. *Those* guys, I thought. I left it there and we got back to work.

We were having a blast coming up with angles and talking about booking philosophy in general. We established our schedule, which would become commonplace for the next few years— 24/7/365. The guy didn't sleep and would call me at all odd hours, and whenever I called him, he was up. If I called him at seven in the morning on my way to the store, he answered on the first ring. If I called him at eleven at night when my kids fell asleep, he was still up. He told me to call him at any time, day or night. He still lived with his parents, and I wondered how many times he woke them taking calls.

Though Paul had taken the burden of dealing with the talent out of my hands, he was becoming famous for his disappearing acts. The guy told me to have everyone call him, but then he wouldn't answer the phone. One time Pat Tanaka called me saying I'd given him the wrong number to Paul's house, that it was a Spanish restaurant. I shook my head—I knew Paul well enough to know it was him doing some accent and saying, "There no Paul here." I saw Paul's strategy for handling the myriad wrestler issues—avoid them. Tanaka was furious, and I'm sure Paul was pissing himself laughing about it.

I would always say "we" when I spoke to the boys in the locker room, keeping that solidarity with Paul. It seemed the right thing to do—he was their booker, and I wanted him to know although I was the owner, our authority was in alignment. One day Paul pulled me aside.

"Hey, buddy, I want to talk to you about the 'we' thing." Paul thought it was actually adding confusion having the workers seeing two people in charge. "Tell them it's all me," he said. "I'll take the heat for decisions they don't like when they come to me. The decisions will still be yours, but let's not tell anyone."

That worked out well for me at the time. Managing my growing wrestling company, plus Carver W. Reed and my wife and three kids, was beating the shit out of me. Do I now think that was entirely the reason for Paul's suggestion? I can't say for sure. However, if I had to pinpoint one moment where the door was opened to the public thinking ECW was Paul's company, it was that. Many times I've replayed my telling Paul the talent was driving me nuts and his friendly offer to send them his way.

Paul and I had a great thing going. We talked all week, pitching wrestling angles to each other and just goofing around. I can't overemphasize how Paul and I would make each other laugh until we couldn't breathe. We were becoming best friends in the only way two workaholics could—bonding over our work. Paul had no other friends at all. He worked, then went home to his parents. As for me, it was Carver Reed all day, every day, then on the phone with Paul. I'd get home and spend some time with family, which Paul would interrupt. I'd get him off the phone until ten or eleven, when my family was turning in for the night, then it was Paul again. The next day I'd call him on my way to work. Ironically enough, I had a big, fat car phone like the one he used in his manager gimmick.

Paul was an only child and I had two sisters. Leslie was my best friend growing up, and I never felt lacking in that way, but at this point in my life, it was like I'd been delivered a brother. I cherished our time together, though I knew it would soon come to an end as the Crockett network deal loomed over us.

In late '93 we began to add a lot of new faces to the shows, both from Paul's New York connections and elsewhere. He brought down Tazmaniac and Tommy Dreamer from New York, and we'd added Sabu, Mike Awesome, Axl and Ian Rotten, the Pitbulls, and more. Terry Funk kept coming back for us, as did Kevin Sullivan and Jimmy Snuka. Our cards had gone from six or eight matches to ten and twelve. I wondered how many of those names Paul was planning on taking to Crockett when he finally left. But in the meantime, we were flush with talent.

Some concern blew through the dressing room with this influx of new workers. I heard grumblings from my guys who were there when we ran our first shows at Mike Schmidt's sports bar. They were concerned they would be edged out. Larry Winters came to me and said he was uncomfortable with the direction things were headed and didn't want to take chair shots every night he worked. I got it and I didn't blame him one bit. Guys like Rockin' Rebel and Sandman were hanging on but, in truth, Paul did want to replace most of the original crew with the new talent. I insisted that Don E. Allen remain. He was an undersized mensch who would do anything asked of him. His size, or lack thereof, was the only thing that prevented him from being a main eventer. He was also a great guy, and I used him as my right-hand man throughout many years in the business.

Paul came to me one day and said, "Sit down."

"Um, okay," I said as I sat.

"No seriously—sit down."

"I'm sitting! What?"

He sat beside me and leaned in close, intensity in his eyes. I thought he'd bite my face off.

"Fuck Crockett."

"Pardon me?"

"Fuck Jim Crockett," he said. "My heart is with ECW. I don't care about the network anymore...it's you and me, Tod. I'm all about ECW now."

Just like that, the Crockett move was no longer, and Paul's booking was for us and us alone. All that talent that he'd brought on as a tryout for Crockett—now all ours. He'd decided to make ECW his home.

I didn't know it at the time, but the Crockett decision had actually been made for Paul. Crockett had thrown in the towel on his network and moved to Texas to start an NWA territory there. But Paul's version is much more endearing, and a nice boost to my ego. He never came clean on that, but I found out on my own when I eventually met Crockett for lunch. He told me all about his plan to relaunch the NWA from Texas and proposed my hosting the world heavyweight tournament in my territory since ECW was the only NWA member with a TV broadcast. Though I didn't see much value in resurrecting the NWA, who was I to tell him that. Besides, the publicity in hosting a tournament would do us good. And, ultimately, it meant that Crockett's dream network was dead and Paul E would remain booker for me.

I was happy to keep him. He worked incessantly, largely because he had no life, but that was fine for me. I knew everything was in good hands while I was handling the other stuff, and we always collaborated on the booking. Though we never let the talent know it, we were booking together seven days a week.

I broached the topic of salary again. Now that Paul wasn't leaving for Crockett's network, he needed to be paid for his work in Eastern Championship Wrestling. He refused yet again.

"Pay me when I make your company profitable." I couldn't do it. I could not let him work all week long, booking with me, cutting TV shows, and sleeping on the floor under the damn editing deck without pay. I drew the line and told him if he wouldn't accept a salary, then I was gifting him 49 percent of ECW. He thought a 50/50 split was better, but I told him the company was mine and as much as I loved him and everything he was doing, there had to be one final decision maker. I founded ECW, so the buck would stop with me. He accepted it.

The reality was we were still losing money every month, but we were improving in other ways. We were putting on good shows, and our fans were amazing. We closed out 1993 with a big card called Holiday Hell at the arena the day after Christmas. You could feel something coming just around the corner. For us, that "around the corner" would happen on February 5, 1994.

Our February card was a regular monthly house show. We didn't bring in any big outside names other than Terry Funk. He'd been working with us pretty regularly and was involved in our heavyweight title angles. Our lineup looked pretty much as it had for the previous few months. But there was an energy in the packed building that night I hadn't felt prior.

We also managed to create a new match for that show. Our main event was something we dubbed a "Three Way Dance" for the heavyweight title between Funk, Shane Douglas, and Sabu. All three wrestlers would compete against each other at the same time. It proposed a unique challenge for the three participants in that they had to tell a story from three simultaneous perspectives.

It led to creative spots like the now famous double headlock. Those three guys put together what was the prototypical match of that sort. Three-way matches, called by various other names, have since appeared in all federations. But that one between Funk, Douglas, and Sabu was the first. History was made.

Our amazing audience was right there for the ebbs and flows of the entire sixty-minute match. I hadn't seen crowd reactions like that from any federation. Wrestling writer Dave Scherer told me a spectator's wife seated beside him passed out from the heat and fell through the bleachers, down to the floor. When Scherer told the guy, he couldn't even take his eyes off the match.

"Fuck her," he said.

Though I would've liked a happier ending to that story, it's undeniable that the fans' passion helped make that match. More telling was what I saw upon arriving at the nearby Marriott after the show, wherein Paul and I were greeted by a couple hundred fans. They began cheering for us, chanting, "E-C-W! E-C-W!" We had no wrestlers with us, and they weren't chanting our names; they were mentioning the company. This was next-level stuff. They were cheering us like we were the stars. Maybe we were.

We stepped into the packed bar and thanked everyone for a great show. The place exploded, and Paul and I couldn't help but exchange glances. We were both speechless—something was happening.

We went upstairs to smoke a doobie and process the scene downstairs and that night's show, which felt perfect. Smoking pot was another commonality I shared with Paul. It relaxed us. We finally sat down and put our feet up.

"No one gets a reaction like that," I said. I knew something had changed, and Paul agreed. WWE and WCW might get some fans waiting at the bars to see the wrestlers. Ring rats, a crude term for wrestling groupies, were customary in the bars and hotels, but not fans waiting to thank the owner and booker. This was special.

"Tonight we crossed the line," Paul said.

* * *

Paul and I always came up with titles for our bigger shows after the fact. Something would happen to trigger a phrase, and that would become the show's title for the videotape. When Paul commented that we'd crossed the line with that February 5 card, the title of the show was born. It was clear our popularity was growing, as evidenced by our getting an unprecedented order of twenty-five tapes from Japan. Word was getting out.

It was coming time to deal with Crockett's NWA relaunch and the tournament. Paul and I had to get busy if we were to proceed with the plan and crown an NWA world champion in ECW. Tournaments are usually the way new or vacant titles are awarded, but we didn't have the budget to host twenty or thirty names, especially if we were flying people in. We slated a show at our main building for summer 1994 as the night we'd crown the NWA world champion and make the announcement. As predicted, ECW got some ink as a result.

A few days after the announcement, we got some ink again when Dennis Coralluzzo, a member of the NWA himself through his South Jersey promotion I'd helped out with Kerry Von Erich, said the tournament was not happening. He was quoted in the wrestling media as saying he was the "deciding vote" and he was giving it a thumbs-down.

There was no real vote as far as I knew, and Dennis's preemptive strike wasn't really a surprise to me. For the past year, as ECW grew in popularity, Coralluzzo had been trying to sabotage us. Before we'd begun garnering national recognition, our gentlemen's agreement to stay in our respective states staved off any conflict. At first, I didn't know who was responsible for the calls to local fire departments reporting oversized crowds at ECW shows. We were never shut down, but we'd get a visit from fire inspectors who tried to count the crowds. Good thing many of our fans came just at bell time.

There were also a few occasions where new venues would get tapes of our most violent or sexually provocative angles with a note from a "concerned citizen" saying they didn't want this smut in their wholesome city of Dover or Montgomeryville. There were too many incidents for it to have been coincidental, and if it were some religious group on a mission, they would've proudly identified themselves and publicly chastised us. So I figured it had to be a competitor. I was putting two and two together, and one night I got confirmation courtesy of ECW's security head, Mark Shapiro.

During a monthly show in Philly, Mark called me to meet him at the door. He'd nabbed two guys flattening fans' tires in the parking lot and was holding them for me. I headed outside and was surprised to see Coralluzzo and his flunky Gino Moore. There was now no doubt in my mind that Coralluzzo was behind the efforts to shut down our shows. That was shitty enough, but to flatten our innocent fans' tires was a new low, even for independent wrestling. If he had a problem with our mounting success, there were a lot of ways in the free market to compete for our business. But he couldn't, so he thought crippling our fans would do something. That fan might've relied on their car for a job that they now had to miss, or they might've had an important doctor's appointment early the next morning for their kid. It was classless.

"What do you want me to do with them?" Mark asked as the oversized Tweedledee and Tweedledum sheepishly looked everywhere but toward me. There was a moment of skepticism as to their guilt as I looked at the two and realized they'd have to actually bend down to flatten a tire. Given their conditions, a jury might've found reasonable doubt.

What I should've done was call the car owners to the back door, show them their tires, and let them have ten minutes in the alley with the two stooges.

"How stupid are you?" I asked Dennis. "Couldn't you get one of your ten-dollar opening match guys to come over the bridge and do this?"

Dennis kept his head down and started biting his fat thumb, a habit that made him look like an awkward creep and not the promoter of a local, independent South Jersey wrestling company.

"Just get them out of here," I told Mark and headed back inside.

"Thanks, man," Dennis called after me. "Really, thanks, man." He was carrying on and I just went back to work.

Now, flash forward to my hosting the NWA heavyweight tournament. He'd resurfaced like the undead and planted a story in the sheets saying he would sink the tournament as the deciding NWA vote. Neither Paul nor I thought the NWA thing was a very big deal beyond the press we'd get. Hosting the NWA world champion in 1994 was like having the stiffest dick in the nursing home. Basically, who gave a shit? Crockett's having asked me to do it was actually the best indicator that we no longer needed the NWA affiliation. Clearly, the NWA needed ECW.

I stood with some egg on my face, as we'd already made the announcement, so I tried to convince Dennis to go along with it.

"Dennis, come over to Philly for the tournament. We'll wear tuxes and I'll put you on commentary as one of the NWA representatives." I decided not to reference my not having him arrested for acting like a two-bit juvenile delinquent in our parking lot last year but rather appeal to his ego. "Remember, we have TV. You'll be in the center of the ring with me presenting the new NWA world title."

Eventually he was on board and wanted to talk about who would get the title. I had to shut that down fast—I wasn't going to have this debate over a hundred wrestlers to whom he owed favors. This was my TV show; therefore, ECW was making the choice of champion. I'd share mine and Paul's decision with him, but unless there was a very good reason I wasn't aware of to veto it, he wasn't getting final say. I did promise that our selection would be someone who would work well with all of us.

Eddie Gilbert brought Shane Douglas into the company before he left, and I never let him go. I'll admit when Eddie first pitched him to me, I furrowed my brow.

*Shane Douglas? Of the Dynamic Dudes? Seriously?*

The Dynamic Dudes, comprised of Shane and Johnny Ace, were WCW's attempt at bleached-blond teenybopper heroes in the mold of the Rock 'n' Roll Express and the Fantastics. I was at the Philadelphia Civic Center as a fan watching them get booed out of the arena as the Philly fans cheered their opponents the Freebirds. They didn't know what to do. All the Dudes' comebacks, designed to excite the crowd as the heroes battled back, were laughed at. People talk about Philly being a "heel town," and that's what they mean.

I told Eddie my reservations in hiring Douglas, but he told me I had it all wrong.

"He ain't no babyface," he said. "Shane could be a great heel." I hadn't thought about him that way. So Shane came in as a heel on his first night with ECW. He came at a good time—we'd just started TV and were looking to fill time. We were using the same names every week, so any new blood Eddie could find was always welcome. I just didn't have high hopes for long-term use of the Dynamic Dude.

Boy, was I wrong.

Everything about Shane Douglas was different as a heel. It was so authentic—he knew how to be cocky and arrogant, yet dangerous at the same time. He wasn't the cowardly big mouth— he backed it up in the ring. He could wrestle, or he could brawl. His in-ring skills were fantastic, and he also looked great. But when he took the microphone—holy shit. He could talk like few workers I'd seen. He needed almost no direction at all. No one had been treated to seeing what Shane could do on his own, as a heel.

He had it all. After watching him work for a couple of months, it became apparent that with the right push, this guy could be huge. We made him ECW's first star.

Shane also had that innate sense of where the cameras were at all times. This is something a fan might not realize, but it's so much easier to edit video when a wrestler is performing his moves positioned in the best angle of the hard camera. The same is true of his turning and making a face in view of the handheld camera. Their moves and expressions are also being shown in the best way possible, so they're getting over too. Shane was like that—he'd drop a leg, cover someone for the pin, then roll over on his side and laugh right into the lens of the handheld, which he knew was two feet away when he positioned himself for the pinfall.

A few years later, our TV show needed some extra content because we were coming up short on matches for that week. We'd used the same footage on three of the last four broadcasts, and we literally had zero content. We asked Shane to cut a long promo, something that would feature him alone in the empty arena. He agreed to come in and concoct something. We told him not to be afraid to go along with it, hoping for a useable fifteen minutes after editing, if that was humanly possible. Shane, not a stranger to the sound of his own voice, gave us the task of cutting his *sixty-minute* promo down to forty-eight minutes for television.

An hour, without stopping. Find someone who can go five minutes without a script today.

Paul and I agreed Shane was ready to carry the company and was the natural selection to win the NWA world title tournament. A couple of weeks before the event, Paul suggested a name change. He said the "Eastern" thing could become problematic down the road. He saw us growing and thought we needed to be poised to play worldwide, and a regional name kept us down. I was open to it and he suggested the word "Extreme." Didn't sound particularly interesting to me, but remember it was 1994.

"That word is going to be *everywhere* soon, "Paul said. He referenced the rise in popularity of extreme sports and said it was going to carry right through popular culture among young fans. I don't know how Paul did that shit, but he was able to predict the future, and he was right every time I can remember. This was a remarkable skill for a guy that didn't leave the house and was socially inept discussing anything other than wrestling with the average person. After my mother met him, she asked why he never looked anyone in the eye. My brother in business was like a savant, and I was glad he was on my side.

Revealing the new identity of our company would have to happen with a bang. Where better than the NWA world title tournament? Press would be there, and it was sure to get major coverage. Anything that happened that night would make the wrestling news.

Little did anyone know just how far we would run with that.

* * *

I began to feel used by my fellow NWA members. I'd stuck my neck out in starting ECW after the collapse of Joel Goodhart's TWA, and I succeeded against all odds. I incurred the financial risk, learned to produce TV, dealt with the snowstorms, hired a star booker and lost him in the throes of addiction. I worked day and night, keeping the day business going to finance the night business. Now, with ECW in the spotlight and gaining the momentum only rocket fuel provides, the NWA affiliates wanted me to put on a tournament to lift their flailing promotions. It was clear what I was doing for them, but what were they really doing for me? For ECW?

Then there was the matter of our fans' flattened tires. Throw in the calls to fire departments resulting in the inspectors asking me to count the heads in the venues with them. The wrestling business is parasitic, built on bloodsucking. So many are either drawing life from someone, or someone is drawing life from them. I felt the teeth of Coralluzzo and Crockett pressing against my neck, and I recoiled.

For the two days prior to the tournament, Paul and I talked nonstop about how to handle this crowning of Shane Douglas as the NWA world champion. Paul first proposed using that tournament to lift ECW to the heights. There was only one way to do that, and it wouldn't be pleasant. We'd come to the conclusion that Shane would indeed be crowned a world champion, but of Extreme Championship Wrestling instead of the NWA. That NWA belt meant nothing, and by our supplanting it with the ECW belt, we'd be making a statement to the wrestling world. By doing it in the ring and on television, it would probably be perceived as our screwing the NWA. But I honestly didn't see value in that organization. It was beyond life support—it was less of a screw job than it was euthanasia.

But there were issues to work through. We first had to get Shane to go along with the plan. He was to win the tournament by pinning 2 Cold Scorpio, then accept the NWA title. After that, according to our plan, he'd have to publicly renounce the NWA world championship for the ECW world championship. We pitched it to him, and he needed a little time to consider the potential blowback he might face, professionally speaking. Paul looked him in the eye and said, "This is going to be the greatest night in the history of wrestling, and you'll be the only one in the ring."

Then there was the matter of the wrestling business at large. I certainly thought the value of the NWA banner had eroded, and Paul didn't give a shit about anything unless it could get us ahead, but others might not feel the same. Hard-liners and old-timers might think we were shitting on the history of the business and reject ECW out of hand.

But so what? Isn't that what I wanted? I'd always been anti-establishment while working *inside* the establishment. I owned a business on conservative Jewelers' Row and had men smashing chairs over each other's heads at night. If we were going to do this, we would have to live and die by that credo of being rebellious to the core. It wasn't a put-on—ECW would have to be where lifers gathered to say "fuck you" to the world. We certainly couldn't lure workers here with money, so we'd have to do it with a unique sensibility.

Paul and I spent three hours in his hotel room picking apart the possible repercussions. The only thing that worried me was the possibility of offending Terry Funk. He was a former NWA world champion himself, and he'd worked hard for us. Terry's presence in ECW gave us credibility, and he was the first big name I'd wanted to bring in. The ring veteran announced for me, wrestled for me, and was there for me. I didn't want him to bail on us, and I didn't want to hurt him. I guess I was ready to say "fuck you" to the world, minus Terry Funk.

We decided it was worth the risk. Shane was on board too, and we would be rebranding the company Extreme Championship Wrestling. I was glad Paul had suggested that name—we would keep the same letters, like marrying a second wife with the same initials so you could keep the bath towels.

The tournament we put together consisted of only eight wrestlers, which meant we could get the whole thing done in one night with just seven matches. The workers were Shane Douglas, 2 Cold Scorpio, Dean Malenko, 911, Chris Benoit, the Tazmaniac, Osamu Nishimura, and Borne Again. Only three of those names were regulars on our roster. I wanted to create a sense of importance to this tournament, with talent flown in from all over the world. A tournament with the same eight names our fans saw every month would lack status.

Everything was in place, and Shane, Paul, and I walked around before the show with this colossal secret we didn't share with a soul. Coralluzzo was there in his suit, ready to fill his role as

NWA representative for the tournament. His radar was definitely up. He was on edge all night, and I suppose I would have been too if I were walking into a dinner party hosted by the guy whose business I'd tried to derail so many times. Dennis was running around following Shane all night, flapping some NWA contract in front of his face trying to get him to sign it. No paperwork in the world would have indemnified anyone from the tidal wave that was to come.

The tournament went off as planned, and after a belly-to-belly suplex, Shane pinned Scorpio for the win and the title. I was sitting beside Coralluzzo at ringside the entire night, and when that bell rang, my heart was off to the races. I knew what was coming, and I was sitting inches from the guy I'd be screwing in five minutes. I kept reminding myself this was the final act of a violent opera in which he'd sung the first aria.

Shane was handed the NWA title, and he walked around the ring relishing the moment. He picked up the microphone and began the perfect promo, as he usually did. He started out by acknowledging the NWA champions of the past by name, shouting out Dory Funk Jr., the "real Nature Boy" Buddy Rogers, Ricky Steamboat, "fat man" Dusty Rhodes, and, finally, reluctantly for Shane, Ric Flair.

Then shit got real.

"They can all kiss my ass!" he screamed into the mic as he threw the NWA belt down like spent trash. "I won't accept a belt handed down to me by an organization that died, RIP, seven years ago. 'The Franchise' Shane Douglas is the man who ignites the new flame of the sport of professional wrestling. Tonight, before God and my father as witnesses, I declare myself the Franchise, the new ECW heavyweight champion of the world." He held up our ECW title belt and the fans cheered. "So tonight, let the new era begin. The era of the sport of professional wrestling. The era of the Franchise. The era of ECW." The arena then resounded with chants of "E-C-W! E-C-W!" That, for me, was like watching Da Vinci paint the *Mona Lisa* in person.

Not so much for Dennis Coralluzzo, though.

Halfway through that promo, Coralluzzo started nervously chewing his fat thumb again. "Hey, man," he said to me as he sensed where the promo was going, "he's pissing on the belt, man."

"Nah," I said, waving it off. "It's probably part of an angle he wants to do."

Dennis listened more. "Uh, no, man—he's pissing on the fucking belt."

Then Shane threw the NWA belt to the ground. "Well, yeah," I began, "it does kinda look like that...but let's see where it goes."

Well, we all know where it went—right up Coralluzzo's ass. He flew into the dressing room, enraged. It took everything in me not to blow snot out of my nose from busting out laughing. Paul E was there and came up to Dennis, arms outstretched, talking in his most soothing tone.

"Dennis, will you relax?" Paul said.

"No, I won't relax!"

"Dennis, we're going to put you on TV again."

"You are? When?"

Watching Paul work people is like watching a boa constrictor swallow an elk—you just can't believe the carnage being delivered by such a calm and calculating reptile.

"Don't you see, Dennis, this is great for you." Paul then switched into intense storyteller mode. "You're going to cut a promo for the cameras tonight saying you will strip Shane of the NWA belt! You'll be making yourself the kingpin of the entire NWA."

"Yeah?"

Coralluzzo looked as dizzy as the cartoon coyote as Paul led him to a corner to film his promo. We stuck some gimmick microphones into the frame to simulate a formal press statement. Coralluzzo reinforced his authority as an NWA representative overseeing the tournament and said he was heading immediately to a conference call with fellow board members Jim Crockett and Steve Rickard, where they would decide on stripping Shane of both belts, since Eastern Championship Wrestling fell under the umbrella of the NWA. He ended the brief press conference and walked off camera. Cut.

The problem was Dennis actually thought the NWA was a real thing and had some power to dictate to Eastern Championship Wrestling whether or not Shane was a champion. He seemed satisfied with his promo, and we told him it would be airing that Tuesday. He left Philadelphia wondering how we might all play this angle out over time. My promo, shot moments after he left, would answer that in definitive fashion.

We didn't show him any footage before the show aired, so Dennis turned on SportsChannel at six o'clock on Tuesday to see Shane's glorious in-ring promo, followed immediately by his promo wherein he threatens NWA actions against Shane.

Then came my promo, where I folded NWA Eastern Championship Wrestling and announced the formation of an entirely new entity—Extreme Championship Wrestling. We were no longer under the phantom auspices of the NWA and therefore bound to no one. Shane was the ECW world champion.

Right after my promo, we shot the closing scene of that week's show where the tag team Public Enemy crept out onto the empty set and stood before the Eastern Championship Wrestling banner. Johnny Grunge took out a can of spray paint and crossed out the "Eastern" and painted "Extreme" in its place. That was the end of that. No NWA. No Coralluzzo. We'd put them both in the electric chair, and Johnny Grunge and Rocco Rock threw the switch for the world to see on national TV.

Professional wrestling would literally never be the same.

## CHAPTER 5

# EXTREME

The dirt sheets covered our dramatic secession from the NWA, but there wasn't any significant reaction from the mainstream wrestling world. This just confirmed my feelings about how insignificant the NWA had become by 1994. I didn't even hear from Crockett, the catalyst for my starting the tournament in the first place.

The guys in our locker room were surprised by what we'd done. They were even more excited to be a part of something that had officially been branded as counterculture. Shane was strutting around like he'd been planning the screw job for ten years. I didn't blow up his spot and tell the boys he didn't know if he was going to go along with the plan until a few hours before the show. He'd done such an amazing job he could rewrite the story any way he wanted.

For ECW, it was back to work as usual. We'd recently begun running shows every weekend, sometimes even multiple shows. Our fan base grew to justify the addition of dates, and we wanted to give our workers as many paydays as possible. It was important to keep our core crew working enough so they wouldn't have to take dates from competing local promotions. We wanted our wrestlers to become known as ECW wrestlers. Doing so meant we needed to keep them working and stretch outside Philadelphia, while still being close to home base.

We ran house shows in cities like Wildwood, New Jersey; Hamburg, Concord, and Montgomeryville, Pennsylvania; Yonkers, New York; and Dover, Delaware, among others. New fans got to see the wild and crazy antics they'd been watching from the safety of their homes, up close and personal. Many of our die-hard Philly fans also followed us around like we were their favorite rock band.

We had talent from everywhere coming in and out of our arena. We put the high-flying Mexican *luchadores* on before it became the cool thing to do in WCW and WWE. That brings to mind a particularly embarrassing exchange. I was in the locker room at our Gangstas Paradise show in September 1995 when I saw Don E. Allen, a good worker from my bar show days, walking into the locker room followed by a kid. The ECW locker room is no place for a minor, and is probably no place for most self-respecting adults either.

I called over to him. "Donnie, are you friggin' crazy?"

"What's wrong?"

"You can't bring kids into the locker room."

He turned and looked. "He ain't with me."

At that point the five-foot-five Mexican *luchador* Rey Mysterio Jr. introduced himself to me. Oops.

Some of the stars that began to emerge in our company, sometimes referred to as "ECW Originals," made their big strides at that time. The first of these seemed to be Sandman. His surfer gimmick and surfboard were not long for this world, and Paul and I had a difference of opinion about how to handle him. The two of us were able to come up with angles without much disagreement, though there were times we weren't on the same page. The evolution of Sandman's character is a good example. The more I came to know him, the more I realized the surfer gimmick was wrong. I thought he'd gotten as much as he could out of it, and eventually

I told Paul I was going to have Sandman be more like himself in the ring. I thought he should avoid being a character entirely and just go to the ring as a badass brawler type you might meet in the bars of South Philly. Smoking, drinking, and fighting—that was his business.

So why don't we have him do all three in the ring?

"No way," Paul said. "You can't smoke in the ring."

"You can do anything in a ring." I thought back to the Tigra and Peaches match where Angel's top came off. Eddie was the one who convinced me you can push the limits of what could be done in wrestling. This may shock you, but the leash on morality is longer in our sport than in most places. Tits, cigarettes, blood, beer—all fair game.

Paul didn't agree, but it was my money and I made the decisions. Sandman took it and ran with it, and so did Paul, shooting Hack's segments all in black and white long before the New World Order did it on WCW TV. It was truly a team effort, all three of us galvanizing and making it work. It got him over and made him different from everyone else on the show.

We turned our attention to some of the other guys on our roster too. Taz was still running around as the Tazmaniac, some odd cross between the missing link and a bouncer at a Queens strip club. He hadn't gone full Brooklyn goon yet. 2 Cold Scorpio had debuted in June 1994 and, thankfully, became a regular for us after the NWA World Title Tournament. Sabu was a hardworking risk-taker who seemed to be made of rubber. He flew all over the place, landed hard, and bounced back. He was either impervious to pain or didn't let us see him suffer. 911 was a massive presence who couldn't really work, as is often the case with giants of the business, but we'd eventually help him find a cool niche in the company.

Some of the guys from my bar show days were still hanging around. Tony Stetson and Rockin' Rebel were there doing jobs—losing to the emerging stars. It was clear that guys like them, Don E. Allen, and Ray Odyssey were being outpaced by the ECW thoroughbreds. Add to that, we would continue bringing in bigger names from the outside and it was clear most of my bar guys were not long for this world. Though I could see it coming, Paul E was the first to say it, telling me they had to go. But in the meantime, they could still get some work and help get Sandman, Shane, and Scorpio over.

Bob Artese was still doing the ring announcements, but if it were up to Paul E, that would've ended too. I don't think anyone would say he was the best ring announcer, but he was who I wanted and thought the company needed. The fans loved him, and how many wrestling shows have you been to where you cared who the ring announcer was? Bob was part of our show, the *whole* show, just as the guy who mopped around the ring was. I'm not kidding—our faithfuls in the audience dubbed him Mop Guy and he, along with Bob, became recognizable parts of a Philly show without even trying.

"Bob stays" was my declaration to Paul each time, and he'd just grumble and walk away.

There were some ECW staples that fans may not realize were already in place before our emergence as Extreme. Back in June of 1993, I walked into the dressing area early to find a little guy with glasses sitting in his underwear, bleeding from the elbow, and there hadn't even been a match yet.

"Hi," I said. "I'm Tod Gordon, and this is my building you're bleeding all over in your tighty-whities. And...who the hell are you?"

He scrambled to get dressed. "I'm sorry, I'm sorry! Paul told me to come down here for a tryout. I was just getting dressed. I'm sorry, sir." His name was Joe Bonsignore, but he would soon become Joey Styles for us. He was bleeding after tearing his arm getting out of a cab with no interior door panels. He looked like a kid, with slicked hair and big glasses, but that innocence would later contrast with the violence of the product. He was a natural. His calls would later become iconic, from his signature "Oh my god!" to the always welcomed "Catfight!" when two of our lovely ladies began tearing into each other. He created little gimmicks in his interplay with wrestlers with whom he was conducting interviews. He'd slink backward from Taz, in fear for his life from a guy the same size as him. He'd act continually annoyed by the goofy and inept Stevie Richards. Joey was the perfect fit, and we'd never have known it if we judged the book by its cover. Or underwear.

Cactus Jack—more commonly known as Mick Foley—quickly became a name closely associated with Extreme Championship Wrestling. He debuted for us in June 1994, just two months before we rebranded. A funny Mick Foley story comes to mind when I think about the screw job and Dennis Coralluzzo. When Cactus first started working for us, I'd ride with him occasionally. He may be one of wrestling's most insane and dangerous characters, but Mick is soft-spoken, polite, and lives as clean as a rabbi. Cleaner—rabbis drink wine.

On one ride, I began bellyaching about Coralluzzo trying to get a particular show canceled. Mick knew Dennis and asked what I was talking about. I told him about the phone calls to fire inspectors and venues and how we were having a potential issue with one of the shows Mick was booked on. We might have to cancel it.

"Pull over at the next pay phone," Mick said. I did and he hopped out and walked over and dropped a quarter in. Within five seconds he was bitching Dennis out and using profanity, which I'd never heard him do before.

"You're going to fuck me out of a payday," he yelled. "You're taking food off my family's table, and I take that personally." He went off.

Tommy Dreamer was another name who was with us before Extreme. He'd been there for nearly a year and couldn't get over with the fans. Paul was so invested in Tommy, I started to wonder if he had pictures of Paul with farm animals. Tommy first came into the federation with the gimmick he was using in the indies in and around New York. He wore suspenders and had this bouffant hairdo that will get you booed in South Philly or blown in a bus station men's room. The minute our fans saw him, they hated him. Even after Paul took him out of the suspenders and threw a shirt on his body, the crowd still mocked him.

That all changed on August 28, 1994—the night after the NWA tournament. Tommy was booked in a Singapore Cane Match against Sandman and, upon losing, Tommy took the ten vicious lashings valiantly, yelling, "Thank you, sir, may I have another!" as his back welted. Hack wasn't going light on him either; it was brutal to watch. That display of balls changed the crowd sentiment, and Tommy was a major babyface from that night on.

Our locker room of misfits was ready to follow their two crazy bosses into the unknown and build some of the most memorable moments in wrestling history.

For better or worse.

\* \* \*

The ECW Arena is another iconic totem to the era of Extreme, and we were actually using it from early on in the Eastern days. It became the spot for our TV tapings just after the Cabrini College debut shows. It was originally called Viking Hall and used primarily for the storage of the elaborate floats used by the South Philly Vikings charitable organization in the Philadelphia Mummers Parade. It was a large warehouse, nothing more than a cold, empty square, used for storage, bingo, and little else.

A local Joe Pesci type named Carmen "Butchie" D'Amato ran the place for the owners, two lawyers I rarely saw. Butchie, known widely as Fucking Butchie, was a larger-than-life character with a gravelly voice out of a Cagney film—one with tommy guns.

Fucking Butchie charged us $1,000 per month for the arena, plus any damage we were responsible for. He was able to fix almost anything himself, which saved us some money by not having to call in a contractor whenever one of the four-hundred-pound Headhunters was thrown through a wall. That actually only happened once.

The place was always in some state of disrepair whether or not we were busting something up, which, admittedly, was fairly frequently. There was a leak in the roof for which we were not responsible but still affected our shows. Butchie would put down buckets to catch the flow from fifty feet above. Every time I asked about it, it was "being fixed."

"They called someone," Fucking Butchie would tell me, referencing the owners. "They're supposed to be coming before your next show."

The only thing that came before our show was more buckets. The fucking roof leaked all five years I used the place. It took a while for the shock to wear off that lawyers would lie to me—about five seconds. Fortunately, no one slipped and broke their neck. Fans and wrestlers alike just got used to stepping around the puddles for five years.

Weather conditions were always horrendous there. Summer shows were unbearable from the heat of the building itself; now pack eight hundred bodies in there and you're working in a big oven. There were some nights I'd be backstage for eight or ten hours straight without needing to take a piss. I'd sweat everything out over the course of the night. I could at least poke my head out the back door for some fresh air, but those poor fans were all packed in there for the duration. Their energy never seemed to wane, though.

Our advance sales were always low for the Viking Hall shows. I'd go into every card biting my nails that no one was going to show except the hundred people that bought tickets at Carver

Reed. The day of the show would come, and I was already on the hook for $10,000 in expenses and we would only have a few thousand dollars in advance ticket sales. Fortunately, on the day of the show I'd round the corner and see a line of fans stretching two blocks long. We always had a big walk-up crowd.

As charming as the signage on the building was—Bingo/Wrestling—I thought we could do a little better. Back when we started running the location regularly and it seemed we had a following, I asked Fucking Butchie about a name change. I threw him a couple of bucks and he agreed to make us a new sign himself, which he did for a fraction of what we would've paid retail. When fans pulled up to the building, they'd be able to see ECW Arena now, rather than bingo, Cozy Morley, or Spinal Tap.

Those fans kept coming to the Arena for years. They were joined by a growing audience from other parts of Pennsylvania, Jersey, and Delaware, plus people who drove down from Massachusetts or up from North Carolina, never to miss an ECW Arena show. We always cut it close to breakeven, but as long as the business could sustain itself, that was all I needed. The fan base was growing, and I could see this was a different breed of fan. *Everything* was different with ECW, from the unique commitment of the workers, to the dedication of our fans, to the synergy between me and Paul. We had lightning in a bottle, and the fans made it happen. I thought back to when Eastern did TV tapings and we'd asked workers to bring their families, wives, and kids to the shows to fill the seats. Now, the newly branded ECW Arena was so packed our workers could barely walk to the ring.

\* \* \*

Our locker room came to be known for our camaraderie. It was true—ECW's sense of brotherhood was an organic thing. It came out of our workers who weren't getting a break elsewhere finally being noticed for their talent and hard work. This company was chugging along like the Little Engine That Could, and everyone there knew it was due to our collective efforts. The locker room knew that our success depended on the person next to you, and the person next to them, and so on.

Wrestlers from the big companies would pass through ECW and comment on how invested each of our workers seemed in each other. One night, Road Warrior Hawk passed a bunch of our talent standing around our little twelve-inch monitor watching what was happening in the ring.

"Why is everyone watching?" he asked the group. "What's about to happen?"

"Nothing," someone said.

Hawk looked at them like they were crazy. He couldn't understand that they were watching each other's matches because they had genuine interest in what the rest of the team was doing. That was us. That was ECW.

It wasn't without some division, as is the case with any family, but anyone who got shit in our locker room deserved it. It didn't happen often, and when it did, it was usually the result of inflated egos as the company really took off. Later on, when Taz got his push and started a wrestling school in New York, he decided he and "Team Taz" needed their own private dressing space. Everyone just laughed at the goofy attempt at a power play. More on that later.

Anytime someone got out of line they were corrected pretty quickly, and that was it. Like the night Rockin' Rebel came to me complaining he was one of the only guys from the Eastern crew who never got a belt. I told him he could win the battle royal we were having that night that was to decide our champion's next opponent. Within a few minutes, I saw him telling his girlfriend in the stands. He also told Francine, a new trainee at our ECW wrestling school whom he would've liked to make his girlfriend too.

That was all Paul and I needed to see. We privately told every worker in the battle royal that Rebel was to be the first one eliminated. He came to the ring strutting like a peacock. He had no idea what was coming, and when that bell rang, nineteen workers rushed Rebel and forced him out. He was protesting as they were doing it, yelling, "Stop! I'm going over tonight!"

"You sure are," some workers said as they threw him over the top rope. He didn't come to me with complaints or questions. He knew why it happened; he should've learned that lesson in wrestling school, but he was obviously absent that day. That's okay—I was happy to teach it to him. He was a piece of shit anyway. He went on to do notable things like killing his wife and then himself, leaving his little children to find their bodies in the morning.

No one ribbed each other in the ECW locker room. No one ever messed with anyone's stuff or shit in anything. We heard about all that stupid stuff going on in the big federations. They all talked about wrestling being a brotherhood, but they didn't know what that meant. Most of them would fuck each other over in a heartbeat for a segment on TBS or USA Network. So many of them did. We had no cliques or shit stirrers.

Paul and I always listened to the workers; they had a voice in ECW and took ownership of what they did. No one was told they'd have to be a rooster or a garbage man. Though not every worker's idea was a good one, and you can't run with them all, if you don't listen you might miss some good stuff. Take, for example, Sandman. Hack lived the business and absorbed everything around him like a sponge, giving him as great a mind for the business as any of the boys, and better than most.

One of the best examples of this was "Funk in a Box"—a clever reveal of Terry Funk's return to ECW during one of Sandman's matches against Cactus Jack. Sandman had a concussion and couldn't wrestle, so we needed a replacement for him. We knew Funk had to make a surprise return, so we planned to bring him out during the match somehow, ostensibly to face Cactus as Sandman's replacement. We'd planned to have him come out of a box sitting at ringside, which is a classic wrestling ploy, so much so that wrestling manager and historian Jim Cornette famously proclaimed anything that comes out of a box instantly gets over with the fans. Sounded good to us! We'll have Sandman get thrown in a big box, and when Cactus reaches in to pull him back out, he'll be pulling out Terry Funk instead.

We added a fun little swerve to it. Hack would first open the box to reveal DC Drake, one of the Eastern originals and, quite honestly, a disappointment for fans expecting a worthy opponent to Cactus. Drake was dispatched in minutes by the ferocious Jack. Then, after the fans were booing and shitting on the match, Sandman could get thrown in the box, and Funk's reveal would happen. We told Hack the plan.

On the night of the show, Hack arrived at the building with two sets of identical, loud American flag pants—one for him and Terry Funk each to wear. He had two red T-shirts as well. Cactus would reach into the box and retrieve who we all would think is Sandman, in his loud and easily recognizable sweats, though his face would be shrouded under a blanket. Cactus would continue to work with "Sandman" until he pulled off the cloth and revealed Funk. It was the addition of that twist, the identical outfits, that gave us an audience explosion from what was already a guaranteed pop. Plus, the earlier disappointment from the DC Drake reveal added fuel to the combustion. But that's Hack—always thinking, always working an angle until it was perfect. Paul and I knew that our greatest asset was not only our workers' bodies, but their minds too.

\* \* \*

ECW wouldn't have become what it did without our fans. Every performer says that, every popular rock band, and it's true every time. But ECW's specific brand of fan—smart, dedicated, passionate—clicked with our product in the way that makes something more than the sum of its parts. There were regulars who attended the monthly ECW Arena shows and got their same seats each month. They, like everything else we were doing, were becoming part of the show.

I did my best to keep a polite distance from the fans. I was still part of the ECW show and couldn't cross that line. But I did come to know a few of the regular fans more intimately. One guy called himself Mr. ECW, which was fine. But then he had business cards made up that said Mr. ECW. That was not cool. I thought it might make people think he was working for us in some official capacity, and who knew what shit this guy might've done out there in the world. I had no reason to believe he was a social miscreant, other than the fact he was at our shows each month, but I knew he couldn't be walking around with an official business card with our company name on it. I told him so.

"I made a thousand of them," he said.

"Throw them away. *I'm* Mr. ECW, and you're in the front row. Get it?" He did. As a consolation, I let him hand me a cookie sheet that I smashed over Fonzie's head during our match at the Arena. He was elated.

Paul Meles was another guy fans came to know as an ECW regular, dubbing him "Sign Guy" because he held up handwritten signs at every show. He was always seated across from the hard camera, and his signs were on TV every week. He must've brought thirty signs to each show and had one ready for anything we did. They were clever and always drew our attention. Sometimes he held up shit that no one was supposed to know. I never figured out where he got his news from, but his ear was pretty close to the ground to have known some of the things on his signs.

Sign Guy used to buy his tickets at Carver Reed, and one day he came in and said, "So, you're bringing in Rick Rude?"

I'm telling you, *nobody* knew about that except Paul, me, and Rude. The boys didn't even know until he showed up, but somehow Paul "Sign Guy" Meles had the inside track. I played dumb and didn't sell the question, but I was thinking, *Holy shit, how does he even know this?*

During Cactus Jack's feud with Terry Funk, Meles held up an infamous sign that read "CANE DEWEY." Dewey was Cactus's toddler son and that wasn't public information, but somehow Meles had gotten the name. He then created the sign that asked a Singapore cane–wielding wrestler to beat Cactus's child. When Cactus turned heel, he referenced that sign in his promo as evidence that the fans were not worth suffering for. It was a brilliant stroke by Mick, choosing the fans as the ones who turned him into a bad guy.

That heel turn was another example of an angle being improved due to a worker's contribution. Paul and I thought it was time for the turn, and we told Cactus. He balked.

"Me, a heel? In Philly?" He realized the problem we already knew we had. It would be practically impossible to turn our fans against Cactus Jack. He was already vicious and violent, and the people loved him for that. Making him commit dastardly deeds would likely just get him over more. We had to find a way to make him hated, and we posed the challenge to Mick.

"Let me work on it," he said. Then about a week later he came to me. "Tod, I got it. I'll refuse to do anything hardcore. I'll pick up a chair, and tease it, then have second thoughts. I'll see the fans calling for the chair shot...and I'll drop it. Then I'll start to grapple with all my opponents." It was brilliant. By not giving fans the dirty tactics they wanted from him, Cactus would piss them off. He knew that just insulting them on the mic wouldn't irritate smart fans, but depriving them of what they'd paid to see from him would annoy the shit out of them. Needless to say, Cactus's stroke of genius wound up being the perfect way to turn the next-generation fan against a wrestler.

I liked the challenge of booking for fans as smart as ours. They read all the sheets too and knew the inner workings of the business. When 2 Cold Scorpio eventually left us for WWE in 1996, I had some fun with our audience. When the news of Scorp's signing hit the sheets, we scheduled a "Loser Leaves Town" match between him and Devon Storm on his last date with us. The crowd naturally expected Scorpio to lose and the up-and-coming Storm to get the push, but we had him beat Storm in less than a minute and send him packing. Scorpio wasn't satisfied and sought another challenger, prompting JT Smith, my guy from the bar shows who'd had the misfortune of being painted white in the ring, to answer the challenge. Fans thought this would be the send-off for Scorpio, with JT getting the run now, but they reeled when he beat Smith in thirty seconds, also sending him out of the federation for a time. The crowd was really popping now, and Hack Meyers came out next, only to be quickly dispatched as well. Finally, Louie Spicolli came out and beat Scorpio in his fourth match of the night, but not before we'd had some fun and tricked the smarts, further endearing them to ECW.

If you listen to fans, they'll create angles and gimmicks for you. The aforementioned JT Smith was a perfect example of this. One night, JT blew a spot in the ring. Years before ECW, wrestling fans would not have even noticed the mistake, but our sophisticated fans started the chant, "You fucked up! You fucked up!" Yes, in wrestling, that's what sophisticates do.

I pulled him aside after the match and said I thought he had a gimmick there. Just what every pro wrestler wants to hear—your niche will be the guy that messes up.

"If you can make the mistakes look real," I said, "I think they'll pop when you mess up." I told him to trip on the ring apron the following week and we'd see if the fans picked up on it. Our crowd didn't disappoint. "You fucked up!" rang out, and JT had his new gimmick. Fans came to expect it on each show. Our cards were like *The Rocky Horror Picture Show*, with predictable fan partici- pation for things like JT's blunders and calling out Hack Meyers's punches thrown and received with a corresponding "Shah!" and "Shit!" respectively. And just as *Rocky Horror* fans showed up with props, so did ECW fans, albeit carrying frying pans and cookie sheets to be used as weapons by our wrestlers. I don't think any other wrestling federation ever encouraged fan participation to that degree. Our front-row fans would light up when their personal cookware was wrapped around Balls Mahoney's head.

After a while I figured JT might end up killing himself falling out of the ring or off the top turnbuckle, so we needed some- thing else for him. South Philly is a heavy Italian stronghold, and it could be rough for a black guy even driving through that part of the city. There was a fair amount of racism there, and I thought having JT come out to Frank Sinatra songs might be enough to have him work heel. The first few times it worked like a charm—fans were booing him to death. Then after a few months, something happened. The gimmick grew on the fans, and they started popping for the entrance. Just like that, we had a black fan favorite coming out to Sinatra in South Philly.

Our buildings were filled with five hundred co-bookers nightly.

* * *

Our TV shows also became a defining element of our product. Public Enemy's spray-painting the word "Extreme" on the ECW banner was more than practical. It was proving symbolic as the show became more edgy and street. We were using contempo- rary '90s grunge music from bands like Alice in Chains and White Zombie on our shows without a thought given to copyright. We were lucky—we never heard from a band or publisher. Paul added a cutty, whip-around promo format he called the "Pulp Fiction," so named for our use of the song "Misirlou" that was featured in the Quentin Tarantino film. Paul was very in tune to all things pop culture, and we used his suggestions all the time. That's the kind of *cool* that Sullivan and Gilbert would not have been able to bring to the table. Or Gilbert and Sullivan, for that matter.

In the early days of Extreme, Paul and I worked through all the promos and angles during our phone calls throughout the week. We had everything down before we arrived at the building for the tapings, and most of our talent was able to take a promo concept and just run with it. Paul and I valued charisma as much as anything else, and workers like Shane Douglas and Raven could nail promos on autopilot. And if you don't believe me, just ask Raven.

We shot our promos after the ECW Arena shows. It made logistical sense to work that way, since everyone was together in one place. Additionally, we could incorporate anything that happened at the show into the promos. The only tough thing was we wouldn't start until after midnight. The bars all closed at around two in the morning, and the guys were usually itching to get the hell out and start the party. The guys that shot first could get out, but anyone scheduled down the list could be there until three o'clock.

I noticed one of Paul's quirks during our late-night promo sessions, in regard to his ordering of particular workers' interview segments. He was fine staying at the Arena until 4:00 a.m. He had no friends and no life outside wrestling. I don't say that as a flippant jab—Paul literally went nowhere for fun and lived with his parents. He was in no rush to get back to a hotel or the bars after a show, because he didn't party. As far as I knew, I was the only one he smoked weed with. One night during a show at the Montgomeryville Farmer's Market, he made me drive around the parking lot for twenty minutes so we could polish off a joint before going inside.

Though Paul was fine shooting promos all night after a card, most of the guys were not, and I noticed Paul would schedule the talent's promos based on how he felt about particular workers. Ian Rotten, whom Paul hated for no discernible reason, was consistently slated to record nearly last every time.

"I hate the fucking guy," Paul would mutter to me privately when Ian's name came up.

"Why?" I asked. "He doesn't bother you."

"I just can't stand him." He never explained beyond that, and he kept Ian sitting on his big ass until three in the morning on promo nights. He did the same thing to Jason, keeping him around until he nearly face-planted from exhaustion. He'd worked in the ring for us and waited around the Arena watching hours of promos before his thirty-second spot was up.

Joey Styles's commentary was a big part of our TV show's identity. The spectacled, gel-haired nerd hosting our shows each week was in stark contrast to the gritty violence on-screen. Most companies would have opted for a rugged ex-wrestler to do that job, but that was just too predictable. Joey Styles was like our viewers, firmly on the outside, being invited into the raucous party inside.

Joey's voice-over commentary of the matches ran from start to finish in each segment, right over the ring announcements of Bob Artese. That was a Paul E move, as he hated listening to Artese's announcements. He had Styles start the commentary as soon as each segment began and drowned out Bob's voice. Paul had a real hard-on for him. He called me one night and said he had nightmares where the only thing that he could hear was Artese saying, "Shaaaane Douuuuuglaaaaaas."

One night Paul was in the ring giving Artese a cue to announce a surprise entrance. Paul stood beside Artese and whispered instructions, but Bob didn't say anything. Paul then covered his mouth and said it louder, which also got no response from Artese.

There was a worker standing behind the curtain waiting for their announcement, and Artese stood like a statue beside a flustered Paul, who began calling the spot even louder. It would've gone much more smoothly had Artese let us know he was deaf in one ear. He eventually saw a furious Paul's mouth moving and turned his head to the good ear and finally got the message.

Artese was hosting the ECW hotline when it launched. This was a 900 number that charged by the minute for inside scoops from our locker room and spot shows. Bob was doing it for free from his house and probably never even got reimbursed for his expenses. Soon, Paul asked Joey Styles to replace Artese for a 50/50 split of whatever the phone line brought in. We had Joey plug it on the weekly TV show, and naturally fans wanted to hear the voice they heard on TV each week when they called. Fans loved Joey. At shows he got a bigger pop than me, the owner of the damn company. He was very good at what he did and deserved the accolades.

There were times I could tell Joey wanted to be in that ring. He was not a wrestler, though, and I'm glad he never made the mistake of thinking he could be. However, this kid was tough as hell. One time in Matt Radico's office, Rockin' Rebel and Joey were going back and forth and Joey had heard all the "oh, look at the tough guy announcer" he was willing to stand. They mixed it up and had to be separated.

But Joey's most famous locker room incident became part of wrestling lore when the man believed to be one of the toughest in any locker room, WWE's JBL, was hit and taken down by Joey. He'd had enough of JBL's bullying, and his Italian temper kicked in one night in the WWE locker room. A lot of wrestlers lived vicariously through Joey when they heard he'd closed that big mouth on JBL, for one night anyway.

Our TV was hitting the demographic we targeted, we had an arena with a crowd full of regulars every month, and our spot shows were catching on. But the thing that best defined our product was the amazing group of guys and gals I was happy to hand a check to every weekend. You'll now get to know them as I had, and I know they'll be as unforgettable to you as they are to me.

# CHAPTER 6

# THE POSSE

My tightest-knit group of workers, dubbed "the Posse," consisted of me; Sandman; his wife Lori, who would work as manager Peaches; Bill Alfonso (herein "Fonzie"); 2 Cold Scorpio; and Nancy Sullivan, while she was there. Kevin Sullivan rode with us for a short time until he went back to WCW, but he left Nancy in Philly with us for reasons I don't know. That was fine with me—Nancy was like a sister to us, and she fit right in. It wasn't planned; she was road tested and could roll with us wherever we or our conversation went. She was actually instrumental in Scorpio and Fonzie becoming part of the Posse, having worked with both of them in Florida and WCW, respectively. She vouched for them, saying they were good guys, trustworthy, and they'd fit into our crew. We opened the door to them, literally and figuratively, and they never got out.

Nancy was sweet as anything, but she knew the business from knocking around it with Kevin. She carried a switchblade in her boot, though I don't think she ever needed to use it. Everyone loved Nancy. When the night was over, she'd say goodbye and head to her room. She never partied with us, never fucked around with the boys, and never got into any trouble. Nancy never opened the door to her personal life either. She was the quintessential lady in a business where that's as a rare as a Rhodes Scholar.

We would ride to the shows in the back of Hack's van, with him at the wheel. He had only one rule for riding in the Sandman van— no radio. He wanted us to talk. It resulted in our being immersed in stories from the business, our lives, and everything in between. We shared a million laughs with about as many six-packs and joints. I was never closer to any group of people in my life, and the same likely rings true for the rest of the Posse.

Fonzie came to ECW on the heels of having refereed everywhere imaginable. He reffed some of the most iconic matches in history and would regale us with those tales as we rode. He was modest about it, though—so much so that we didn't know he was involved in some of those matches until months after he was riding with us. Take, for example, the classic steel cage match between Lex Luger and Bruiser Brody in Florida. This was a match wherein the always difficult Brody would not sell any of Luger's offense, causing Lex to become so fed up that he just climbed the cage and left. Someone referenced it while we were driving to a show in the Sandman van, and Fonzie commented from the back.

"Yeah, I was the ref for that, daddy," he said, invoking his catchphrase used on camera and off.

The van fell silent. Fonzie had been riding with us for months and never talked about reffing one of the most notorious matches in the Florida territory's history. The same thing happened for years when someone would bring up a big Dusty Rhodes angle or major title change and Fonzie would reveal he was the ref. We were shocked every time, until we weren't.

Then there was the time Hack almost drove off the road when Fonzie said he once punched the legendary Dusty Rhodes in the face. At first we thought it was part of an angle—Dusty hits the ref, the ref hits Dusty, or something stupid. But Fonzie was just fucked up and being driven home by his booker. Stranger still was the fact that Dusty was doing Fonzie a favor by going two hours out of his way to drive him home to Tampa. And when they arrived at Fonzie's house and Dusty woke him from his stupor, he leaned over and punched Dusty in the face as hard as he could.

"I don't even know why I did that, daddy," Fonzie said, recounting the story that now had everyone in the van pissing ourselves. To his credit, Dusty apparently rolled with it.

"Fonzie," Dusty had said, "I'm gonna let you live, 'cause I know you're fucked up." That's what it was like riding with the Posse— you never knew what was going to come out of someone's mouth.

I would become close to some of the other guys that would occasionally ride with us, like Sabu and New Jack, each eventually becoming known as "one of Tod's guys" when there was some splintering in the locker room. Some workers were designated as "Tod guys" while others would be seen as "Paul's New York guys." But my core was the Posse, a whole other category, and we remain best friends to this day, with one tragic exception to be covered later.

I was still working at Carver W. Reed in the daytime, so on Fridays I couldn't head out to shows until I shuttered the store. My Posse would pick me up in the Sandman van at four in the afternoon with a cold bottle of water waiting for me. That always meant something to me, and I know it sounds stupid—a one-dollar bottle of water, so what? But the fact that the Posse was thinking about the one guy they hadn't picked up yet, who might've had a hard day at work, was significant to me. If it was WWE, someone would've pissed in the water or put thirty-five crushed Xanax in there so I'd pass out and they could shave my eyebrows. But I didn't have anything to worry about with the Posse. We looked out for each other.

* * *

## SANDMAN

I could easily fill this entire book with stories of Sandman's exploits. Since he wouldn't remember half of them, I'll dedicate this chapter to just a few highlights. I'll be referring to him as Hack, which is what everyone in the business called him. Never once have I ever heard him called anything but Hack or Sandman. When asked how he got the nickname and why, he said his brother called him that as a kid and he had no idea why. Everyone in his life has called him Hack since.

We were the odd couple. My whole persona was the suit-and-tie businessman, with intellect being my greatest weapon. Hack's persona was the guy with no shirt regardless of the weather, back-pocket snot rag (his term for what actually was a washcloth), and being the loudest guy in the room, any room, including the locker room.

As I mentioned earlier, Hack was banned from the first shows I ever promoted at Mike Schmidt's bar. Getting him out of that first jam would be the first of too many to count. We basically hit it off from the jump, and I proudly still call him my best friend thirty years later. From the outside, fans think he's just some bar-brawling drunk, but that couldn't be further from the truth. Besides our being born on the same day, we both share an intense love for Philly's four major sports teams. When we weren't locked in a debate about one of them, we would ride and test each other's knowledge.

"Name the starting lineup and batting order of the [whatever year] Phillies."

"Who did the 76ers get in the Wilt Chamberlain trade?"

It was endless.

In his home life, he was a phenomenal father who was totally involved in his kids' day-to-day lives. He immersed himself in the History Channel and National Geographic Channel and was always interested in learning. No ride was complete without him turning to Scorpio, Fonzie, and me with a question like, "Do you know how many years this planet has left if we don't do something about the fossil fuel situation?"

We would all stare blankly as he told us the answer. As I said, not the guy you'd expect when watching him pound six-packs, but it does better explain our friendship.

Hack hit his stride when he shed the surfboard and traded the surfer gimmick for no gimmick at all. Hack's no-frills brawler became as much a character as anything that could've been drawn out on paper. He smoked, drank, and beat the shit out of people after first victimizing himself by guzzling an entire can of beer and smashing the can against his own head. And that was just during his ring entrance; he was often bleeding before the bell rang.

Hack is truly one of those closet geniuses whose wisdom shines through despite his repeating every story a hundred times and meeting you for the first time every time he meets you. I don't think Sandman would mind my telling you he's been in rehab for alcohol and drugs. Then again, odds are he wouldn't remember that I wrote it a few seconds after reading it, so no matter. Hack's challenged memory could be a result of either too many concussive chair shots to the head, the years of chemical abuse, or more likely, both.

When I first started ECW, Hack wasn't much of a drinker. Even later on with Extreme's busy road schedule, he would ossify himself on the weekends and didn't drink or smoke during the week. He was the classic case of the weekend alcoholic. Eventually, years later, he adopted the weekend lifestyle as a full-time gig.

It got him in trouble from time to time. One of those times involved the Bruise Brothers, twins Ron and Don Harris. They were a huge tag team, each of them six foot five and three hundred pounds, and they were both badasses. One night I noticed they'd added some new ink to their arms in the form of Nazi "SS" emblems. I couldn't believe these two were walking around with them in front of their two Jewish bosses. I went to Paul and asked if he'd seen it. Paul's mother was a Holocaust survivor, and he was as dumbfounded as I was. Eventually they put bandages over the ink while they worked, and I believe they've had them changed into a different design now.

One night they were scheduled for a tag match involving Sandman. One of the brothers had just had stitches put in his head, so he requested that Sandman not cane him there. He'd take the whacks everywhere else but the head. Wouldn't you know it, the bell rings and Hack starts whacking them both everywhere, including their heads. After the match, Hack was outside the building getting some air and both brothers came out and started beating the shit out of him. There were no words exchanged—the door opened and fists and forearms were flying. Hack didn't know what hit him. He was yelling, "What? What'd I do?" as he was being beaten. They didn't answer, just let their fists do the talking. New Jack, of all people, ran out and broke it up.

"They asked you for one thing," I said to him later, "*one thing*—hit him anywhere but the head. Anywhere! Cane the shit out of them, just not the head."

"Fuck." Hack just shook his head. "Why do I do those things?" Was he now going to start some introspective journey into his laundry list of fuckups and what was behind them all? I helped that process along.

"Because you're a drunk," I said. It didn't require Columbo to solve that one.

My personal relationship with Hack allows me to tell you that he is also the most stand-up, loyal, honest friend anyone could ask for. If someone offended me or became aggressive toward me, he took it as a personal shot at him. If I was ever stuck somewhere hours away with no ride back, he is the only person I know that I could call in the middle of the night and he would jump in his car and come get me.

I learned how truly funny he was at one of our first ECW Arena shows. At the time, we had to wrap our shows and clean up by 11:00 p.m. so the old ladies of South Philly could have their Saturday "Midnight Bingo." Fucking Butchie knew how to get the most bang for his buck out of that building. To be fair, it was primarily a bingo hall, and these tough-as-nails broads that looked like Cactus Jack took this shit seriously. Anyway, we'd packed up and were headed out the back exit while the fierce bingo competition was in full swing when Hack turned and yelled, "Bingo!" The women started tossing their cards down, thinking there was a winner.

Monday morning came and I got a call from Fucking Butchie. "Hey, Tod," he starts. "Not for nuttin', I love the guy and all, but you gotta tell Sandman he can't ever do that again 'cause it brought a ton of shit down on me." Butchie must've been trampled by walkers that night.

Hack was known for his three-day benders with no sleep. On one such occasion, he was wandering the dance club–laden South Street and was waved over by a bouncer.

"Sandman!" the guy exclaimed. "No line for you. You wanna come in?"

He did, and the bouncers seemed genuinely surprised to see him there, which was weird. He lived in Philly—it wasn't like the pope had walked in. Within minutes Hack was dancing on the tables while the customers chanted, "Go-Sand-man! Go-Sand-man!" He shook his body to the beat and looked out over the crowd and noticed something was missing.

Women.

Hack had danced his ass right into a gay bar and got up on the tables, thrilling the crowd. He didn't miss a beat, literally or figuratively, and twirled a napkin overhead and gyrated his way off the tables, into the kitchen, and out the back door.

There was only one occasion when Hack's drinking got in the way of our friendship. It was actually the only time he and I had a beef. We organized a weekend-long event called Cyberslam in 1996 to give internet wrestling fans, a new trend at the time, special access to our wrestlers. The event featured a card on Friday night, then a Q&A with fans and a convention all day Saturday, culminating in an ECW Arena show that night. Hack was slated to go on the Q&A panel early Saturday afternoon. However, it seemed Hack pulled another bender. He was still awake and rip roaring on Saturday morning when I saw him, red-faced and growling in that sandpaper voice of his. Fonzie and I were in the first Q&A slot, then Sandman was to follow us a half hour later. I'd organized the event, and shortly before start time, I was running around the hotel making sure everyone was ready for their time slot. That's when I saw Sandman going to bed.

"Hack, don't lay down. We have that Q&A gimmick coming up."

"I'm just gonna lay down for a minute or two."

Mind you, it's 11:45 and he's due on the dais at 12:30, and this is the first time he's slept in a day and a half.

"Hack, I need you to be ready for 12:30. We have a lot of people here."

It was true. In addition to our regular fans, we had people fly in from all over the world. People paid to see these guys, and now Sandman was jeopardizing his appearance. As I went to argue that fact more, I saw that he'd stripped down and dropped onto the hotel bed, naked. I rethought the discussion and turned to Fonzie, who'd come upstairs with me. Hack would obviously be missing his spot at the fan Q&A, so I had to think of someone who might be available to fill in. I knew one of our tag teams was around.

"Okay," I said to Fonzie. "I'll replace him with the Eliminators for the second slot today."

Hack leapt up like the bed was on fire.

"What?!" He was boiling mad and screaming at me. And naked. "You're replacing me with the Eliminators?!" He'd forgotten he was at a convention and thought I was firing him. He stumbled across the room and charged me. Naked. "You wanna replace me?!" He started swinging at me, and I stumbled backward into the bathroom. It was pretty tight, and there was nowhere to go unless we planned on showering together.

Fonzie tried to jump between us. I was successfully ducking his sloppy-ass swings, thank god.

"The convention, man!" I yelled back. "The convention!"

"What fucking convention?" Hack said. Fonzie got him to step out of the bathroom and I was gone. I was dizzy from the fiasco, but I had to fix the Q&A. Our fans had turned up in big numbers, and we were the first federation to recognize the internet wrestling community. It was important that we got good word of mouth from this weekend. Despite the shock and pain of my closest worker friend going ballistic on me, naked, I had to get to work. The next time I saw Hack was at the ECW Arena show that night. He came up to me as soft as a puppy.

"Hey, buddy."

I laced into him. "Get the fuck away from me."

"What? What's the matter?" He had no recollection. Fonzie walked him outside and told him about the whole ordeal in the hotel room that morning. Hack slinked back over to me with watery eyes.

"Hey, Gordon—"

"No. It's not that easy. Everything is *not* cool." I walked away and avoided him.

Cactus Jack was another one who'd had enough of Sandman's drinking. Hack was especially careless with Cactus one night during their feud, and, in return, he whaled Sandman with some ungodly chair shots that left him concussed. We didn't think about CTE, aka chronic traumatic encephalopathy, the long-lasting effects of repeated concussions. That syndrome wasn't officially on the radar until 2002, and I don't think I ever saw Hack put his hands up to shield himself from a chair shot as long as I've known him.

Sandman was on another planet after Cactus's chair shots. Long after his match was over, he'd find me in the dressing room and ask me how long until his match. I told him once or twice that he was already done, but by the third time he asked, I started giving him different times—"two more matches, Hack," then later, "eight more matches." He'd walk away and wait for his match each time. I had to call Lori and have her take him to the hospital.

Cactus eventually came to me during his feud with Hack and said he was done working with him as long as he continued coming to the ring drunk. Cactus was always willing to sacrifice his body for a show and never complained about anything, so I knew this was a genuine concern. Their next match was at a small-spot show, and I spoke with Hack about it. He was sober for the match but, in typical Sandman fashion, he used that discussion as part of the angle by taking the microphone and calling Cactus a pussy for coming to me about it. I was so pissed about that. How could he do that to one of the biggest stars in the building, going public with that?

Having said that, Sandman worked sober that night at my request, and the match absolutely sucked. Paul and I watched in awe at how his work rate changed when he wasn't drinking. Everything in the ring seemed cautious and at half-speed. It was the shits.

Years after ECW we worked an indie show in Buffalo, New York, where I tagged with Hack against Sabu and Fonzie.

Sandman began his post-match celebratory ritual of pouring beers somewhat into his mouth but mostly all over himself. He motioned across to me, and I stepped over and took a cold one from his hand. Fonzie and Sabu were next, and the four of us stood saluting each other and guzzling. Then Hack looked down to ringside where Cactus was on commentary for the video-taping. He pointed down to him and the *god no, not me* look came across Cactus's face. But Hack waved him in, and Cactus knew he couldn't ignore the pop of the crowd. He got in the ring, reluctantly opened a beer, and took a virgin sip.

No way Hack was having any of that. We pointed at Cactus, and the crowd chanted, "Drink! Drink!" It was a rib—we knew Mick didn't drink alcohol. Within seconds, Hack had him backed into a corner and was standing on the ropes, hovering above him, wielding a couple of silver cans. Cactus, ever the crowd pleaser, tilted his head back and hated every moment of Sandman saturating his face with the brew. Cactus was pumping it out of his mouth and down his beard as the foamy tsunami erased his face. He did the job, but I could tell he was not happy about it. I'm sure part of it was Cactus having planned to wear that same shirt for another week or so.

That instance of Hack pouring beer into Cactus's mouth would have paled in comparison to what could've happened on one particular trip in the Sandman van. Hack was riding in the back— we never let him drive after a show for aforementioned reasons. During the ride, he was pissing in a bottle to eliminate the delay of restroom breaks and wound up filling the bottle pretty quickly. The triangular rear window didn't open enough for him to dump the bottle, so he called up to Cactus, who was riding in the front passenger seat.

"Cactus, here." He handed him the bottle.

"No, thanks. I don't drink beer."

"It's not beer, it's my piss. Throw it out the window."

Had Cactus decided to be polite and take a swig so as not to offend, that ride would've taken on a whole new vibe.

When Hack's wife Lori wasn't on the road with us as Peaches, she'd beep me incessantly to check up on him. This was before cell phones, but I had a car phone and she knew I'd be able to get back to her wherever we were. After eight to ten beeps a night I'd be fed up.

"Stop it, Lori!"

"Where is he?"

"I don't know." In actuality he was ten feet from me snorting bumps of coke off a hotel table. Lori would end the inquisition and let me off the phone.

"Thanks, Gordon," Hack would say and go on with the night of debauchery. Anything to help out a friend.

One day while at work I called him and he answered out of breath.

"Hello?"

"Yo. It's Tod."

Then, a response came from Hack that no other living person would utter.

"Oh, hey, buddy. I'm in the middle of fucking my wife. Can I call you back?"

"Nah, I'll wait. Shouldn't be long."

Sandman popped huge and told Lori what I said.

"Asshole!" she yelled with a laugh.

"Oh, well, that's done," Hack said, now giving me his full attention. "What's up, buddy?"

For all his exploits, I have to say Hack has remained my best friend. I've had others in my life that have lost that distinction, but Hack has always been there. It might sound strange, given his in-ring persona and out-of-the-ring exploits, but he's been the most honorable worker I've ever met. He was known in the locker room as "Tod's boy," and people have groused that was the reason for his pushes, until people did some basic math and realized he hadn't won a match for two years. He refused to go over, telling me and Paul that others needed it more.

"I can get my heat back after a loss with a six-pack in the ring," he said more than once. "Get someone else over." Very few people knew that side of Hack. So if you're someone who pinned Sandman some night, you might've been given that win by Hack himself. Chances are Paul and I wanted you to job to him.

## 2 COLD SCORPIO

Charles Scaggs, aka 2 Cold Scorpio, might very well be my favorite person in the world. He's certainly one of the nicest and most loyal—a true friend for life. I love the guy from the bottom of my heart, and my kids do as well. He's stayed in my home so many times that we refer to one of the bedrooms as "Scorp's room," just as we do Ally's, Becky's, and Charlie's. He is also an amazing talent in the ring, a rare breed that can go toe-to-toe with any style of worker.

Hardcore brawl? No problem.

High-flying *lucha* style? No problem.

Chain wrestling? Name it and he does it well.

Promos? Well, not so much. You see, Scorp mumbles. I call him "the Bumble Bee." There are times during conversations when I have no idea what the hell he's just said, so I simply nod. Other times, I ask him to repeat himself a dozen or so times before I get it. And when he talks Carny, forget it. For those not in the know, Carny is an affected wrestler language from the bygone days of having to protect the secrets in the business. You would stick an "iz" sound in the middle of words you didn't want laypeople to hear. Saying, "Give this book a good review" would come out as "gizive thizis bizook a gizood reviziew."

When Scorp spoke Carny, he wound up adding a "z" sound to every syllable of every word. Thus, the Bumble Bee. He was generally indecipherable to start with, and when he whipped out the Carny, everyone in the Sandman van would *buzzzzz* along, laughing our asses off. He was good-natured, though. He rolled with all of our joking, so he was a natural fit to the Posse.

Even when we could make out what the hell Scorp was saying, we were often still in the dark. We were riding to a show one day and he's looking out the window when he says, "Johnny Lunch- bucket on the right."

I thought he was hungry. "What?"

"Johnny Lunchbucket," he repeated. "Up ahead."

Now Hack is turning to me with a furrowed brow. "What the fuck is he saying?"

I was no closer to understanding. Not sure why Hack thought I, of all people, spoke jive. I just shrugged.

Then we passed the police car on the shoulder.

"Did you mean the cops?" I asked.

Scorp nodded. "Told you—Johnny Lunchbucket."

I didn't ask for an explanation. I was too busy gasping for air with my head thrown back to the heavens, laughing like I would die. Sandman keeps barking, "Johnny Lunchbucket!" between his raspy cackling. Scorpio didn't elaborate—he just sat in the back of the van, chilling. Why find a code word for police when you're out of earshot of the cops? Further, is "Johnny Lunchbucket" really an efficient way to let Sandman know about a speed trap? And what the hell is a "Johnny Lunchbucket" anyway? But that was Scorp.

And man, could he smoke weed. It went on all day long; I don't know how he functioned, but he did just fine. You'd never know just by talking to him at breakfast that he'd had four joints so far that day. All of us in the Posse would smoke, but it was this guy's oxygen.

The Posse came through for Scorpio in a big way when he was trying to sleep with a woman EMT who worked the ECW matches with her husband. Scorpio would flirt with her, so she was well aware of his intentions. When she finally got a taste of Scorpio, no pun, it seemed the old saying proved true—she didn't go back.

The issue of her husband working beside her at our shows persisted, though, so we all had to come up with creative ways to distract him. Scorpio would let us know they were going off somewhere in the building to get it on, and Fonzie would fall down and fake some excruciating back pain. Or Sandman would call for the guy and tell him some weird shit, like he was seeing colored spots. We'd do everything we could to keep this guy tied up so his wife could ride Scorpio in a closet.

What people don't know about this laid-back guy in the corner of the locker room is that he's a legit badass. During a WCW road trip in Japan, all the workers were miserable from seemingly endless bus rides. Unprovoked, Road Warrior Hawk began riding Scorp mercilessly, and my guy just sat there and took it. The joking went on way too long and started to have some racial overtones directed at Scorpio, who is black. He confronted the taller, heavier Hawk when they stepped off the bus. Hawk barked something at Scorpio and before it reached Scorp's ears, he'd knocked Hawk out with one punch. The sight of Road Warrior lying unconscious kept the boys from ever picking on Scorp again.

Another example of his toughness came during the infamous Arn Anderson/Sid Vicious scissor fight in a hotel. The legendary confrontation saw Sid confront and stab Arn in the doorway of a hotel room. Blood was spurting all over as the other wrestlers kept yelling at them to stop. Only one, however, literally jumped in between them to break it up and took a slice or two for his good troubles.

Yeah, that's Scorp.

Throughout his whole career, Scorpio has had a long and successful run in Japan. His flight over usually had a layover in Amsterdam. I mentioned previously that he's a world-class pot smoker, and his time in Amsterdam was more fruitful, as the

Netherlands was one of the first countries to decriminalize marijuana. He walked into a café with chalkboards as far as the eye can see, listing all different types of pot and hashish for sale. He was like a kid in a candy store. He returned and told me the news.

"Oh my god," I said, contemplating the menu. "What did you get?"

Ever the worker, Scorp said he knew the place was holding out on the *really* good stuff. He said he walked over to the cashier and whispered, "What have you got under the counter?" Imagine for the first time in his life being able to buy weed legally, having a choice of over a hundred strains, and wanting to know what he could buy illegally. That, my friends, sums up the mindset of a wrestler rather perfectly.

Worker or not, I trust Scorpio more than anyone in the world, both with my family and with me. I recently had a potential health scare that thankfully turned out to be insignificant. But when Scorpio heard about it, he offered to drop his life and fly up here to move in and take care of me. He's one of a kind.

## FONZIE

Bill Alfonso came into the company playing an official, sanctioned by the state athletic commission to clean up ECW, a tailor-made heel for our fans. Paul and I didn't tell anyone about the angle, and on his first night he walked into the locker room at the ECW Arena wearing a suit and tie. He mostly stayed out of sight until Sandman laid his eyes on him.

"Who the fuck is this?" he yelled to the room.

Fonzie introduced himself.

"Why are you wearing a suit in here?" Hack asked. "Look at this shithole!" His confusion was well justified. Fonzie played it up, walking around asking when he could talk with Vince McMahon and asking where catering was. Meanwhile, there's a guy shitting in a box in the corner. I knew I'd click with Fonzie.

We'd planned a two-month angle, and Fonzie was playing it to a T. The skinny heel with a rodent-faced snarl went to the ring and told fans he was there to clean up ECW or shut it down altogether. Though he had no connection whatsoever to Greg Sirb or anyone else on the Pennsylvania SAC, they probably would've liked to shut us down from the first night Sirb heard about Angel baring her breasts in the ring.

After appearing in his power suit, Fonzie had a shirt made with Pennsylvania Athletic Commission stitched on it, underscoring his role on camera. He began restricting the action in our rings. Fans hated him and would throw shit at him as he stopped 911's popular chokeslams, saying they were not pure wrestling. He was taking away the one thing about our product that defined us, and the fans were bloodthirsty over it. They'd wait for Fonzie outside with sticks and boards. We had to smuggle him out of the arena with the ring crew late at night after the ring was broken down. We knew the angle would be hot, but we had no idea to what degree.

Fonzie would eventually hit his stride as a hyperactive heel manager who blew a loud whistle incessantly, driving both fans and anyone near him—including wrestlers and this owner—crazy. But before that, he was just a representative from the state looking to clean us up. Obviously, our talent knew Bill Alfonso and knew this was a work, but I really don't think the majority of our fans did until he began getting physically involved in matches, like clotheslining yours truly. I suspect that's when it became a wrestling angle to the fans. Fonzie was eventually chokeslammed himself by 911. Fans knew it was part of the show but lapped it up anyway. If Greg Sirb of the actual state athletic commission was assaulted in the ring, I think our fans expected there would be severe repercussions for us. We'd be sued, shut down, and the press coverage would be massive. But this was just another wrestling angle, a damn good one, if I do say so myself, and it was all leading to a match against me.

One of Fonzie's great heel moments was during the long-awaited Taipei Death Match between Ian and Axl Rotten at Hardcore Heaven '95. Both men came out with shards of broken glass covering their taped fists and prepared to pound each other into bloody pulps, as was the promise of that style match. Before the bout, I appointed Fonzie as a special referee for the match, challenging his law-and-order style. Well, it backfired, as the angle went. When Ian's forehead showed just a speck of blood, Fonzie examined it and stopped the match for blood. The crowd saw red and went nuts. To get Fonzie out of the building, we created a diversion by having the Gangstas and Public Enemy come out and brawl in the aisle. Once Fonzie was gone, I got on the mic and officially restarted the Taipei Death Match between the Rottens, with an ECW ref, and the crowd went home happy, having gotten their serving of blood and guts.

Fonzie was great to have around for the weird shit that would come out of his mouth. He didn't intend to be funny most of the time; it was just how he talked. He'd say he was headed to the Acme's to pick something up.

"Acme?" I'd say.

"Yeah. The Acme's."

"It's called Acme."

"That's what I said. The Acme's, daddy." He had no idea. Why correct him?

Fonzie had the greatest stories, and they'd fall out of his mouth at the most random times. Just two years ago I brought up the oversized wrestler Giant Gonzalez, and Fonzie mentioned he'd managed him in WWE, traveling with him and functioning as an off-camera handler of sorts. Gonzalez was a former Argentine basketball player, standing at nearly eight feet tall, and needed help with the myriad things a life on the road brings. Fonzie was awakened by a late-night call in his hotel room from Gonzalez, who said he needed Fonzie to help him right away. Fonzie got to the room and was treated to the scene of Giant Gonzalez in the buff and a young lady in the bed.

"What do you need me for, daddy?" Fonzie asked. "Seems like you're doing just fine here."

"I need you to fuck her," he said. "I'm too big. You go first." Talk about a manager servicing his client. Gonzalez must've had a sewer pipe in his pants and needed Fonzie to get things going before he tried again. Fonzie, ever a dutiful and dedicated manager, did as asked.

Fonzie has been in the business since 1978. That's forty-four years as I type this, and that culture permeates his everyday life. We would pull up to a crowded diner, scan the packed parking lot, and he would say, "They drew a nice house tonight." My favorite Fonzieism would happen whenever we lit a joint on a road trip. The first time we offered him a hit, he said, "Let me just take a 'cop hit.'"

The rest of us asked what the hell a "cop hit" was, and he matter-of-factly explained he would take one hit to prove to everyone else in the car he wasn't a narc. This was especially hysterical because he asked for that same cop hit on *every* trip we took, even though he'd been riding with the same people. He'd take his cop hit to loosen up but saved his real smoking until after the matches were over.

You never knew what to expect from Fonzie when we traveled. We landed in Pittsburgh after an early-morning flight that followed a grueling night. When my Posse got to baggage claim, I noticed only Sandman and Scorpio were with me.

"Where's Fonzie?" I asked the guys. They didn't know; I figured he was in the bathroom. We waited at the baggage claim for a while, with no luggage and no Fonzie. Finally, the light signaled our baggage would be coming down the chute and the carousel began to turn. As we looked for our bags, we saw Fonzie on the carousel, curled up and sound asleep. As he got closer to us, bags began tumbling down the ramp, around and onto Fonzie. When he was delivered to where we were standing, Scorp and Hack pulled him off like a suitcase.

Fonzie was also a fiercely loyal worker. When WWE came to town and we were slated to do our invasion angle with them, Paul issued a strict edict that no one from our company was to be seen in the crowd at the Spectrum that night, as it would tip fans off to our surprise appearance. Everyone followed the dictate with one exception—Joel Gertner. Gertner was a heel manager who was disliked by fans, and not particularly popular in the locker room either. I don't recall him having real heat with anyone, but I never saw him in any social situations, and no one I knew really hung out with him.

Word got back to us the next day at our show in Allentown that Gertner had been unable to contain his wrestling fandom and was seen sitting in the cheap seats at the WWE card. I just rolled my eyes at the news, too hungover from the previous night to care. But Fonzie came up to me upon hearing the news.

"Can I smack Gertner in the face?" he asked.

"Yeah, because *that's* a great solution," I said sarcastically. Fonzie didn't read the tone, or only heard the "yeah."

"Good," he said as he bolted from me. "I got the office."

By the time I realized he thought I was serious, he was already at the table where Gertner was sitting. Before I could get to them, Fonzie smacked Gertner clean off his chair. I don't know what was funnier, the slap or Sandman's explosive reaction to seeing it. When Gertner got up, Fonzie said he should be thanked, as Gertner would now be spared being hit by one of the larger guys. Fonzie was old school like that.

Spending a couple of decades in the wrestling business also makes one resourceful with regard to health care. Wrestlers are independent contractors; therefore, there is no employer of record to provide a health-care plan. Fonzie hurt his shoulder in a match with me in Trenton, New Jersey, one night and needed to have it examined the next day. The layperson might head to a doctor, but Fonzie went right to the Acme's, where he summarily stepped up on a shelf and pulled the entire display down on himself. The store manager was attentive, quickly calling an ambulance to shuttle the injured shopper to the hospital, where his care was most generously covered by the supermarket chain.

Here it is, twenty-eight years since the Posse became friends, and I don't think I have ever gone three days without hearing from Fonzie. He most often sends me pictures from our time in the ring together, but every now and then I get a video of him catching a huge fish, or an alligator coming out of the water toward him to steal said fish.

Hack, Scorp, and Fonzie have the same love for each other as they do me. Anytime they've had a booking together in the last fifteen years, I'd get a video of the three of them saying, "Wish you were here, Todster." Pretty unique and enduring relationship for four older guys.

# CHAPTER 7

# THE WORKERS

Though the Posse was the band of workers closest to me, I came to know and respect so many others who created memories for our incredible fans.

## TAZ

Taz first appeared in ECW in 1993 as Tazmaniac, brought down from New York by Paul E. He tagged with Kevin Sullivan at first and was unable to find footing as that animalistic hybrid character. He looked the part—short, squat, and thick. It got easier when he dropped that gimmick and just became Taz, a fully human singles wrestler.

Taz worked hard in the ring and was always reliable. He wasn't a partier and took his role in the company seriously. Perhaps a bit too much so. He first came into the company pretty humble—grateful for the job and that we'd put him with Kevin Sullivan. Over time, he started believing the gimmick he was playing of some dangerous thug, stomping around the locker room and scowling like he might kick some worker's ass if provoked. I'd been around plenty of legit tough guys in a locker room; that was just part of the business.

The problem in this case was that the couple of times I'd seen Taz in an actual confrontation with another worker, he didn't exactly come out with the upper hand. Matter of fact, it's a good thing his being slapped across the face by Rob Van Dam after being told to pick the hand wasn't televised. That would spotlight the drastic difference between the character Taz was portraying and reality.

Taz and 911 were having an issue backstage at a show in Florida. 911, real name Al Poling, is about six nine and over three hundred pounds. When he stepped to Taz, who was seated in the locker room, he cast a shadow that covered him completely. Al is normally a placid guy, but he'd had enough of Taz mouthing off to him and it was time for Taz to put up or shut up. Those present in the locker room that night watched in silence as 911 stopped just a couple of feet from Taz.

"If you're feeling froggy, then jump," Al said. The room looked to Taz, who didn't exactly leap but was instead snatched out of his seat by one of Al's massive arms. There was Taz, held up about nine feet in the air, his feet dangling just like in a cartoon. Fortunately for all involved, Al Poling is a sweetheart of a guy. I don't think he has manslaughter in his heart, or it would've been a very different story for Taz and my company.

Everyone dressed in one big space in the ECW Arena, which probably contributed to the sense of camaraderie on our roster. When Taz was getting one of his singles pushes, he commandeered a little room under the stairs, away from the communal area all the wrestlers shared. He'd decided this would be his private dressing room and eventually invited Perry Saturn and Shane Douglas in, granting them exclusive access to the six-by-fifteen-foot junk closet. It was the first time anyone in my locker room wasn't part of the boys. It wasn't a big deal—guys like RVD, Sabu, and Sandman just laughed at it. It was a joke to the rest of the locker room.

We put Taz with a legit tough guy for a high-profile angle when we brought in UFC shoot fighter Paul Varelens. He was there to face Taz in a "shoot fight," which was anything but that. Taz was set to beat this legit combatant in the center of the ring on TV, which would certainly give any pro wrestler a nice rub. We had to ensure Varelens would go with the program and not make this an opportunity to show the world how tough UFC guys were compared to pro wrestlers. We asked our old pal Missy Hyatt to stay close to him, keep him happy, and let him know how important it was that her friends come out of this looking good. Why Missy and not, say, Hack Meyers? I don't know—just seemed like a better choice. I knew our plan was working when, during our press conference for the match, I looked out to the front row of press and saw Missy there. Varelens was beside me, so I knew he shared my vantage point as Missy opened her legs to cross them and showed she wasn't wearing panties under her skirt. I breathed easier, confident our star would dispatch Varelens easily and get that tough-guy push.

However, the ECW fans are not so gullible to fall for such a ruse. Even if they were, the fact that Taz had three ECW wrestlers standing ringside to protect him if Varelens actually started fighting certainly tipped them off. It was such a bad look—Varelens standing in the ring alone, and Taz in his corner growling as Perry Saturn, John Kronus, and Shane Douglas stood behind him. After their rip-off shoot match, the fans weighed in with deafening cries of "Bullshit! Bullshit!" Like I said, you can't get one over on our fans. It was salvaged a bit when we used it as an angle wherein Taz acknowledged ripping the fans off, thus bringing more heel heat.

Well, what Paul Varelens couldn't do, maybe Leon Spinks could. Fans never got to see it, but the pro boxer was tapped to give Taz a rub after a fortuitous encounter in the hotel bar. Upon returning from a show, a handful of the boys and I had gone in for a nightcap when we saw a familiar figure slumped over the bar, his hoodie drawn tightly around his face. It was unmistakably Leon Spinks. We said hello and he popped huge for us, slurring that he "loved that rasslin'!" We sat down for a couple of cocktails with our new biggest fan, incoherent as he might have been. He was more than happy to host us.

"Fuck boxing," he said. "That's as fake as wrestling. They set up the whole Ali thing, you know."

*Do tell*, we all thought as we quieted enough to hear a syringe drop. What he meant, he went on to explain, was his upsetting Muhammad Ali for the heavyweight title in 1978. We all had our suspicions about boxing, but here was a big confirmation right from the horse's mouth. Spinks was nodding in and out right there at the bar, but he was clear enough to tell us that he was told he was going over Ali as a big underdog, setting up the huge rematch. We were speechless.

"You gotta be on our show tomorrow night," I said. I wanted him to help build Taz, and he agreed. We got Leon frigging Spinks right there with a handshake deal. We asked him if he wanted to come upstairs and watch some of the promos we were going to tape that night. He followed us up and sat in a corner as we turned on the camera and started recording that week's promos. Halfway through the first one, during an apparently exciting part, we hear a "wooooo!" from across the room. Everyone exchanged looks—didn't seem to have come from any of us, and Leon had nodded out again, head down and mouth open, seated in the back of the room. We started the promo again.

"Wooo! Woooo!" came again, more emphatically now. It was Leon, going in and out of his stupor, very excited by the rasslin' promos he was hearing in his sleep. He was fucking up all our takes, though, and we had to keep restarting because the former world champion was cheering as he watched the interviews on the TV in his mind. We eventually showed him out, but not without a promise that he'd come back the following night to shoot the angle in the ring. As long as he didn't wear orange, we would be fine.

At some point during his push, Taz declared that no one was to wear orange to the ring but him. I don't think anyone was itching to do so during this era, but occasionally a new talent would come in and take orange gear out of his gym bag. We'd nudge each other and wait for Taz to stroll over.

"Yo, brotha," he'd say to the new arrival. "Come over here so I can talk to ya." At that point Taz would tell him he needed to secure some new gear for that night, as Taz had an exclusive lease on the fourth color in the Crayola box. It was very amusing.

I can't remember who first suggested it, but all the boys were planning on wearing orange to an ECW Arena show one night. Paul got wind of it and squashed it, pleading with the offenders.

"Come on, guys," he said. "You're gonna piss him off, and I'm going to have to listen to the miserable prick all night long. Don't do this to me." Ultimately, we dropped it.

As promised, Leon Spinks was picked up and brought to the Arena on Saturday. Paul and I weren't sure what we'd have him do; we were planning to sit with him and Taz to work something out. But Leon showed up in no condition to perform. He was barely in a condition to open his eyes, and he was practically carried into the dressing room. Taz said he wasn't working with anyone in that condition, and I couldn't blame him. Any altercation between them would've made the Varelens match look like Steamboat vs. Flair. We told Leon we couldn't use him that night and we'd hook up another time. We gave him fifty dollars and had him driven home.

While this passage might seem like I'm out to bury Taz, that couldn't be further from the truth. Was he a pain in the ass? Yes. Did his tough-guy act rub the boys the wrong way? Yes. But Taz was also a true professional who had great respect for the business and the wrestlers that preceded him. His work ethic was second to none—he was always one of the first to the building so he could hit the weights and prepare for that night. He lived cleanly and worked on his look. It must've been difficult for a guy who worked that hard to look over and see Sandman and Tommy Rich, who, let's just say, didn't care about such things.

Taz's promo skills were also kept under wraps for some reason, and one night during my angle with Fonzie, Taz grabbed the mic to turn heel and stunned us. Paul and I were shocked at his abilities to cut a promo and wondered why we'd never given him a mic a year earlier.

## TERRY FUNK

Here is someone the absolute opposite of Taz, and if anyone had the right to be a puffed-up asshole, it was Funk. But he wasn't. He was humble and gracious, and that reminded me not to take shit from other workers with five years in the business, three months in front of a camera, and a fan base that could fill a DMV waiting area. There was Terry Funk, who'd been in wrestling rings all over the world for thirty years and was as gracious and egoless as could be. There was one time he reminded me he was Terry f'n Funk, and it was actually kind of funny. When Eddie Gilbert left me high and dry, I approached Terry about booking for us while he was doing color commentary for our TV shows. He chuckled and smiled.

"Oh, Tod," he began in his *aw-shucks* drawl, "you can't afford me." He patted me on the shoulder and went back to work. My naivety makes me laugh now—we didn't have TV for even a single year, and I'd just asked one of the sports' all-time legends to follow Eddie Gilbert in booking full time for us. It was pretty unrealistic.

Terry elevated guys like Shane and Public Enemy. He made them. "They're good boys," he'd say whenever I thanked him. I think he saw his time in ECW as a mentor role more than as talent. I was so indebted to Terry. We all were. One night, Terry Funk—former NWA world champion and icon the world over—told me, "I'll always be ECW first." It floors me as much now as when he said it. He did so much for us.

Terry was a kind-hearted guy despite his years of brutal, bloody battles in the ring. I doubt he had any genuine dislike for another human being, but Paul E certainly tested his patience at times. There was one time Terry no-showed us but was kind enough to call and tell me in advance that he was planning to do it. Is that even technically a no-show?

Terry had been calling Paul for days prior to the show. He was trying to get details for his flight into Philly for his main-event match tagging with Cactus against Public Enemy. Terry was trying to work out the travel arrangements on his end, and Paul would not answer his phone or return Terry's messages. It was a common thing with Paul, being deliberately unreachable. Paul waited until the night before the flight to send Terry his ticket, at which point Funk called and told me he wasn't coming.

"What?" Paul said when I told him, acting surprised. You'd think the ten messages Terry left on his machine all week would've been a tip-off. Regardless, Terry wasn't coming, and we needed a replacement for the main event we'd been building on TV for months. We went through the list of names...Sandman, Taz, Saturn. Paul was being pretty indiscriminate about whom to select—he felt anyone that we'd gotten over would be accepted by the fans, and he was probably right. Ultimately, he selected 911. But I saw this as an opportunity to do something really different.

"Mikey," I said.

"Mikey? Nooo." Paul rejected it out of hand for every reason he should have. Mikey Whipwreck was five foot seven and maybe a buck and a half of high-flying energy that our big stars had the privilege of throwing all over the Arena before pinning him. But he had an underdog appeal, and fans went crazy for him. He'd eventually get so popular with fans that he'd hold all three titles in ECW. I pitched replacing the legend Funk with Mikey, and slowly Paul seemed to see what I was getting at. Fans would expect someone like Sandman to come out and put up a good fight, but any regular wrestler from our locker room would disappoint fans who'd come to see Funk. By going in an outlandish direction and doing an outlandish finish like having Mikey and Cactus win the tag team titles, everyone would forget that Funk wasn't there. Paul eventually saw the light and ran with it.

For that idea, Paul bestowed on me the most backhanded compliment that I'd ever gotten.

"You know what, Tod, you're a great crisis booker." He was still my close friend at the time, but I could've knocked him out right there. Like it would have killed him to leave it at, "You're a great booker." It had to be qualified by that weird-ass "crisis" thing.

Funk was one of those veterans who had a good handle on how the US health-care system worked, and didn't work, for wrestlers. One of our younger guys was sitting with Funk complaining about a neck injury, which Funk astutely told him was nothing to ignore. Compression spinal injuries are common from workers getting dropped on their heads every night, and ignoring a seemingly innocuous pain could have consequences. The worker said he didn't have insurance and it would likely be too expense to handle.

"Do the rental car deal," Funk said.

The kid was perplexed, as was I. The worker told him he didn't need a ride to the doctor. Funk smiled and slid closer—*listen up, grasshopper...*

"Get a rental car and buy the top insurance," Funk said. "Might cost you fifty bucks, but it's worth it. Then, leave the rental place and run that sumbitch right into a stop sign. Grab your neck and wait for the ambulance."

Genius.

Funk did so much for us at ECW beyond medical consulting. He was a great help to me from the first day I brought him in to do color commentary beside Jay Sulli, which alone should be a penalty for misdemeanor crime. He never avoided risk in his matches for us, even when he probably should have. Terry was in his fifties and doing moonsaults and a host of the most risky stuff ever done in a ring. Terry Funk helped define ECW, and I like to think ECW helped redefine Terry Funk.

## SABU

The phone rang at my store in the fall of 1993.

"Tod Gordon?" a quiet voice asked.

"Yes."

"Sabu."

"Fine, thanks, and you?"

"No, it's Sabu."

I first saw Sabu when Joel Goodhart was running TWA. Some time had passed, and he gave me a call to see if I would book him. I remembered him doing some cool stuff, particularly how fast he could scale a steel cage. He looked like a frigging squirrel. I asked him how much he wanted, and he said two hundred. I agreed to give him a shot and within a couple of months he was my world champion. It was very apparent this guy was something special, and more importantly in wrestling, different.

That's the holy grail in our sport that runs every week of every year, without an off-season, across dozens of global federations. If you can be authentically unique, you'll work forever. At least you used to work forever when there were more than a couple of companies. Sabu was like that. After his first match for us, he slid a table into the ring, set it up, and dove through the damn thing, breaking it into a million pieces, and sold a hurt leg. People, myself included, were like, "What the fuck?" Soon enough, it evolved into Sabu putting his opponents through tables.

One night while Sabu was off doing a tour in Japan, Rocco Rock slid out a table and used it in his match. This created hard feelings between Sabu, Rocco, and Paul E. But eventually, tables were coming out in every other match, to the point where the image of someone going through a table could've become our new logo. If you have any doubt Sabu was an innovator, take just the tables in a wrestling ring for starters. I've been put through my share of tables, and I can tell you firsthand it's effective and safe when done correctly and agonizing when done incorrectly. Correctly would mean a clean break, across the center, with your upper torso taking the bump through the table. Incorrectly would mean how Sabu landed on me one night when the legs of the table gave out and the table didn't break, rather dropped flat onto the Rostraver Ice Garden floor, which offered no cushion whatsoever.

Fonzie, my on-camera archenemy, saw that botched spot and ran over to me looking for the "Iggy," meaning my squeezing his finger gently to let him know I was okay. I'd seen NFL players get the wind knocked out of them, but I didn't know the paralysis it caused until that night. I was unable to move and couldn't reciprocate Fonzie's finger squeeze. As he is not one to overreact, Fonzie broke character and began running around ringside yelling, "Todster is dead! We killed Todster!" I was eventually able to tell the referee I was fine.

When Sabu first came in to ECW, we had him wear a Hannibal Lecter mask and get wheeled to the ring on a gurney by 911. Sabu was immediately resistant to doing that, citing a wrestler doing Dr. Hannibal in Japan and he didn't want to infringe on his gimmick. I told Sabu no one here knew about Dr. Hannibal, and he'd do it a hundred times better anyway. He agreed to try it out and see how it went, but he never fully committed to it. After a handful of appearances, the mask and the gurney were gone, but it really didn't matter. Sabu was over in a way I'd never seen before. He wasn't babyface over, and he didn't have massive heel heat—people just loved watching him work. He put his body in danger seemingly in every match. His matches were loaded with high-risk aerial moves that he seemed to pay the price for every night.

Just Sabu's use of a folding chair is a hallmark of his innovation. People had been whacking each other with them in wrestling rings for years, but Sabu used it like a fulcrum to launch himself. He never seemed to get the credit for everything he'd created, except from the boys who knew firsthand and made money off it. It really bothers me. Everything the Dudleys did, going through tables, flaming tables—there *were* no tables before Sabu. Did he get a bunch of awards for it? I don't think so.

Part of Sabu's problem was how introverted he was. He's shy and the furthest thing from a braggart. But if he'd blown his own horn a little louder, he might've gotten the money and the credit he deserved.

## RAVEN

Raven—called Scotty by all—is a self-proclaimed member of Mensa, and the only thing in more abundance than Scotty's wrestling intellect was his desire for everyone in earshot to know about it. I once told him if he was one-tenth as good as he thought, he'd be a legend.

Scotty was one of those guys filled with ideas about wrestling angles. He'd proudly announce to the room that he was as smart as Paul, then he'd lay out his match for the night. It was actually his idea to put Stevie Richards with him as a wayward groupie in tight jean shorts, and Stevie was perfect in the role. Scotty had been lobbying us for some time to create the Blue Meanie. He was a big *Yellow Submarine* fan and thought the character would work in a wrestling ring. Call him crazy, but it did once we capitulated and let him go nuts with his ideas. That led to the Blue World Order, and the rest is hardcore history.

Scotty's chatter was omnipresent. It seemed wherever you were in the dressing area you could hear him talking, unless, of course, he was getting a blowjob in the parking lot, in which case you couldn't find him when his match was on. The guy had a rat a minute. He was nuts.

The character of Raven got over with the fans, borrowing from the sensibilities of a generation embracing grunge music and movies like *The Crow*. Scotty played that well but also embellished it with comedy by putting his wayward flock beside him. He had an innate ability to know what fans would react to; he was smart like that. Damn it, I said it again.

Scotty is the type of guy who will get legitimately mad if you are beating him in a meaningless game of trivia. I experienced it firsthand on a car ride when I stayed neck and neck with him during the game. It bothered him so much, which made it all the more fun for me. He didn't often ride with the Posse, but he was a Philly guy and lived five minutes from my store, so he'd occasionally catch a ride with me.

Scotty had his battles with Percocet, as did half our damn locker room, but not quite to his level. There were days when the brilliant one would be whacked on pills, but you'd never know it watching him in the ring. I don't know how these guys got all those pills, but I do know a foot doctor moved in with Scotty at one point. His name was, rather perfectly, Dr. Mark, and he actually served as the ECW ringside doctor for a while. Yes, our ringside doctor was a podiatrist.

The Raven that I see at conventions today is clean, sober, and his usual snarky, smartest-guy-in-the-room self.

## TOMMY DREAMER

My feelings on Dreamer have changed over the years, but when Paul first brought him down to Philly, he was a great guy. He'd come up to me and say, "Mr. Gordon, I just want you to know I would die for this company. I would do *anything* for you." He said it more than once when we were trying to get a push going for him, and he wasn't bullshitting. That guy was open to all sorts of risk in the ring. He took a ball shot one night from the Bruise Brothers that required surgery.

He was smart too—a great benefit to a promoter and booker. There was an informal pecking order regarding who got to come up with their own finishes. Paul trusted guys like Raven and Dreamer because they understood the nuances of the business and their suggestions were usually winners. They could run it by Paul, and he'd ultimately let them do it. Raven would always casually drop references to Dreamer's "fat ass" whenever he could, being the incessant ballbuster that Scotty was.

"Paulie, can Tommy do his fat ass drop?" or "fat ass" this or "fat ass" that. Scotty tortured him with the references. Amazing what you can get away with as a Mensa member.

Dreamer was also a selfless worker, as evidenced by how he handled his feud against Raven. Very few people in the business would agree to a program where they lost every match against their opponent for a year, much less encourage it. Kudos to Tommy for that, as it resulted in a great payoff.

I mentioned earlier that Tommy finally won the fans over by taking the ten brutal lashings from Sandman. I think Paul tried everything in the book before that, to no avail. To make matters worse, Dreamer was horrible on the microphone. We had to put girls around him all the time to distract from the fact that he was opening his mouth. But honorably taking Sandman's vicious shots made his career. Fans came to see him as Mr. ECW after that, though it was quite a price to pay. I never thought he was that talented, and truthfully I don't think Paul did either. But when he found that niche—taking endless abuse and brawling with the best of them—it became his calling card. As time went on and he got more experience, Tommy went on to become a terrific worker.

If we asked the locker room to elect a team captain, I think Tommy would have been a good choice. He was straitlaced, didn't mess around with drugs, and was responsible inside and outside the ring. He always had a calm demeanor, which was good to have in a locker room that could sometimes get out of control. One night during a show in Jim Thorpe, Pennsylvania, someone lit up a joint in our locker room, which was not much larger than a walk-in closet. Paul E got hot.

"Who the hell is smoking here?" he said, looking around the group of guys. The sight of Freebird Terry Gordy trying to play it off with his hand behind his back and a huge plume of smoke emanating up from behind his head was hilarious. Tommy was the one who stepped in and pulled Gordy aside, respectfully telling the veteran that smoking weed was frowned upon in the locker room. That's what I mean—Tommy had that touch where he could correct one of wrestling's Freebirds in an independent locker room and make it sound like friendly advice.

## NEW JACK

Jack and his tag partner Mustafa came into ECW as the Gangstas in June 1995 and upped the ante on violence, controversial promos, and felonious incidents almost from the start. New Jack was without question our loosest cannon on the roster. Though Jack was only playing a gang member on our shows, it was murky just how much of that character existed in Jerome Young. It seemed he was ready to throw down all the time. Some of the shit he did in the ring to others as well as himself was downright scary, from slicing another wrestler's head with an X-Acto knife to plunging through stacks of tables to the concrete ECW Arena floor.

Jack was fierce on the microphone as well. One night he cut a fifteen-minute promo in the ring and kept the fans popping for the whole thing. It was so badass he became an unintentional babyface right there. That happens sometimes when someone is so villainous that fans would rather watch them than the heroes sent to dispatch them. Later that night at the bar, I told him he was wasting his time in wrestling. He should be a hype man for the biggest clubs in the country, walking around with a white suit and a microphone. He'd make far more money than I was paying him and he'd be more famous.

Drugs and alcohol became another calling card for New Jack, adding to his unpredictability and danger. But believe it or not, when I met Jack in '95 he was as straight as an arrow. He drank some but didn't touch any drugs that I knew of, until Sandman's wife Lori pulled him into a bathroom one night. Seems Jack showed up drunk, and she told Jack she'd be able to get him right again. A few snorts later and New Jack's heart rate soared to the stratosphere and pulled him out of his drunk.

It's not good for you and it could kill you, but it works.

We invited New Jack to ride with the Posse a few times when he came into the company. At some point during a ride to a show in Jim Thorpe, he pulled out a bottle of Mad Dog 20/20, which looked like a harmless fruit drink.

"See this shit?" he said to us in the Sandman van. "They say n****s can't drink this. Makes 'em all go crazy. Y'all white people can drink it, but n****s can't." I thanked him for the warning and he proceeded to down the bottle. He was in rare form by the time his match against the Dudleys happened. After it, he waited crouched in the locker room and ended up whacking Dances with Dudley in the head with a legit blackjack, splitting him open instantly. I didn't even know he'd had the weapon on him. It spilled into a messy locker room brawl that was not very ECW, with Jack and the Dudleys hammering on each other.

The fight brought everyone down. It just wasn't us, and it took the air out of the whole locker room. When we piled back into the Sandman van after the show, you could cut the tension with a knife. No one was speaking; everyone just stared out the windows in our own worlds. The silence took on a life of its own.

New Jack was riding with us, and he wasn't speaking either. I was upset about the whole thing. The part of my company I was most proud of was the respect for each other's boundaries. Tonight had shattered some of that, and the Posse was feeling it. I dealt with the silence for about twenty minutes, but I decided I had to break it from my perch in the front seat.

"Well, I'm sure glad Mad Dog doesn't make n****s act crazy." It was one of the only times in my life I'd said that word, but the entire van cracked up. Within thirty seconds, the windows were open and we were all smoking and laughing.

The next morning, I was sitting alone in a diner near the hotel when New Jack walked in. Taz and Perry Saturn were sitting across the room eyeballing him hard. Jack headed to my table and I shrank. I knew he was going to ask to sit with me as the other two glared. Sure enough, he asked and I had to decide who I'd rather have hating me—two guys across the room or one within arm's reach. I opted to let him sit and just dealt with the guys boring a hole in my head with their eyes. They finished their breakfast while grumbling under their breath the entire time.

Mustafa, New Jack's partner in the Gangstas, was normally a quiet guy and definitely the one to take a back seat to the explosively gregarious Jack. In a very out-of-character outburst, Mustafa was arrested for going ballistic in a hotel stairway. He had a psychotic moment and started flipping out, and the cops came to cart him away. I later found out that he'd smoked pencil shavings that night. I guess he was out of weed and had resorted to opening a sharpener, rolling the shavings, and smoking them. I'd never heard of that, and I don't know where he did, but I can now unequivocally state it's extremely unsafe.

New Jack could've been so much more in this business, but the demons got hold of him. Everyone eventually heard all the stories and didn't want to deal with him hurting someone. But he had a sensitive side too. He literally cried on my shoulder when his wife left him, and he trusted me never to tell anyone about it. I didn't until just now. Jack inserted himself into my group here and there, but I tried to keep him on the periphery. There was just too much drama all the time, like when he was in our hotel room one night going after Fonzie, saying he was going to throw him out the window. I don't know what Fonzie said to set him off, but that was life with Jack.

## BWO

The Blue World Order was a tongue-in-cheek takeoff of WCW's New World Order faction of villains. Theirs featured headliners Kevin Nash, Scott Hall, and Hulk Hogan; ours featured non-head-liners Blue Meanie, Stevie Richards, and Nova. They appeared as Raven's flock of flunkies and always intended to draw a laugh. As goofy as it was, the bumbling trio got over with our fans as a smart though not faithful parody of what a major federation was doing. They were the Three Stooges beside Raven's dark, brooding persona. It was insane.

Stevie Richards was the worker in whom I saw the most potential. From the first day I saw him, I thought he could go the distance in the business. He had the right look at the right time—a Shawn Michaels type without having to mimic him. Shawn was on top of the WWE at the time, and that athletic but not steroided body was what companies now wanted. He moved great in the ring too, and I saw so much in him. When Paul first started booking, I told him to watch tapes of my early Eastern shows so he could see what I was talking about. I told him that Stevie was a young Shawn who needed a little training, but I wanted to bring him back in.

"He has the look," I explained. "He's lithe, and it's clear he has natural talent."

"Fine, fine, if you want." Paul didn't seem nearly as jazzed as I'd hoped, but I didn't yet know how important it was for him to find talent himself. He'd stew when I found someone and he didn't. It was all so silly—this was one company. Who cared which one of us found a guy that drew money? Well, *he* did.

Stevie came back to ECW in 1994. In addition to being a talent in the ring, Stevie is a really responsible guy and just overall pleasant to deal with. I put him in charge of ECW ticket sales and moved him into an office I furnished above Carver Reed. Gabe Sapolsky, a journalism major from nearby Temple University, was already up there making our newsletter. Gabe was a huge fan and reached out with the proposition of creating a newsletter that he would run himself. He'd just take a percentage of whatever we made. He seemed like a good kid, and his being a journalism major at Temple gave him some creds as far as writing a coherent product.

Gabe and Stevie worked above me during the day while I did my split-personality thing downstairs, grading diamonds for Carver Reed and booking venues for ECW. Stevie didn't want to use his gimmick name while taking calls for tickets, and fans knew wrestlers' real names by that point, so he created a persona. If you called the ECW ticket hotline in the mid-'90s, there's a good chance your order was taken by none other than Lloyd Van Buren. Not John Smith, not Dave Jones. That's Stevie's sense of humor for you.

I never hung out with Stevie—he was straight-edged and didn't party. But he'll always be one of my favorite guys to work with. To this day I get holiday messages from him; he's probably the most responsible person to have ever gotten famous for wearing Daisy Duke shorts.

The Blue Meanie character, brought to life by plus-size wrestler Brian Heffron, was a parody of a character from the Beatles animated film *Yellow Submarine*. Brian was another outlier in the business—polite and gentle in everyday life. He was actually a front-row ECW fan before pulling out his belly, painting his face, and getting into the ring. He started as Meanie and has stayed with that character ever since. It was too memorable to abandon.

Some of my favorite skits were shot with the BWO in my office at Carver Reed. I had them chasing each other around my desk, shooting each other with fake guns, acting generally like idiots as I'd come into the scene and do my famous, "Richaaaards!" Meanie was a sight as Bluedust, a takeoff on Dustin Rhodes's WWE character Goldust, sprawled across the top of my desk like a massive pinup model. They were hilarious and added the much-needed comedy to our hardcore show.

## CACTUS JACK

I picked up Mick Foley for one of his first shots with us in Hamburg, Pennsylvania, and we drove alone in the car together. It was a chance for us to talk a little and for me to get to know the guy I'd hired. I was a huge Cactus Jack mark from his WCW work, and I had no problem telling him so, as he later recounted in his autobiography. We left Philly and headed for Hamburg.

I've already mentioned my difficulty with directions, and that day was no exception. I blame it on the good conversation more than anything else, but the ninety-minute ride started to seem quite a lot longer. Cactus must've noticed too.

"Hey, Tod," he said, "I thought the show was in Hamburg."

"It is."

"Do you normally go through Delaware to get there?" He pointed up at the sign that indicated we were headed to the first state in the Union. We'd started out in Pennsylvania and our destination was in Pennsylvania, yet here we were paying the toll into Delaware.

"It's a shortcut," I said. "I like the back roads."

Cactus nodded along and accepted it, probably because he was too polite to call me an idiot.

That night, Cactus worked with Sabu, who used an ungimmicked beer bottle to smash over Cactus's head for the finish. The only problem was the damn bottle wouldn't break. Sabu whacked him, then whacked him again, and again. The thumping of the bottle could probably be heard in Delaware as Sabu went harder and harder each time in an effort to bust it on Mick's skull. It finally shattered and Sabu got the pinfall.

Cactus's last night with us was nothing short of brilliant, absolute Mick Foley to a T. He unexpectedly took the mic and cut a promo in the ring, announcing it was his last night and saying he had two people to thank for his time in ECW. Paul and I exchanged a glance as we stood beside each other atop the "eagle's nest," the perch where we ran production.

"There's two guys back there that need special mention," Cactus announced. "Two guys sitting in chairs right now, that are the lifeblood of ECW. Let's face it—without them there would be no Extreme Championship Wrestling. One of them is a creative genius, and the other one is a visionary who saw what he wanted to accomplish, and went about forming ECW. So right now, I'm going to bring them out here."

The crowd cheered in anticipation as Paul and I stood. We prepared to scale the steps down to the Arena floor in what was sure to be a milestone moment for us.

Then Cactus yelled, "Here's Stevie Richards and the Blue Meanie!" They ran to the ring as Sinatra's "New York, New York" blared over the speakers on Cactus's last show before heading to WWE, the New York territory. I was both shocked and amused—it was such a moment as the three of them did the famous Fargo strut around the ring. Find video of that and look at every fan's face—smiles, laughter, absolute joy. That's what Mick and ECW were all about—giving the fans what they wanted, even if they didn't know what that was.

Cactus was also aware that we might've been giving the fans too much of what they wanted. Paul and I were talking with him one night about the direction of the product. Workers were taking more and more chances, and fans came to the Arena expecting to see us outdo ourselves each month. That was becoming impossible given the insanity happening in the ring. There was a time when going through one table got a huge pop from the fans. Then it was two stacked tables, then flaming tables, and eventually New Jack going off the eagle's nest through a tower of tables. We had barbed wire, barbed-wire baseball bats, thumbtacks, and shards of glass. Guys were leaping from unsafe heights, and if we didn't slow things down, we'd be out of surprises.

In preparing for his match that night, Cactus looked at us and said, "The only thing left is the Daffy Duck bump."

Paul and I lost it—we knew exactly what he meant. He was referencing an old Looney Tunes cartoon where Bugs Bunny and Daffy Duck were trying to outdo each other's magic tricks. The finale is Daffy Duck blowing himself up and Bugs applauding, saying, "You're right, Daffy. That really was the best trick ever."

To which Daffy's heaven-bound spirit replies, "Yeah, but I can only do it *once!*"

That's what Mick Foley meant, peeking out from under the Cactus Jack persona and reading the business as the very smart worker he is.

## SHANE DOUGLAS

I already detailed how great I thought Shane was, both on the mic and in the ring. I am so fortunate, as are you, that Eddie Gilbert brought in this member of the Dynamic Dudes back in Eastern, and we were able to hang the company on his back. He made the transition with us to Extreme and, as was to be expected, the WWE soon came calling. Shane left us and headed for New York as they say, becoming Dean Douglas, the evil professor.

If you're thinking that sounds like an ill-fitting character for Shane, you'd be right. All of us cringed as they took the egotistical, entirely hateable "Franchise" Shane Douglas and put him in a light blue academic gown and shoved a paddle into his hands. Shane didn't need that kind of help—he was his own character and could get over the old-school way. But 1995 was the age of cartoonish gimmicks in WWE, and I knew that Shane was sunk. He started there in mid-1995 and was gone by Christmas.

In retrospect, I wonder if it was entirely the failed character that sealed Shane's fate. Shane's a real bright guy who was actually a legit schoolteacher for much of his time away from the ring. If you asked him for the time, though, he did have a tendency to explain how the watch was built. That would likely be followed by references to Stonehenge and early primitive timepieces and sundials.

Late one night after a show, Paul, Shane, and I sat in a hotel room bullshitting. Paul and I were going over details from the show and we'd basically forgotten about Shane, who was sitting at the table reading the newspaper. During a lull in our booking talk, we were reminded of Shane's presence.

"Pig futures are up twelve percent," he said, his nose still in the paper. It was a fine reminder that it had gotten quite late and it was time to break up our powwow.

A few months after Shane left us, I had to call JJ Dillon in the WWE's talent relations office regarding our booking one of their wrestlers. I happened to ask how my guy Shane was doing for them. I barely got the words out before JJ cut me off.

"You want him back?" he shot.

"What?"

"Shane. You want him?"

They couldn't get rid of him fast enough. His last show for us was June 9, 1995, and in January of 1996 he was back in our ring. I don't know if he went there with an attitude, having just been

ECW's world champion, or he'd been too diligent a messenger as soybean futures took a nosedive. I didn't care—I loved working with Shane and was glad he came back home.

## PUBLIC ENEMY

How do you not love a guy who searches the Yellow Pages for the category "Hookers"? It happened when I roomed with Johnny Grunge one night. I kept watching TV and told him he should be looking under "Ho's."

He went quiet for a few minutes except for the flipping of pages.

"Not there either, boss."

He was sweet and playful, big and fluffy, but man oh man, did he seem to be going in reverse sometimes. I loved him—he was so genuine, and he fell in very easily with my Posse when we were together. I don't know how I became friends with this big hick from Louisiana, but we hit it off. Johnny and his tag partner Rocco Rock made Public Enemy our most prominent tag team for a good while. They came to the ring to the ubiquitous '90s tune "Here Comes the Hotstepper" and had the crowd dancing hip-hop with them, despite Johnny having no rhythm at all.

Rocco, real name Teddy, was great on promos. He had this intensity he could turn on and off during a sixty-second spot. Teddy was trained by Samoan Afa and worked around the globe as the Cheetah Kid. His aerial abilities earned him the moniker "Flyboy," and he and Johnny made the Public Enemy both a fearsome and funny team. It was a delicate and rare balance, but they had it down perfectly. They weren't a comedy act like the Dudleys, but they weren't straight hardcore like the Gangstas either.

Though they were fun in the ring, it was outside the ring where they were most amusing, particularly Johnny. One day he lumbered into the locker room, shuffling his feet and looking tired as ever.

"Damn," Teddy said. "Where were you last night?"

"Picked up a ho last night," he said and began describing a not-so-romantic tryst. The guys began moving in closer when he started describing every curve of his date's body as the clothing was removed. Soon enough, he recalled, his pants were down and he was being serviced—the best he'd ever had, he said.

"And while I'm getting my dick sucked real good," Johnny said, "I look down and see him playing with *his* dick." With that, he walked off.

Everyone in the room stopped. Jesus. Did he kill the guy? Run out of there with his pants off? Well? He'd just stopped talking and started putting his wrestling gear away. Everyone rushed him.

"What did you do?" we yelled.

He shrugged. "I told him, 'As soon as I cum, I'm beating the fuck out of you.'" The room exploded.

Gotta love Johnny.

When Public Enemy left us to work for WCW, I got a call from Teddy the day after their first show.

"I think I'm going to have to pack up and get another job," he said.

"What's happened?" I asked. In wrestling, there are a few ways to get fired as soon as you start. A promoter will deal with you if you have a shit match. Maybe it was your opponent, maybe it was nerves. That's an easy fix. But there are some nonnegotiables, like if you injure someone, or show up too impaired to work.

Or if you steal the WCW production truck.

Shortly after getting to the arena for Public Enemy's first WCW show, a TV taping, Teddy looked around for his tag partner, who had disappeared without a word to Teddy. It turned out Johnny had gotten into town and rushed to the arena without leaving time for the really important part of the day, which was finding a place to get drugs. He must've realized that only after arriving at the venue and, as a result, he took the WCW production truck to score.

The postscript is even funnier. Dusty Rhodes was booking at the time and got wind of the theft. The following day, he ribbed Johnny good when the WCW crew was riding to the next venue on a bus. Dusty arranged for the bus to make an unscheduled stop, and a fake police officer stepped onto the bus and pulled Johnny off. When Johnny asked why, the "cop" said they'd gotten word Johnny had stolen the production truck the night before.

Johnny protested, "Yeah, but it ain't stealin' if you bring it back. It's borrowin.'"

You gotta love Johnny.

## THE LADIES

I owe so much to the women who helped solidify the ECW brand over the years. Some stayed longer than others, but all were important to the overall mission. Tigra, Angel, and Peaches were our earliest workers. They were there from the beginning when we hadn't yet established an identity to protect. They helped us set that mold for women to step into down the road.

As I mentioned, Nancy Sullivan was there early on, first with Kevin Sullivan, then on her own. We had her managing Sandman for a while, and as great as Nancy was on camera, I remember her most for how she was off camera. She was one of the first members of the elite Posse, and as you've read, not everyone qualifies to ride with us. She earned that distinction by being so smart and cool. Everyone loved Nancy, but more than that, they respected her. It wasn't just a general respect for your fellow worker—she got Terry Funk–like respect from the boys. She slid into that sister role right away, and she and Missy Hyatt brought years of experience to ECW, which made dealing with them so easy.

Well, Nancy, anyway.

I first saw a glimpse into Missy's complicated love life when she asked me if I could customize a gold pendant for her. She ordered the jersey number of the particular Chicago Bear she was dating at the time, and we fastened it onto her necklace. Not long after that, she asked if I could change the number—she was now dating Buffalo Bills quarterback Jim Kelly, so she wanted the pendant changed to the number 12. A few months later there was a hockey player, so she needed the 12 changed to whatever his number was. Then it became a J for actor Jason Hervey, whom she began dating. This worked out well for us at Carver Reed—she ended up spending $600 on a $100 pendant.

Missy landed on Sandman's radar when she first came into ECW. "I'm gonna fuck Missy Hyatt," Hack said, devoid of ambiguity. He was a huge mark for her. I told him he was nuts, but he was insistent. A few months later, we were working a show in Glenolden, Pennsylvania, across the street from a cemetery. During the show, I stepped outside the building for a minute when I heard my name being called. There was no one in the parking lot, but I could make out something across the street in the graveyard.

"Yo, Gordon!"

It was unmistakably Hack's voice. I stepped closer and could see him in the cemetery, as well as Missy Hyatt bent over a headstone. He was behind her and giving her the business.

"I told you so!" Hack yelled again and he kept plowing. It was endearing, his need to share his conquest with me.

Another time we were at a show in New York when I stepped into the bathroom we were using to change. There were about eight workers in there, and I kept hearing this *thud, thud, thud.* I walked past the sink area and there was Hack standing behind Missy again, her head bonking against the side of the sink. I stopped in amazement—why wouldn't she just lift up her head? She turned toward me.

"Hi, boss," she said and her noggin was driven into the sink again and again. The shit you see at work.

Francine and Beulah were ECW-made and quickly became fan favorites. Francine saw the ad for our wrestling school on TV and came down to be trained. Once she started working for us, she often sat in the dressing room corner during the shows, minding her own business. She wasn't being rude; she was just keeping to herself, which she, no doubt, thought was the polite thing to do. But the boys eventually told her she needed to watch the monitor, study the business. She didn't have to jump into everyone's conversation, but it would benefit her to watch more. She took that advice and got more involved after that.

Beulah was another wallflower in the locker room. She'd sit off to the side until Tommy Dreamer called for her, then she'd go to work. I'm trying to remember if I'd ever said more than three words to her, and I don't think I did. When she worked with Raven and Tommy Dreamer, Paul would give them the booking for their matches and they would go off to work out Beulah's involvement with them. She was easy breezy.

I think our best female worker was Sherri Martel. She was such a pro and looked great in the ring. She bumped like one of the boys and was down for anything. Luna Vachon was great also. My introduction to her was a testy one—literally. On her first night she was in the dressing room with Nancy, and I went in to speak with her. Nancy introduced me to Luna, who extended her hand as I had done mine. The difference was Luna bypassed my hand and instead reached between my legs and grabbed. She shook my balls hello and in her trademark gravelly voice said, "Good to meet you."

"You too," I said in an unnaturally high-pitched voice.

Anyone looking to make a memorable impression with their boss on a first day of work might want to highlight this passage. It cannot be overstated how different the wrestling business is from the rest of the world.

## THE DUDLEYS

The popularity of this faction of inbred mountain men came out of nowhere. What started as a simple tag team idea, modeled after the Hanson Brothers from the hockey film *Slap Shot*, became an ever-growing list of tongue-in-cheek comic characters that fans absolutely ate up. The two original Dudleys were Snot Dudley and Dudley Dudley, whom I'd modeled after Nicely-Nicely Johnson from the Damon Runyon musical comedy *Guys and Dolls*, continuing the long tradition of wrestling bookers looking to Broadway musicals for inspiration.

Once we saw the Dudleys were getting over, Paul and I had a great time coming up with characters for their extended family. We tossed around anything and everything that came to mind, and some of it actually made it to the ring. It didn't matter if it didn't get over—we could shitcan one cousin and just introduce another next week. Fans began expecting them to come out of the woodwork. The workers behind the Dudleys were either guys looking to come to ECW or friends of existing workers looking for bookings.

Next to join the clan was Big Dick Dudley. There was also the undersized Spike Dudley, Buh Buh Ray Dudley, and D-Von Dudley, who feuded with his own brothers for allowing themselves to be made fools of. Dances with Dudley was a real stretch as we tried to capitalize on the popularity of the film *Dances with Wolves* by introducing a Native American inbred brother. Sign Guy Dudley was a challenge to our front-row fan Sign Guy, and they'd antagonize each other by holding up dueling signs at shows. Man, we had fun with that one, and so did the guys. The promos were pandemonium as all of the characters started competing for mic time, unleashing their ticks and accents all at once.

Eventually Buh Buh and D-Von reconciled and formed a formidable tag team that actually outlived the extended family gimmick and followed them into WWE and, with a slight modification for trademark reasons, TNA (Total Nonstop Action). The Dudleys gimmick was one of those gambles that could have landed as either the stupidest thing ever to hit the ring or a ton of fun for the workers and fans alike. Thanks to the gifted workers under the eyeglasses and tie-dye, it was the latter. Buh Buh became a great heel and caused near riots as fans rushed the guardrails to get at him. His fiery promos were so effective and helped make the Dudleys what they became.

## MIKEY WHIPWRECK

Before Mikey became our five-foot-seven high-flying sensation, he was part of 911's ring crew. Once the ring was set up, Mikey and his friend Paul Lauria would mess around in it, doing crazy flips off the top turnbuckle. One afternoon I was at the Arena early to put out one of the many fires that would crop up—sound guy can't make it; lights blew out; it's raining in the ring—and I saw Mikey and Lauria screwing around in the ring. It looked like Cirque du Soleil.

Paul E and I got to talking later, and I told him about Mikey. In usual fashion, Paul immediately had a great idea for a character.

"Let's use this kid," he said, "but instead of making him a job guy like he looks, let's have him keep winning. Every week he can keep winning by accident."

It was brilliant. The fun would come in our finding ways for Mikey to surmount impossible odds and get his hand raised against ECW's Goliaths. We'd have him complain each week, practically crying, saying he was in agony from getting his ass kicked and didn't want to wrestle anymore. He would beg us not to book him ever again, saying his mother would put him out of the house if he came home with another black eye. The problem was, Mikey kept winning championship belts and defending them successfully, no matter how accidental via disqualification or countout. He won every week without pinning anyone. We modeled his on-camera persona after Hardy Har Har from the Lippy the Lion cartoons.

When we were coming up with a name for Mikey, Paul suggested the Ultimate Worrier. I liked that, but we ultimately went with

Whipwreck, which was based on an independent promoter named Dennis Whipwreck. We had some fun using local promoter names for characters, like Whipwreck, Joel Hartgood for Goodhart, and Dino Sendoff for promoter Dino Sanna.

Most people don't know that Mikey's persona was part shoot. He was still living at home up in New York, and he came up to me off camera about a black eye.

"Mr. Gordon," he said, "I can't go home with this eye. I don't know how long I can do this." He was a skinny eighteen-year-old kid, and we had him getting his ass kicked by giants like Curtis Hughes. I felt bad for him, but he was so perfect and he didn't really want to stop wrestling. He was just complaining about it. That served his on-camera character perfectly.

Our lovable loser would step into the ring each week and get destroyed. He'd be tossed into the audience, where he'd be counted out, but keep the title belt.

"No!" he'd yell in the post-match promo. "Please take this belt from me!"

The ring announcer would declare him still champion by countout, and Mikey would try and give the belt to his opponent. In his interviews he'd plead, "Mr. Gordon, if you have a heart, please take back this belt." It was hilarious and, like any great wrestling angle, partially true. It catapulted Mikey to one of the top babyfaces in the company.

## 911

911 began his time in ECW as Sabu's handler during the short-lived Hannibal Lecter gimmick. He was friendly with Rocco Rock, and his owning a wrestling ring got him in the door. My advice to anyone looking for steady work on the indie scene would be to forgo paying some broken-down wrestler to train them and buy a ring instead.

911 caught fire as a quasi enforcer, doling out his dreaded chokeslam to worthy recipients. That one simple moment in the ring each night got him over like a god. When some injustice would occur in the ring, 911's unmistakable theme song "Frankenstein" would blare out in the arena, its deep guitar chords driving the crowd to their feet. They watched with perverse glee as the chosen victim was snatched eight feet into the air and single-handedly driven down, practically through the mat, by 911.

911 was the aforementioned Al Poling, the strong sweetheart of a guy who lifted Taz practically to the ceiling. We were using his ring at the time, and watching him assemble it with the crew was transfixing. I'd watch eight guys carry a huge metal post into the building, then five minutes later Al would pick it up by himself and walk it into place. He could probably snap anyone in the locker room in half with little more than a grunt.

Eventually we had 911 chokeslamming everyone. One night we had a guitar player mess up the national anthem, and "Frankenstein" cut in as 911 stomped to the ring. He snatched the guy up and delivered a chokeslam, as he had to Santa Claus and so many others before that. When there was a shitty match in the ring and the crowd became bored, they'd chant, "Nine-One-One! Nine-One-One!" even before we'd planned to send him out. We'd get the hint and the fans would get what they wanted—911 stomping to the ring, chokeslamming all the in-ring participants, and ending the dreadful match.

911 was popular for doing that one little gimmick, and he probably could've done it for five years. But Al blew it when he became intoxicated by the cheers and wanted to actually wrestle in matches. He didn't know the business—he was setting himself up to blow a great thing by exposing how unskilled he was as a real worker. We had him work Ron Simmons in his first foray into wrestling matches. I'm not sure you could actually call what took

place in the ring a "match." If it had been Simmons's audition tape, he never would have worked in the business.

We tried a few more times, then eventually moved him into tag team matches with Rey Mysterio, where his time in the ring could be cut dramatically. Even still, 911 lost his shine when he ceased to be a special attraction on the card and just kind of drifted away after that.

My favorite 911 moment didn't happen in a ring. We were on a flight to Florida when Al started lamenting to passengers in the adjacent seats about his late wife. Here's this hulking biker dude, fighting to get the words out as tears welled in his eyes. People in the row ahead of him turned around to offer a sympathetic ear. People in the aisle next to him came over to add support too, as Al told them he'd recently lost his third wife. It was especially hard, he said, because he'd had three wives die. He told them he lost his first wife when she ate poison mushrooms.

"Oh my god," came the hushed gasps around him.

He fought through tears. "Then my *second* wife died of the same thing—she ate poison mushrooms." He stopped and looked out the window.

More gasps, then a concerned old lady leaned in. "Is that what your current wife died from also?"

"No," he said matter-of-factly. "Blow to the head."

"What happened?"

"She wouldn't eat the poison mushrooms."

With that, the entire section of the plane broke into hysterics. He sold the damn thing so well. I was impressed.

My affinity for a good rib kicked in a few months later when I was at Lulu Temple running a show with ECW. I was in the back kitchen area with the local Shriners whom I'd come to know from running shows there, and I thought I'd go for it. I started putting on the crocodile tears, saying my first wife had died from a poison mushroom. Some old Shriner put his hand on my shoulder.

Early babyface run.

Charles Gordon, passing the baton.

Terry Funk. One of the first believers. I'm forever grateful. (Courtesy of George Tahinos)

Eddie Gilbert was one of the first of many co-workers gone too soon. (Courtesy of George Tahinos)

My first world champion, taking a quick break between joints.

With Blue Meanie and Cactus Jack, aka Mick Foley, clearly not at Gold's Gym.

Chilling with Bob Artese, our one and only ring announcer. (Courtesy of George Tahinos)

The Posse.

You try working a forty-hour week at Carver Reed and running ECW. (Courtesy of George Tahinos)

The chaos in the locker room during Hack's "blinding." (Courtesy of George Tahinos)

Hack played this one perfectly, in the ring and out.
(Courtesy of George Tahnios)

Paul Heyman. (Courtesy of George Tahinos)

Joey Styles and Tommy Dreamer. (Courtesy of George Tahinos)

Buh Buh in my face. Lotta finger pointing from those New York guys. (Courtesy of George Tahinos)

Me and Sabu. And his uncle. (Courtesy of George Tahinos)

Facing off with the worst State Athletic Commission officer ever. (Courtesy of George Tahinos)

There were few people more loved and respected in our locker room than Nancy Sullivan. We were destroyed at her passing. (Courtesy of George Tahinos)

If only it was this easy to block Jasmine out.
(Courtesy of George Tahinos)

"To the man that discovered Paul Heyman... WHAT
AN ERROR."

My partner in crime, Leslie.

Working like a dog.

Becky, Charles, and Ally.

Me and Adrienne on our wedding day.

With Becky...

and my first grandchild, Max.

"I hear you, brother. My wife just died too. Cancer." Everyone was so solemn; I couldn't continue the joke. I said I was sorry to hear it and left them standing as I headed out of the kitchen before you could say "second wife." 911 pulled off the rib in front of twenty passengers on a plane—no one's wife died there. I try it with five Shriners, and I hit the cancer lottery in the first ten seconds. It was shorter lived and more disappointing than 911's wrestling career.

## BENOIT, GUERRERO, MALENKO

Wrestling shows need variety on the card. Imagine watching a film consisting of only car chases. You'd be falling asleep an hour into it, so pacing is important and wrestling shows are no different. ECW was known for its blood and guts, but we couldn't be *all* blood and guts. We wanted some comedy on there, and we usually looked to Public Enemy, the Dudleys, JT Smith, or Mikey for that. But we also wanted some wrestling, real grappling.

Dean Malenko, Eddie Guerrero, and Chris Benoit were three smaller guys who could pop our crowds as big as a barbed-wire and flaming branding-iron match could, maybe bigger, and they could do it with just wrestling. Our fans were smart, and while they enjoyed the thrill rides on our show, they also deeply appreciated the in-ring workmanship of guys like them. They were smaller, nothing to look at if they passed you in an alley, like 911 or Mike Awesome would be. But the excitement and frenetic pacing of their matches was something to behold, and they got love and respect from the ECW fans.

The three guys came to us in different ways. I'd already been using Malenko since the NWA heavyweight title tournament that Shane won. He beat Malenko in the semifinal match before beating Scorpio in the finals. I needed some talent that worked Dean's style to put with him and maximize that special ingredient in our shows.

Eddie Guerrero was a name I'd always heard, and I eventually saw tape of his legendary matches with Art Barr in Mexico. He was part of the legendary Guerrero wrestling family, and he joined us in March 1995, primarily to work Malenko. He mixed it up with Scorpio for a few shots, but 90 percent of Guerrero's workload was Malenko. Guerrero was gone in August of that year but had some classic matches for the ECW TV title.

Chris Benoit was working mostly in Japan when he came to us in August of 1994. He was with us for about a year and spent time tagging with Malenko, and also working matches against guys like Sabu and Chris Jericho, among others. Benoit, Guerrero, and Malenko all left in August '95 for WCW, where they began spotlighting what they called the junior heavyweights, which Kevin Nash, the WWE heavyweight champion, began calling the "vanilla midgets."

Our crew of scientific grapplers kept mostly to themselves in the locker room. They weren't partying with the boys, and I'm not even sure where they went after shows. They were in their own world.

I called Malenko the Warner Brothers frog, the one in the classic cartoons that performs Vaudevillian acts for only his owner. Malenko was animated and funny in the locker room. He had a good personality and the guys liked him, but once that microphone came on, he went mute. So we labeled him "the Shooter" and gave him Jason as a manager to speak for him.

Those guys added something very unique to cards that might've appeared a little monochromatic without that style of worker.

## VISITING WORKERS

Kevin Sullivan, Jake the Snake, Marty Jannetty, Hawk, Kerry Von Erich, the Steiner Brothers, Terry Gordy, Steve Austin, Cactus Jack, Stan Hansen, Abdullah the Butcher, Eddie Gilbert, Tatsumi Fujinami, Doug Furnas, Rey Mysterio, Konnan, Rick Rude, Brian

Pillman, Eddie Guerrero, Scott Hall, Jerry "the King" Lawler, Jim Cornette, Steve "Dr. Death" Williams, Arn Anderson, Bobby Eaton, Don Muraco, Jim Neidhart, Nikolai Volkoff, Tommy Rich, Jack Victory, 2 Cold Scorpio, Ron Simmons, Davey Boy Smith, Chris Jericho, and Terry Taylor.

How's that for a list of wrestlers? You know what they all have in common? Every one of them came through ECW's doors.

I brought in guys that I wanted to see as a fan. That guided 99 percent of my decision making in ECW, and it usually worked because I was one of them, one of the fans in the bleachers.

I scored early when I got Stan Hansen and Abdullah the Butcher to come in for the tag match against Kevin Sullivan and Terry Funk. Having Hansen was a big deal because he wasn't being seen anywhere except Japan at the time. His uncontrolled entrances overseas were a thing to behold, as fans scattered when Hansen swung his bull rope in all directions through the crowd. He was set to do that for us too, culminating with his wrapping ring announcer Bob Artese in the rope. The only problem was Stan was blind as a bat; he couldn't see the tip of his nose without glasses. I was holding the microphone ready to interview him, when he walked right past Artese and wrapped the rope around *my* neck and started throttling me. I was gagging and trying to tell him it was me, Tod! It wasn't fun.

Speaking of Abdullah the Butcher, I want to say that despite his reputation for being difficult to book, we never had a problem. We quickly came to understand the one rule mentioned earlier about booking Abby and Hansen—they don't lose in front of the cameras, lest they damage their reputations in Japan. That was fine with us, allowing them to work out their own finishes. I loved using Abby and did it whenever I could. The bloody brutality of his matches popped our crowd every time. He was known for gouging and goring his opponents until they flowed like stuck pigs. One night long after Abby had worked for me in ECW, he said, "I always wanted to cut you and Crockett," referring to Mid-Atlantic promoter Jim Crockett. There are very few careers in which you can say that kind of thing to a boss and it's not really inappropriate.

My favorite Abby story occurred when we brought in the Headhunters, the aforementioned eight-hundred-pound tag team. One of them was literally thrown through a wall during a match at the ECW Arena, leaving a hole you could pass a Volkswagen through. As the drywall dust settled and the camera shot through the gap into the dressing area, there sat Abby with his giant tits out, struggling to get a sock on his foot. He glanced up casually, saw the camera filming him through the hole, then calmly stood and walked out of frame. I was disappointed we didn't get the conclusion of the sock deal, because that was a cliffhanger worthy of a Netflix series.

Ron Simmons, the first black WCW world champion, was a former football player and built like a cement mixer. He came in for a short run and told me on his first night that he didn't want to do a job—lose a match—in Florida where he was living at the time. He asked to speak with me outside and told me, rather intimidatingly, that he didn't think losing for $500 was going to happen. He thought $700 would make it more palatable. In truth, a couple hundred bucks isn't a big deal, particularly when a 250-pound monster is standing alone with you in a back alley. But giving in to those kind of holdups sets a bad precedent. Word spreads faster than herpes in a locker room, and soon enough, ten wrestlers on your card will be asking for an additional hundred bucks to lose.

"I don't have the extra money, Ron," I said. "I understand you don't want to job here, so I'll just get someone else to do the match." I suppose it was calling his bluff a little, but I really wasn't going back into my pocket. I'd rather lose him for the night than open that Pandora's box in my locker room. He said he needed a minute to consult with his wife, Lottie. He got on the phone and put on this whole show, hemming and hawing with her. In the end, he tells me they've agreed that he will do it because he likes me. Perfect. We were very friendly after that first night, having established our boundaries.

Tully Blanchard was another guy that lasted only a short time in ECW. He walked in the locker room on his first night and looked around.

"Do I even know anyone in this company?" he said to no one in particular. Eventually he took up with Shane Douglas and Paul E, both of whom he knew from WCW. But he never gelled with our locker room. There were no incidents per se, but he just wasn't one of us. Our fans were even tougher on him. One night the entire audience stood and literally turned their backs on Tully, showing their disapproval of his work.

Years later I was able to use that event for a great rib when around 2015 I did some work for the shoot company Kayfabe Commentaries. After my current coauthor Sean Oliver and I finished shooting an edition of their show *YouShoot*, I saw Sean and his crew sitting at dinner with Tully in the hotel restaurant. I knew Sean was aware of the Tully incident with our fans turning around on him, so I decided to have a little fun. I sat at the end of the bar, right across from their dinner table. I waved to Sean and ordered a cocktail. As he listened intently to Tully, I saw him eyeing me as I walked around the restaurant, stopping at tables, chatting briefly with fans. Sean was probably wondering what the hell I was doing.

I returned to my martini and waited for their dinner to wrap up. When it did, I texted Sean that I'd just told the restaurant to stand up and turn their backs on Tully as they walked out together. Sean read his phone and went whiter than he normally was. For the next five minutes I watched Oliver, who'd already paid the bill, delay the group's exit. They'd eventually have to leave and, whenever that would happen, he'd realize no one was standing or turning their backs. I'd really just said, "Hello, how is your meal? Good to see you," when I walked the room. But until Sean and Tully headed out, I greatly enjoyed the tension and soon realized I was sitting alone at the bar and laughing like a ghost had just told me a great joke.

Just as Tully didn't really fit in our locker room, the same was the case for the Steiner brothers. During their brief time in ECW, they'd sit in a corner playing cards, not integrating with the rest of the room. They'd say, "Hi, boss," each time I passed them. When we put Taz with them for a six-man tag, he sat with them and played cards in the dressing room that night. He even said, "Hi, boss," when I walked by. It was hilarious. I knew the Steiners wouldn't last long, but that was okay. We brought in talent for short runs knowing we never intended on keeping them.

Freebird Terry Gordy was another worker we brought in for only a few shows to get that crowd pop when someone unexpected walked through the curtain. After one show, we were in a hotel room drinking and smoking weed. Present were me, Sandman, Fonzie, Scorpio, Tommy Rich, and Gordy. As we're sitting around bullshitting, Gordy goes catatonic, slumps down with his eyes and mouth open. I seriously thought he was dead, but Tommy Rich told us to relax.

"He'll kick out of it," he said like he knew what the hell he was talking about. To my eyes it appeared Gordy would need to kick out of a coffin. Relax? I'm the owner here. If that guy just dropped dead, it's my ass everyone is coming for.

Sure enough, after everyone else carried on their conversation for five minutes like we weren't supposed to be planning a funeral, Gordy looked up and said, "So anyway, me and Hayes were in Dallas..." It was like he never left us.

Tommy "Wildfire" Rich wasn't an official member of our Posse per se, but he was a great fit for us. I'll call him an honorary member. He was a hard worker and a good guy. He got along with

148

everyone and didn't walk around with an ego, despite being one of the guys in wrestling that could have. He was easy to get along with, funny as shit, and he loved us—he had all the right Posse qualities.

Rich was a partier, to be sure. We were doing a show in Buffalo when he came to me in the dressing room and asked me what number match was currently in the ring.

"This is number four," I said.

"When am I on?"

"You're sixth."

"Okay, good. I have some time to run out real quick."

"Run out where?"

"I need to run down the road to the hood. I seen it when we drove in and I know there's some shit going on there."

Rich barely had time to use the bathroom before his match, much less wander Buffalo to find the sketchiest part of town. He'd apparently seen a prime place to make a recreational purchase when we drove in.

"Tommy, you're on sixth. Why don't you just go during the *seventh* match?" This seemed way too logical.

"Nah, man. Lemme run." And with that, Tommy "Wildfire" Rich went out into the Buffalo cold, looking for his powder or rock gimmick.

I was biting my nails as match four ended and five began. Rich was up next, and I had to think of a save if he didn't make it back from his very important errand. As fate would have it, the bell rang to end match five and there was no Tommy Rich in the building. I found Paul and told him we needed to switch up the order and move Tommy and the FBI, the in-ring faction Full Blooded Italians, down to seventh.

"Why?" Paul said. "They're up next."

"They're working on this big thing for the match and they're not ready yet. Can we send match seven out now, swap the order?"

149

So match seven headed out in the number six slot and that bought us more time. Tommy Rich finally returned and seemed happy, so I guessed he had his hood gimmick on him. What Tommy Rich *didn't* have on him was boots and socks. The goddamn guy walked back into the locker room barefoot and got ready for his match, which took place without the big angle I'd teased to Paul. I never did find out what the hell he did with his boots in downtown Buffalo.

Steve Austin worked with us before he was Stone Cold. We renamed him "Superstar" Steve Austin after his working WCW as "Stunning" Steve. He wasn't with us very long, and I think there was some issue with him and Paul, though neither man expressed that. The first thing that tipped me off was when Paul asked me to make the initial phone call.

"Why me?" I asked him. "Weren't you in WCW with him?"

"Trust me—it'll be better if you call." That was all Paul was giving me, so I called and booked Austin myself. On his first night there, he and Paul E ran into each other in the dressing room.

"Steve?" Paul said, feigning surprise. "What are you doing here?" They hugged and talked, which left me befuddled. Why did Paul want to seem uninvolved in his booking? I never got the answer.

But within two or three shows, Austin no-showed us. When I finally got hold of him, he told me the reason.

"I didn't come because Paul lied to my face," he said. Austin had one request for Paul, albeit an odd one for someone working in ECW—he didn't want blood in the ring during his matches. He asked Paul to put him somewhere in the lineup before the blood started flowing. While he didn't mind bleeding himself, he didn't want to be rolling on a mat with other workers' blood. Paul told him that was not a problem, done deal. When Austin went out for his match, the mat looked like we'd rented it from the set of

*The Texas Chainsaw Massacre.* The previous three matches all had blade jobs.

Paul and I were still tight, and I thought both his mind and work ethic would get us to the next level. But I was seeing his casual relationship with the truth and his inability to forge relationships with any human being other than me. I was aware I held the purse strings, so that might've been a reason for the bond. But when we talked, I really felt a connection, something beyond wrestling, and we made a pretty damn good team there too.

"Why didn't you talk to me?" I asked Steve. I was the one who wanted him there in the first place, but this was the flip side of Paul having told the workers to deal with him instead of me. When he first suggested that, it succeeded in taking a great weight off my shoulders. But it also kept me out of the loop with the boys. In the Austin instance, I would've put him on early so as not to come in contact with blood. Paul had a tendency to agree with anything someone asked, then do what he wanted anyway.

"Paul, before I come to ECW I want a trapeze artist in the dressing room."

"Done!"

That's a condensed summary of every wrestler's potential conversation with Paul E. He'd probably also tell them he had a connection to Ringling Brothers.

There was only one worker I can recall who worked for us but never stepped foot in our dressing room. We booked Jim Cornette to do a run-in for us and clear the ring with his iconic tennis racket. Jim initially said he would come up for the angle only if Paul apologized to his NWA compatriot Dennis Coralluzzo for what we had Shane Douglas do to the NWA belt. It was these select times I was happy Paul had slid into the more public face of the company. Cornette was no dummy and he knew who owned ECW, but having Paul apologize would've been a much grander gesture than if I did it. After some back and forth it was agreed that Paul would apologize to Dennis, though it would happen in private, not in front of the boys.

When Cornette and Coralluzzo pulled up to the ECW Arena, Paul went outside, stuck his head in the window of their car, and said he was sorry to Dennis. Cornette elected to stay in the car all night and when it was time for his run-in, someone was to go get him. We agreed and when it was his cue, Cornette got out of the car, came in the rear entrance, went straight to the ring, whacked me and anyone else in sight with the tennis racket, and was back through the crowd, out the back door, and into Dennis's car. Talk about an easy transaction, for both Jim and me. I could think of a couple of workers I wished would've adhered to that locker room schedule also.

Assembling the right talent was a crucial ingredient to our success. They combined to create classic ECW moments that are still talked about to this day. There are a handful of those moments that stick out in my mind as exceptional.

# CHAPTER 8

# MOMENTS

**B**efore we get into the ECW moments that fans saw in the ring and on camera, I want to take a minute to clarify one that's taken on a life of its own. It happens to be the title of this book.

In the years following ECW's closure, the phrase "Tod is God" has become part of wrestling folklore. It was chanted by fans in the ECW Arena whenever I did something in the ring to assert my authority. It got to the point where I'd hear it anytime I came out to ringside for any reason. It then became a complimentary chant whenever something cool would happen in the ring in my absence, similar to the "E-C-W! E-C-W!" chant. Even today, fans write it on my Facebook wall all the time. However, the origin of that phrase has been the subject of some debate thanks to a few shoot interview appearances by ECW workers.

In two separate *YouShoot* appearances, both Sandman and New Jack recount having first heard the phrase during a licentious night in a Travelodge hotel room after a show. (Note: Sandman, licentious means lewd. Note: Fonzie, lewd means obscene.) There are elements of both truth and fiction in their recollections of the night's events. Firstly, it's been reported that a submissive—a woman in her thirties who desired being dominated, sometimes in group fashion—was present in Scorpio's and my room for a night of fun. That part is true. Hack and New Jack also recalled Scorpio making the woman yell "Tod is God!" rather loudly as she was being dominated. True also. I'm sure it did echo through the hallways and maybe a couple of the boys heard it, but that's where their versions part with the truth and become fantasy.

Hack was never in the room with us. He says he was snorting bumps of blow at a table just "being entertained" by Scorpio and the submissive's show. Mind you, Sandman recounts this while sitting on the floor of the *YouShoot* set after having gotten down there to illustrate Scorpio whipping the girl with his freakish appendage and is unable to get back up into the interview chair. Saying Hack's recall is challenged would be putting it mildly.

New Jack's story was embellished even more interestingly. He claims he was let into the room while Scorpio was going at it with the sub as me and Fonzie were sitting on opposite ends of the room getting our rocks off watching the action. He said she was yelling "Tod is God!" thinking it was me laying pipe, and only when New Jack grabbed a lamp and held it over her did she see it was Scorpio. In reality, New Jack wasn't there holding a lamp and Fonzie wasn't there whacking off. These are two very entertaining accounts, but neither are true, and that should've been evident when Jack said she needed a lamp to know the difference between me and Scorpio being inside her.

As for the clever phrase itself, Scorpio didn't invent that on the spot, nor can I credit the submissive for coming up with it. All the credit goes to "Sign Guy" Paul Meles himself. One night he showed up with a sign that read, "TOD IS GOD." The rest is history. The fans in the ECW Arena picked up on it and made it a chant. It is a catchy little thing, ain't it? Well, our crowd saw it and ran with it. It was repeated in the halls of the Travelodge at Scorpio's command, but only long after our fans made it a thing.

\* \* \*

One classic ECW moment we got some heat for was the crucifixion of Sandman by Raven. This was Hack and Scotty's brainchild from the get-go. They worked it out on their own as they usually did for their matches, and Paul and I didn't even know what was coming.

During their match, Sandman was out on the Arena floor when Raven directed his flunkies Stevie Richards and Blue Meanie to tie Sandman to a cross and fasten it to the ring ropes. They even made a thorny crown out of barbed wire and wrapped it around Hack's head, who hung bleeding for all the world to see. Sandman's real-life young son Tyler was there beside his father as part of the angle. It was an effective and horrifying visual, as Scotty no doubt knew it would be. Even our bloodthirsty fans, normally at fever pitch by the end of a match, were shocked into silence by the ritual. It was true ECW.

Parallel to this, we'd invited Olympic wrestling gold medal winner and not yet WWE star Kurt Angle to come down to the matches that night. Kurt was flirting with the idea of becoming a pro wrestler, and he wanted to get a sampling of our product. He picked quite the night. Upon seeing the crucifixion, Kurt apparently began freaking out at the offensive religious imagery. He went into the dressing room and found Paul, wherein he lodged his disapproval of the sacrilegious and disgraceful display, then headed for the door.

I was at ringside after the crucifixion, and when I got back to the dressing room Paul pulled me aside.

"We have a problem," he said. "Angle is freaking out."

"Who gives a shit? He doesn't like barbed wire and blood? This is what we do."

"I know," Paul said, "but there's a religious slant here. We're both Jews and we just crucified a guy like he was Jesus Christ. How do you think that's going to look?"

It was too late, right or wrong. It happened and our fans saw it. Paul may have had a point, but you can't put the toothpaste back in the tube, right? Maybe not, but you apparently can ask the toothpaste to go back out to the ring and apologize to the fans. Paul first asked Sandman to go out, to which he promptly replied, "Get the fuck out of here."

I asked Scotty if he'd do it. He thought it was an awful idea and I did too, but he eventually agreed. Raven took to the ring and addressed the fans.

"Apparently Tod Gordon and Paul Heyman, by my acting without their knowledge, are offended at my use of religious iconography. And apparently I've offended quite a few people in the audience. You people chose to respect Scott Levy's privacy when I needed personal time, so I choose to respect your privacy and your religious beliefs. So to the people I've offended, I apologize."

It was well done by Raven. He framed it cleverly, putting the heat on me and Paul, while still getting himself over with the fans and working in the word "iconography." Classic Scotty.

\* \* \*

There were a couple of ECW angles that I'm proud to say kept fans and writers guessing. Pro wrestling was built on its ability to blur the lines of reality and stir the emotions of paying fans. It ultimately leads to feuds that can last for months or years, and all the associated box office.

In fall of 1994, Sandman and Tommy Dreamer had an "I Quit" match at the ECW Arena that ended in Dreamer taking Sandman's lit cigarette and jabbing it in his eye. Hack dropped down and sold it, rolling around the ring longer than would normally be done for a typical worked wrestling angle. Everyone just stopped. Nancy and Dreamer were in the ring and they froze in panic, unsure of what to do. It looked great. Hack and I talked that angle through extensively, and that pause sold it to the fans, no question.

We came out and tried to help, at which point I uttered my favorite line, "Is there an ophthalmologist in the house?" Thankfully, there wasn't and we continued the ruse, with even babyface wrestlers trying to protect Sandman from Dreamer as he approached. We didn't even tell the locker room that we'd be doing the cigarette deal, and they seemed to be buying it whole-heartedly. Hack and I thought this could be very special, and thus to keep everyone guessing we agreed that not one wrestler other than him and Dreamer could know about it being a work. Someone would've told their wife or girlfriend, and that would've been it. Want to blow someone's surprise party? Tell one wrestler. In India.

We announced to the fans that we will keep them posted on Sandman's condition once he was treated and brought him away from ringside, cameras still rolling.

"Gordon!" Sandman shouted as he held his eye. "Where are you?!"

I moved to his side. "I'm right here, Jim." I never called him by his shoot name, but I wanted the cameras to capture it. It added to the realism of the hectic situation backstage being caught by our cameras. It was so real that if I wasn't in on it, I would've believed it, even being in the business. Sandman was carted from the building through the crowd and into an ambulance. I purposely led him out the front, through the people—I wanted it to seem disorganized and I also wanted fans to see the bloody towel he was holding up to his face.

It was up to him to make this get over outside the ring. Hack agreed to stay in his house and not be seen outside. He was down with that—he knew the business better than anyone. It was over to the point where wrestling journalist Dave Scherer called me and asked how he was.

"I don't know, Dave. It's a bad situation, and I don't know what's going to happen with him. I don't want to talk about it." My reticence kept him guessing and, hopefully, the other writers to whom he spoke. Sandman did no interviews, no press. He didn't even answer his home phone. He simply disappeared for a while.

The angle culminated in our hosting Sandman's in-ring retirement ceremony due to the injury. Hack proudly announced to the locker room that he was wearing his olive-green wedding suit for the occasion. As Sandman and I stood in the center of the ring, Peaches came out displaying a couple of new additions. She'd obviously just gotten breast implants, and she prepared Hack for what he'd see when the bandages were finally removed from his eyes.

"I've changed a little since you've last seen me," she said. I handed the mic to Hack.

"Oh, Peaches, I don't care how fat you got." That unpredictable switch—from violence to comedy—is how we kept our fans entertained. Of course, Sandman would remove the eye bandages himself and attack Tommy Dreamer once he turned his back.

That was one of our trademarks, going from hilarious to serious, clever to shocking, with such ease. I truly don't know if that angle would've been as effective with anyone other than Hack at center stage.

* * *

Our workers' commitment to ECW was second to none. During a four-way match, Pitbull #1 (Gary Wolfe) took a DDT from Shane Douglas, which resulted in his breaking his neck. Gary didn't realize it at the time, but it was a legit break and he had to wear a halo neck brace, which was remarkably intrusive and uncomfortable. In order to ensure total immobility, the halo was screwed into his skull around the crown of his head. I can't imagine living with that for an hour, let alone several months.

But that's not the remarkable level of commitment I'm talking about.

Gary finally had the damn thing taken off at Jefferson University Hospital, which is right across the street from Carver Reed. He stopped by for a visit I'm sure he regretted for a long time. I was happy to see him without the monstrous device, and he was even happier to tell me he'd be able to wrestle again in three months.

"That's great," I said. "But would you mind not taking the halo off?"

He looked at me like I asked if I could fuck his wife. "Why?"

"Gary, I wouldn't make this suggestion unless I thought there was a big money angle in it for you."

"Do you know how much that thing hurts?"

"I can imagine. Maybe take it off at home. But keep it on outside." He agreed as reluctantly as a man could while being asked to walk the plank. I called Paul as soon as Gary left.

"Here's some money in the bank," I said. "Gary has the halo off but no one knows. He's going to wear it in public until he's cleared to wrestle, which should only be a few months."

Only a few months, said the man with no bolts in his head.

Anyway, my plan was to have him come out and wave to the fans in a triumphant return to ECW since the tragic injury. Our crowd knew about the injury being legit, so imagine their horror when Shane Douglas would come out the following week, grab Gary by the halo, and toss him across the ring. Gary would be fully healed by then, but no one in the world would know that. Paul lit up—he saw the same dollar signs I did.

When the prescribed time came, we decided to do it during a match between Shane and Pitbull Anthony, Gary's partner. Gary was at ringside in his halo brace for his partner's match, and after the contest Shane did his thing, further cementing himself as our most despised heel. Gary sold it perfectly and the fans went berserk. I came out first, flying. I dove into the ring and before long a couple of fans hopped the guardrail to get at Shane. We had plants in the crowd ready to jump, but they were beaten to it by real fans.

We'd put the plants there to heighten the tension and drive home the realism, but we didn't count on the pack mentality of our dedicated fans. The rest of the crowd saw them charging the ring and they figured Shane was fair game. Before long, Shane had a real problem on his hands and, by proxy, I did too.

"How do I get out of here?" he asked me in the ring as fans closed in.

I didn't have a reply for him, though "Oops" probably would've been most appropriate. We eventually got him out in one piece. I'd never been so scared in the ring, so I can imagine how Shane was feeling. It's difficult to get smart fans emotionally invested, but so satisfying when something you concocted works so well. Though, it's much easier to enjoy it when you're not out there.

* * *

The blowoff to the Fonzie's state athletic commission deal was my getting in the ring to face him at November to Remember '95, despite Paul always advising me to stay out of the ring.

"You want to be like Dusty Rhodes?" he'd ask, referencing the longtime booker/wrestler who kept himself winning forever. "You wanna own the company *and* be on TV all the time? You know wrestlers hate that, right?" This coming from a 49 percent owner who was on our TV show for twenty-eight out of forty-eight minutes each week. Paul was very good at talking me out of anything high profile that I came up with, convincing me it was bad for business. "What's more important—making money or your ego?" He knew what to say, and he always did it with a slant that made sense. He had a way about him.

However convincing he might've been, the Fonzie angle needed that moment where I get my hands on him. I'd been taking bumps this entire time—my getting revenge on behalf of my company and all our fans was the only logical climax. Win or lose, I had to throttle that weasel for the appeasement of our fans.

Neither Fonzie nor I had any training for the match. We didn't solicit advice from workers about hip tosses or arm drags. How ridiculous would that have looked, us out there trying to have a wrestling contest? Our match would be a brawl; it was the only realistic way to do it. Neither of us was particularly concerned with throwing a working punch. I think I can speak for both of us when I say it was understood we'd go out and pound the balls off each other.

That's not to say we didn't go over the match. We talked about it all the time, even rehearsing some of the spots. It wasn't just a gimmick match, like, "Ooh, the company owner is getting in the ring." We'd invested so much into making Fonzie hated, and now all roads led to this. When the day arrived, I was stoked and a little scared.

But there was one problem—Fonzie was missing. We had adjoining hotel rooms, and when I woke up and stuck my head into his room, I saw his bed was still made and the room was empty. Fonzie never pulled all-nighters without us. Hell, he was usually attached to my hip. Then on the eve of our much-hyped match, he chose to stay out all night. Of all the fucking times.

When he finally bounced into the room, he was bug-eyed and sniffing like a maniac.

"Hey!" he said, all smiles. "Morning, Todster."

"You fucking kidding me?"

"What?"

The symptoms were very obvious to me. "After all your years in the business, you chose last night to coke yourself up?"

"Don't worry, daddy. I got this."

He'd been up all night long partying and dipped hard into the nose candy. I'd been doing it too, but I thought he'd be a little more judicious on the night before our big match. I didn't think he'd fall asleep in the ring that night, but I made sure to hit him hard enough to guarantee it.

We got caught in the hotel elevator together on the day of the matches. Fans piled on and started giving Fonzie some shit, and he was nervous. They followed us out and got more boisterous. Fonzie was grunting under his breath as he strode next to me.

"Todster, tell them it's a wizerk," he said, invoking Carny for "it's fake" at a time when our fans probably spoke it better than I did. "Wizerk, Tod, wizerk."

I yelled, "I'll see you in the ring tonight, motherfucker!" and headed off in another direction.

I went on to do the job that night when Taz knocked me out and dropped Fonzie on top of me, sending the angle in yet another direction by turning Taz heel and putting Fonzie with him. We went on to do tag team matches and also matches where Fonzie and I were handcuffed to each other at ringside. He drove me nuts by blowing that damn coach's whistle in my ear during the matches and I couldn't even walk away. My rage as I screamed at him was not a work. One night during a handcuff match, I was yelling in his face and he cut me off and reached into his pocket. I was ready to take a shot with brass knuckles or something when he brandished a plastic Tweety Bird.

"Pez, Todster?" he said, pulling the head back and offering me a snack. It took everything not to crack up right there at ringside. I don't know if the cameras ever caught that or if it just remains a moment between us two and the front row fans.

\* \* \*

Kimona's striptease is certainly not beside the Piper/Snuka coconut incident or Starrcade '83 as one of pro wrestling's great memories, but it certainly sits on ECW's list. It was a spur of the moment thing that actually bailed our asses out during a very tense night at the ECW Arena.

Kimona was working as a dancer at a strip club when she ran into Raven one night. He convinced her to come to one of our shows, and fans took notice of her. She was a stunning eighteen-year-old Asian beauty, and Paul and I saw how other fans were looking at her in the audience, actually cheering at one point. She was not part of the show in any way, but they'd made her so. We offered her a spot with Raven, thinking she'd be comfortable working beside her new, um, friend.

Raven seemed to be at a strip club every frigging night, and each foray seemed to serve as an impromptu casting call because these girls ended up in ECW locker rooms. It was amazing—whichever club he went to produced a stripper headed for TV the next night. Who would've thought the titty joints in South Jersey and Philly had such an abundance of undiscovered talent?

Kimona debuted as Raven's valet and was eventually embroiled in a bisexual love triangle with Beulah and Tommy Dreamer, featuring a long, passionate in-ring kiss between the ladies. I'm not 100 percent sure who booked that whole angle, but since Dreamer was in it as the object of both girls' affection, I'll give you one guess. He's a horny toad, and the believability of two women looking like Kimona and Beulah fighting over Tommy was challenging. Given his looks and lack of charisma, he might've been the least likely person in the ECW Arena to get two women like that, and I am including Fucking Butchie in that analysis.

Fast-forward a few months to the night we all found ourselves sitting through a ninety-minute delay as our shitty ring broke. The temperature kept climbing in the Arena and when it hit around five hundred degrees, we figured we had to do something before our fans left in disgust and demanded their money back, or worse, started getting rowdier than they already were. At that point,

Kimona suggested she perform for the crowd, doing a striptease to help the suffering audience get through the uncomfortable delay.

Sounded good to me!

Listen, before you judge I'd like to remind you she'd been doing it for a career before she was brought into the company. She saw how tense the situation was becoming, and she did it for one reason—to save our show. She didn't do it to get herself over; she was already over. It wasn't like she'd been asking to do this for months beforehand. She saw the need and raised her hand to help.

I remember Francine sitting in the locker room eating her bag of nuts murmuring about how distasteful it was. There may have been others who felt the same, but I just specifically remember her face as she offered her official disapproval. I wondered how everyone would've liked not having a place to work the following night if the crowd had decided to walk out in disgust from being trapped in a sweatbox with no main event. How dare anyone criticize someone for doing something to save the company. I didn't see Scotty offering to go out and challenge fans to trivia, or Francine taking center ring to read poetry. No one dared stand up and say anything directly to me about it, but I was well aware of the whispers and facial expressions.

It was an amazing and selfless gesture by this young lady who knew nothing about pro wrestling and really owed us nothing. Thank God for people like that.

\* \* \*

One of ECW's more unfortunate moments happened at a spot show in Massachusetts in November 1996. A seventeen-year-old fan named Eric Kulas came to the show dressed in a bus driver's uniform and asked for a spot on the card. He apparently had a gimmick called Mass Transit, and, considering his size, he did bear an uncanny resemblance to TV's most famous bus driver, Ralph Kramden of *The Honeymooners*.

It was not unusual for an indie wrestler to crash a show on the independent circuit and ask for a spot on the card. Of course, showing up at Madison Square Garden and asking to speak to Vince McMahon about your Jackie Gleason deal and getting a spot on that card is about as impossible as anything. But the Wonderland Ballroom in Revere, Massachusetts, is not the Garden, Paul ain't Vince, and therefore Kulas was given a spot in a match against the Gangstas, New Jack and Mustafa.

I wasn't present at the card that night so I can't speak to all that happened before the match, but the facts are pretty clear—the underage Kulas said he was of legal age, got in the ring, and New Jack lacerated his forehead with an X-Acto knife, nicking an artery that caused a fountain of blood to spurt out of the kid while a panicked scene unfolded at ringside. New Jack downplayed the event in subsequent shoot interviews, posturing that some outsider walked into our locker room and was subject to whatever repercussions surfaced. But I know Jack didn't intend to slice the kid as deeply as he had and, incidentally, Kulas had asked Jack if he'd help him bleed since he'd never done it himself.

I can't blame anyone for the accident. Kulas wanted a break wrestling in his favorite federation; Paul E needed a replacement for Axl Rotten, who missed the show. New Jack went too deep on the blade job in the heat of the moment. It was a bad night for wrestling and certainly for ECW, but we hadn't exactly carded workers at the door before that, and I don't think we did afterward.

Footage of the incident garnered attention in tape trading circles, the '90s equivalent of going viral, I suppose. Though I would erase the incident if I could, it did further fortify the image of ECW as the most dangerous wrestling company in the world and gave New Jack's reputation some additional credibility as well.

# CHAPTER 9

# PEAKING

In order to understand ECW, you must understand my original business plan and how it was modified along the way, for better or worse. Our explosive growth cut both ways; it violated so much of what I had planned, but it delivered us the worldwide recognition that remains thirty years later, as of this writing.

I'd planned a local promotion with a tight budget. I used the age-old promoter's recipe of putting one or two names on top of the card to draw a house and then filled the rest with local talent that fans would go home talking about. In time, I thought our roster would be able to deliver the wrestling product I craved—smart and credible. SportsChannel was a fortuitous gift, broadcasting us for free. Tape traders were exchanging copies of our shows with fans in regions that couldn't get the televised product. We were soon being seen all over the country without any financial burden extending us beyond our means.

In time, fans all over the world wanted to see ECW. We began making good money on global videotape sales and our healthy gates in the Pennsylvania and New Jersey markets. Before we knew it, some of the biggest names in the business were wrestling in our rings and our homegrown talent were becoming bona fide wrestling stars. It was all happening too damn fast, and before I knew it the words "pay-per-view" were being floated. I knew that was well into the future—we just weren't there yet.

But the next logical step seemed to be expanding our reach for live shows. In 1994, we stuck our toe in the New York waters, running in Yonkers before a few hundred fans. That posed little risk, as it was a drive-in show for the locals. We could hit New York in two hours from Philly. It worked, and we knew New York was a market we could revisit with ease.

From there we looked south, and at a significantly elevated expense sheet. Florida was a good wrestling state, and as far as I knew there was no one running shows down there besides WWE and WCW. It seemed primed for action, but it meant airline flights for all. This was nowhere in my original business plan, but the promise of mining an open territory blinded me a little. I was aware of the risk, but maybe the gates would've been worth it. In September of 1994, we did a double shot in the Sunshine State, running Tampa and Ocala.

Ocala was home to Dory Funk Jr.'s wrestling school, and we ran a show down there. The Funks were kind enough to let us use the facility for just a piece of the ticket sales. More importantly, that trip gave birth to one of the classic locker room lines Paul and I used on each other for years, often to the point where one of us would choke with laughter.

We were going through a particularly hectic setup that day. We were out of state and getting used to new people and a new space. I had Paul next to me in my ear going on about the schedule, the lighting guy on the truss calling down to us as he focused lights, and I wasn't happy with how the chairs were arranged across from the hard camera when, lo and behold, Marti Funk, wife of Dory Funk Jr., breathlessly bounded into the room. She was a petite southern spitfire who carried a camera everywhere, as she fancied herself a photographer. I think she sold two pictures to Bill Apter's magazines, and I doubt they were ever used. Apter is the kindest man in this business, and I'd bet money even he thought she was a pain in the ass. So, Marti blew into the room amidst the chaos of a problematic setup and an approaching bell time. She found me and Paul, both stressed, and tried to catch her breath.

"Don't worry," she said, gasping. "It's all gonna be okay."

Paul and I looked at each other.

"Don't worry," she said, looking up at us. "Dory's here."

We stopped. The room stopped. Time stopped. Paul and I were frozen in confusion. Marti dropped the words with the gravity of something biblical, and to her it no doubt was. I half expected him to be strapped to a cross when he walked in. Paul and I turned to each other with blank stares as Marti watched our reactions with a disciple's glint in her eye. The savior had arrived.

Paul and I slowly nodded to each other.

"Oh...good to know," Paul said. Sure enough, Dory came in, looked around, and did his mute cowboy thing. We didn't need any help and he didn't exactly offer it, or anything for that matter. But to her, all was now right with the wrestling world.

Because after all—Dory was here.

When Marti and Dory were out of earshot it began almost immediately. "Hey Paul," I'd call over to him. "Don't worry—Dory's here." We said it to each other at least once a week for twenty years.

\* \* \*

Our growing success garnered regular coverage in the newsletters. The wrestling newsletters, a.k.a. dirt sheets, are the closest thing to a trade paper that our industry has, akin to *Variety* or the *Hollywood Reporter* for entertainment. Part gossip, part information, the sheets were the first place one could find out about talent jumps and talent brawls alike. In more recent years, they've all been converted to websites, but in the '90s such news was dropped into your mailbox every week. The *Wrestling Observer*,

*Pro Wrestling Torch*, and *Figure Four Weekly* were among the bigger publications in the industry.

Paul, like Eddie before him, scoured the sheets weekly, exhibiting a level of paranoia that was tiring. They both probably sat around their respective hotel rooms trying to interpret every word of every story and see how it applied to them. I was Paul's best friend and I couldn't figure out why we'd gotten on so well. We shouldn't have—he saw treachery in everyone. I pride myself in being an open book in business, and maybe he sensed that he had nothing to worry about with me.

I did an interview for Wade Keller's *Torch Talk* in which I said glowing things about Paul. There was no denying his effect on our popularity, and his booking instincts were second to none. He called me upon seeing the article and asked me to read it aloud as he turned on his speakerphone and stood beside his parents. It was surreal, this thirty-year-old man asking me to read nice things about him to his mom and dad. They seemed happy, he was elated, and I was just confused, ultimately chalking it up to the eccentricities rampant in creatives. Maybe Salvador Dali did the same shit.

I'd initially asked Eddie to get us in the sheets, which he did rather easily. I thought we needed national coverage, and we continued to have our events and results reported, but we were generally spared the dirt mucked up by the rumor mill of the business. Our guys didn't talk much, so we didn't find our way into the gossipy parts of the sheets all that often. We had a close circle, and we knew we'd be fucking ourselves if we told tales out of school.

There are a handful of wrestling writers who were at the forefront of this kind of journalism. That term, journalism, has been debated and drawn into question, but the sheets were treated as such in our business. Dave Meltzer was the biggest name in that world, penning the *Wrestling Observer*—a tightly packed collection of pages that covered as much of the global wrestling business as was possible.

Dave came to be seen as an authority, and when he began rating our matches, I paid attention. Here was a guy giving our product an official stamp of sorts, calling some matches four-star brilliant or half-star duds. It's part of any creative endeavor—critics rate everything from movies to Broadway shows.

Those critics, however, actually see the product they evaluate.

I called Dave when I saw these star ratings and asked him how he was making it out to see all of these shows, many of them little spot shows without video. To his credit, he admitted he wasn't watching the matches himself. He said he had people at the shows who "he trusted."

"And you just print it?" I said, incredulously. "They say 'one star' and that's what it gets?"

"If that's what they tell me, yeah."

I could only shake my head. That was it for me. How the hell could this guy call himself a journalist? It seemed so irresponsible to sign his name to an evaluation that someone else—and exactly who?—provided. You want to cover the matches, then just print the results. Judging them through some anonymous fans seemed like bullshit. I never spoke with Meltzer after that.

Wade Keller was the writer responsible for the *Pro Wrestling Torch* and brightening the senior Heymans' day by printing my glowing report card about their son. When I first asked Eddie to get us in the sheets, Wade is the guy he contacted. Shortly thereafter, Wade and I started talking. He seemed trustworthy and I respected him, based on what I'd seen and heard. Then he did something stupid.

I opened an edition of the *Torch* and was shocked to learn that I was carrying Ric Flair's bags at a WCW show in the Philadelphia Civic Center. I called Wade as soon as I read it.

"Not only did I not carry anyone's bags," I began, "but I wasn't even there."

"Someone I trust saw you."

"Wade, I'm not lying to you."

"Bruce Mitchell saw you himself."

Bruce was another wrestling writer who apparently needed an eye exam. He'd never met me, so I don't know how he could be so certain he'd seen me. Maybe it was another short, bald Jewish guy. There's more than one in this city, or so I'm told.

I was so angry. I never lied to Wade; I always shot straight. For him to say that I was lying was a big insult. I might not have answered all his questions in the past, but I never lied to him. That was all I needed to never speak to that motherfucker again. It bothers me to this day. I would not have gone to the Civic Center whether or not I was asked to carry a bag for someone. Paul always said not to go to other people's shows; it will sink your credibility as a promoter. I understood that when he said it, and to this day I have never been to a show I wasn't promoting or working on.

A month after this debacle, we were doing a show in Philly and got word that Bruce Mitchell was coming. He must've gotten new glasses and was ready to watch some wrestling. I was coming into the building with Sandman when we spotted Mitchell. Hack starts yelling, "Gordon! Carry my bags, Gordon!" Can't tell that guy anything.

Dave Scherer wrote a sheet called the *Wrestling Lariat* back then. Scherer was one of our bleacher bums—a group of vocal fans that sat way in the back bleachers. They were responsible for starting some of our more famous chants, all classy stuff like "Stevie takes it up the aaaass, doo-dah-doo-dah" for Stevie Richards. Scherer started the newsletter that I thought was most well written, unlike Meltzer's *Observer*, which was rife with grammatical and formatting errors. I told Scherer as much, but also said he needed to decide if he was coming to our shows as a writer or a fan. He couldn't sit there with a critical eye and still chant "You fucked up!" when JT Smith fell off the ring apron.

Scherer was critical of us when he had to be, which was fine provided the information was true. I couldn't tolerate hearsay reporting like Meltzer's star ratings and Keller's Tod Gordon wiping Ric Flair's ass sightings. He was critical but fair, and in the court of public opinion that's all you can ask for. Scherer was always the first writer in line for press conferences, and everyone wanted him there because he didn't screw anybody. I loved him for showing us that respect and now, thirty years later, I consider him a great friend. He still maintains a successful website called PWInsider.com, and it's the only wrestling website I currently read.

Another ECW fan-cum-writer was Mike Johnson. Unlike Scherer catcalling from the bleachers, Johnson was a front row guy. I liked his reporting until he wrote what I considered to be a disrespectful barb aimed at me and Fonzie. His review of one of our matches diminished our efforts to rolling around until Taz came out. The contest certainly wasn't Bockwinkel versus Gagne, but we worked our asses off. We always wanted our matches to work and had spent months getting fans to really believe he was from the state athletic commission, looking to shut down their beloved ECW. Our fans were smart to everything, so it meant a lot to actually string them along.

Fonzie and I never planned to go out and do moonsaults, but we could always pop the crowd. As I mentioned, we never sought training and didn't ask workers for advice. We pounded each other silly. So when I read Mike Johnson's summation of our match at an Allentown house show, it hit me below the belt. Naturally, I devised a plan through my stewing.

Johnson would undoubtedly be seated in the front row again at the next ECW Arena show for our return match. I told Fonzie to throw me over the guardrail once I started bleeding really good, and onto Mike. I'd planned to cling on and get him really drenched. Fonzie agreed, but fate intervened shortly before the card when Mike called the store to order tickets.

"How dare you?" I said to him, unable to conceal my anger and wait for the bloody payoff on Saturday night.

He was instantly apologetic, saying he had no excuse, and I was 100 percent right. That was sufficient for me.

"Okay," I said. "Now we can be friends." Little prick never knew how close he came to going home soaked in my DNA. Today he's a top-notch, well-respected journalist and a close friend.

On a level above the sheet writers sat Bill Apter. Bill was a staple in the wrestling magazine world for decades, covering Bruno Sammartino's matches at the Garden and Starrcade matches for WCW. He covered the sport all over the world and had the respect of everyone who was anyone in wrestling. When ECW began making a real splash, he invited us up to his office. We'd been preceded there by generations of ring greats, so I was psyched to visit. I brought Sandman and Pitbull Gary with me.

Bill did a weird thing in that place—he challenged every wrestler that visited to a match right there on his office carpet. He even had a damn belt that he called the COW belt, for Championship Office Wrestling. If he expected *any* of the ECW guys, especially Hack or Gary, to do the job for his Wonderful Willie character he was in for a surprise. No one in that room was losing to Bill Apter, who stood shorter, skinnier, and balder than me. When Apter proposed the match, telling us that everyone in the business had challenged him for his COW belt, he was the only one wearing a smile. We started grappling as Sandman began knocking ceiling tiles out with his Singapore cane.

"We don't job for anybody," Hack said, and all three of us piled on top of Apter for the pin. We got up and walked out.

Mainstream beware. ECW is here.

Long gone were the days when I had to ask for national coverage. We were in all the newsletters, magazines, and on the websites as the smart fan's only alternative to the big two, who'd both been laying a collective egg. That got our foot in the door, and before I knew it the *Torch*'s Year-End Awards had named me the third most powerful person in professional wrestling, behind only Vince McMahon and Eric Bischoff. That overwhelmed me— three years before this, I was at the Civic Center watching WCW's Halloween Havoc as a fan. Now, I'm looking at a list that has Vince billionaire number one, Eric at billionaire company number two, and Tod from the jewelry store number three. I sat on that list above names like Hulk Hogan and Ric Flair. We were reaching our absolute heights, and along with that came glory beyond my dreams, as well as all the heartbreak lying in wait on the flip side of success.

* * *

Paul and I were simpatico beyond just wrestling. That doesn't mean the partnership wasn't without challenges. For all we saw through a similar lens, there were ways in which we differed. Paul's shielding me from talent seemed to make sense initially, mostly because it came at a time when I was painfully overburdened. I'd become president of the Variety Club while also serving as president of the Pawnbrokers Association. Both organizations required daily work, as well as several meetings a month. I was supporting my entire family through Carver Reed as well, and all of that was a priority. Further, Paul's decision to have just one, singular voice communicating to the boys also seemed prudent. Having too many chefs in the kitchen makes problems, and allowing him to be the face of our decisions was fine with me. In truth, it meant far fewer headaches.

But it also separated me from talent more than was healthy. My Posse and a select few like Sabu, the Pitbulls, and Public Enemy knew I owned the company and was still the final decision on anything, but that was probably murky for others not in the loop.

One example of that was when I gave Taz a raise. He'd been making $200 per show, and I thought he was a great example of work ethic, punctuality, and execution in the ring. His head hadn't exactly swelled beyond his body yet, so I started paying him $250 per show, a 25 percent raise. When I saw him alone backstage the following week, I wanted him to know I valued his work and that's why I raised him.

"There's something extra in your check now," I said.

He just stood there. "Yeah. And?"

"I just wanted you to know."

"Thanks," he said and walked away. It was the weirdest exchange I'd had with him. It was like I was annoying him, no iota of gratitude, no "thank you," no anything other than that snarky response. I shrugged it off and went about my night until Paul pulled me aside.

"Tod, don't talk to the talent about money," he said.

"It's *my* money."

"But you don't get the business. I know how to talk to them about this stuff, so please don't talk business with the boys."

I knew business, wrestling or not, and you say something to your boss when he gives you a raise. I don't care if you're a dock-worker or Hulk Hogan—appreciating the person who hired you is a basic. I had no idea why Paul thought people in wrestling were exempt from such basic decency.

I didn't get it right away, but something began gnawing at me about that exchange. My subconscious started to whisper in my ear, painting an unpleasant scenario. It was suggesting that Taz was unmoved by my telling him he got a raise for the same reason Paul told me not to talk with talent—because Paul must've already told Taz about the raise and that he'd given it to him. It was the only explanation for Taz being confused when I said I gave him the raise. Paul had egg on his face when Taz was given a conflicting version of his raise.

I buried that suspicion and didn't bring anything up. Paul and I were still good, and if he needed to play commander in the locker room, then so be it. I still controlled the purse strings, and things were manageable at the time. Then came a big gamble that offered a sizable jackpot but required our sliding all our chips onto two squares on the roulette board as the wheel was spun.

* * *

Our SportsChannel America deal allowed us to be seen all over the country. We were also on UHF channel 48 in Philly for those that didn't have cable, but the issue with SportsChannel was the impermanence of our schedule. Our times would shift, making it hard for our fans to find us.

We were contacted by Sunshine Network in Florida. That cable network had statewide coverage and by signing with them we could avoid having to look at dozens of individual markets, like a UHF channel in Miami, another in Tampa. With Sunshine, we could deal with just one entity. We'd have the same time slot across the entire state, and their coverage was better than SportsChannel America's in Florida.

Around the same time, MSG Network out of New York came into the picture. Our having TV coverage in New York would be huge—we'd be able to run the city and draw crowds I'd hoped would be comparable to Philly, maybe even bigger. MSG also reached into Jersey and Connecticut, so it opened up so much more opportunity.

The big issue, though, was the money deal. SportsChannel was airing us for free and just pocketing their ad sales. But Sunshine and MSG both wanted payment for the slot, and in exchange we'd be allowed to sell twelve minutes of advertising per week and therefore keep 100 percent of that ad revenue. Not a bad deal if you can fill the twelve minutes with soft drinks, 1-900 chat lines, and magazine subscription commercials. Therein was the risk.

Sunshine and MSG each wanted $3,000 per week. That $24,000 per month was a massive nut for our fledgling independent wrestling company, and if we were to do this, we needed to hit the ground running acquiring advertisers. Paul assured me he had a million business contacts in New York alone, ensuring we wouldn't have to lay out a dime once his people saw we were on TV throughout the tri-state area. He kept mentioning club guys he knew that would be attracted to our edgy product, cutting commercials to fill their nightclubs on a weekly basis. He said he lined up sponsors ready to buy the show once we were on the air and they could see the ratings. I figured Florida would soon follow once we perfected the model in New York, so I inked the deal with Sunshine and MSG. We would now be seen in a consistent time slot on two very visible networks in two powerhouse regions of the country.

This was a deviation from my business plan, to be sure. I'd just committed to $6,000 a week above all the other expenses we incurred regularly. Paul seemed confident he'd lock up our ad sales in short order and didn't seem the least bit nervous. By contrast, I was sweating bullets. Paul looked so confident, though. It was hard to doubt him.

It wasn't unrealistic to think we'd lock down some advertisers. We were ahead of the curve when it came to our TV product. History would prove that our show influenced what WWE and WCW would soon be doing on their TV shows. Cartoonish super-heroes were out, and good guys that acted like bad guys were in. Actually, if you looked at our roster you'd barely be able to tell who was a heel and who was a babyface. WWE's soon-to-come "Attitude Era" product and WCW's NWO faction would borrow shamelessly from the model we'd invented. Looking back, it seemed a no-brainer that advertisers would line up for a show so ahead of its time.

We went on the air in New York and Florida with no ads, but it allowed us to run live shows there. Right away, the New York crowds started a "Philly sucks" chant. Naturally, when we ran Philadelphia after that, the ECW Arena fans started chanting "New York sucks." I looked at Paul as lightbulbs went on in both our heads.

"They're writing an angle," I said.

"I know. Think we can run with it?"

The fans were smart and knew Paul was from New York and I was from Philly. They also knew which workers were my Philly guys and which Paul brought down from New York. We could each have our factions and work angles in both cities for months, maybe a year. It was so organic, like a gift from the wrestling gods. I pitched it to Paul, and he soured immediately.

"I'm not being the heel," he said. I was confused.

"You're not. And you are. Me too."

"But I don't want to be the heel."

"Paul, you're only a heel in *Philly*, just like I'm the heel when we work New York."

"No way. I'm not being a heel anywhere."

Paul had been a heel manager his entire career to that point! I was incredulous. Was it so important that he be seen as the cultish guru so many seemed to fancy him? More important than a windfall of box office money? It seemed so. The fans were handing us an angle, and we'd always listened to them in the past. But this time I couldn't convince Paul we were holding a jewel, and instead we tossed a sack of diamonds in the trash.

* * *

When you finally find that ever elusive success, there's something that will invariably find you—lawsuits. ECW's first involved Terry Funk, Cactus Jack, and a flaming steel chair. Cactus used a towel soaked in lighter fluid wrapped around the chair and lit it before attacking Funk with it. The ignited towel fell off in the scuffle, landing near the guardrail by the audience. A guy in the crowd decided he'd be helpful and inserted himself into the show by reaching through the guardrail and trying to pound out the fire with his hands. As a result, the fan suffered burns. I know, shocking.

A building employee ran down to ringside with a fire extinguisher he must've found beside a fossilized T-Rex turd. The thing had "Property of Bedrock" stenciled on it. When Fred Flintstone activated the extinguisher, nothing but black dust shot out. It was obviously long past its expiration date and did nothing but cover everyone at ringside with soot.

Order was soon restored and the card continued. We found the fan who'd burned his hands and invited him to the back. I was ready to give this guy the VIP treatment and turn his bad night into a...well...bad night that he didn't want to sue anyone over. I sent someone over to the merchandise table to grab some stuff for him, because when I see someone whose hands are still smoking from a fire, I think, *He must want a Sabu T-shirt.*

I introduced him to all the boys and at one point he inexplicably asked the workers if anyone had a cigarette. He sat there smoking and eventually hobbled out of the Arena, well wishes all around for a speedy recovery.

The only other time an ECW event put my heart into my throat like that was at Hardcore Heaven '94. Not so coincidentally, the participants were Funk and Cactus again, and this moment was forever emblazoned into fans' memories via our weekly show opening. At the finish of a Cactus versus Funk main event match, Public Enemy interfered and screwed the finish. Cactus and Funk laid them out pretty good in the center of the ring when an overzealous fan tried to be "helpful." He tossed a chair to them for use on the downed tag team. Upon seeing that, other fans began doing it and within a matter of seconds, dozens of chairs were airborne and covering Johnny and Teddy. Cactus and Funk powdered out of the ring after being pelted by a few as Bob Artese grabbed the mic and began yelling for the fans to stop. It's a miracle no one was hurt and sheer divinity that we weren't sued.

In regard to the fire incident, we were not as lucky. A couple of months after the flaming T-shirt, four certified letters were delivered to Carver Reed, the registered business address of ECW—one to me, one to Paul, one to Funk, and one to Cactus. Signing for that much certified mail is rarely a good thing. We were being sued for $10 million by our friend who, apparently, could no longer ride a motorcycle, have sex, or do anything anymore. He claimed to be destroyed mentally and physically as a result of the burns on his hands. The burns on his hands that he got by knowingly pounding a burning cloth, mind you. His shitbag lawyers thought ten million was a fair price for his pain, and I leaned over to one of them during legal proceedings.

"You do know this company has no value, right?" I said. "If we had ten million dollars, do you think we'd be running monthly shows in a warehouse in South Philly with a leaking roof and fire extinguishers from the Paleolithic era?" They were such tools, blinded by the big money grab they'd cooked up. If they had this guy take the stand and be honest, saying, "Hey, I thought I was helping out, I smacked the burning towel not realizing the accelerant would get on me and now my hands hurt like hell," he probably would've gotten paid. But they unloaded some melodramatic, bad TV courtroom routine saying the guy couldn't even think of fire without debilitating flashbacks.

I almost stood and applauded the bad acting, but the jury did better than that—they gave him nothing. One of the jurors even emailed writer Mike Johnson after the verdict, writing, "Wannabe gets nothing." Mike had used that word while testifying on the stand, yielding an admonishment from the judge.

So, that was the end of that. I'd really felt bad for the guy up until his team began trying to take advantage of us. Their accounts didn't line up with the evidence, nor did they seem plausible based on the injuries. Oddly, there was no tape of that particular match to review, so the jury could rely only on everyone's verbal account.

And no, I really don't know what happened to the videotape.

* * *

As our TV shows were getting more and more attention from fans, but perilously few advertisers, I opened the ECW Training Academy wrestling school. It was a simple operation—we put a ring in the back of the Arena, and our trainers were the Pitbulls, JT Smith, and Rockin' Rebel, who was really just there to try and bed a pretty new trainee we had named Francine.

For a while it was *only* Francine coming to the school. We advertised it on TV but only got a total of four or five students in the entire two years we ran it. We used them as enhancement talent, for example Joel Hartgood and Dino Sendoff. We kept it running mainly because it wasn't costing us anything. Trainers got a piece of any tuition in the rare event a student showed up.

Years later, Taz also saw fit to open his own school up in New York called the House of Hardcore, where he and Perry Saturn trained kids. Taz and Perry started coming to our shows wearing their snazzy new Team Taz shirts. Hey, if your bookers don't give you a faction, start your own!

ECW Training Academy made no money and, in reality, the entire company was always still on the ropes. Profit was elusive, like a carrot on the stick that always seemed so very close. Our merchandise deals were percentage deals, just like Gabe's news-letter, which didn't last long. We had no extra money to invest in anything even if we wanted to. Plus, since the pricey TV deals with Sunshine and MSG, we were now falling behind. Once Paul got that idea in his head to go national, we went from businessmen to gamblers. It was necessary, and I understood Paul was desperately expanding so quickly in order to keep guys working here. If they started working more, they'd start making more, and that might keep them from answering the phone when WWE and WCW started calling.

* * *

Word began getting back to us that the wrestlers in the two major federations were watching us regularly. I'd first heard that from my old friend Kevin Sullivan when I booked Arn Anderson and Bobby Eaton from WCW. Kevin was booking there and put the loaner deal together so I could have Arn and Bobby make an explosive appearance at the ECW Arena that generated the biggest pop I ever heard from our crowd.

"They're all watching you in the locker room," Kevin said. "You don't know what you got there." The night Arn did his run-in for me, I heard the same advice again. After his match, Arn asked if he could talk with me and we headed over to a corner, where he pulled up two chairs. So dramatic.

"Have a seat," he instructed. "You got something here. I don't know how you did it—the audience participation, the anticipation, their chants—but you're onto something here. Don't fuck it up."

I never forgot that. Arn Anderson was serious about the business of wrestling and was a heavy WCW player. He'd worked with and for the greats, and for him to say that to an indie promoter out of Philly it had to be sincere.

I'd heard the same thing about WWE talent watching us too. Vince McMahon had Harvey Wippleman, a manager and office stooge, watch ECW and report back to him every week. Imagine being given that job—"I'm too busy and important to even fast-forward through this one-hour tape, but you seem like you have a lot of time to jack off, so watch this for me." I'm sure Vince wouldn't have liked what he was seeing as we were saying "Fuck WWE and their steroids" on TV.

The truth was, Vince McMahon could've put me out of business rather handily if he'd wanted to. If he'd run a card across the street from each of our shows, that would've been it, particularly when their emulation of our product started to take off and they'd abandoned wrestling clowns, pig farmers, and dentists. I knew we had a segment of die-hard fans that would be lined up to get into our show while mooning theirs, but the large majority of fans would want to see Diesel, Shawn Michaels, and the Undertaker in person. Fortunately, Vince thought we were worth more to him alive than dead, for reasons I didn't fully know yet.

Though no one ever ran a show beside ours to put us out of business, we did have an interesting offer to do that to someone else. I made a call to WCW headquarters to book some talent for our upcoming shows, and WCW president Eric Bischoff asked to speak with me. He got on the phone and in the first and only time I spoke with him he said, "Tell you what, pal, you ever want to run a show in the same town Cornette's running, I'll give you my whole roster." He dropped it like I already knew all the backstage drama that seemed to swirl around a business populated with paranoid predators.

I flashed back to Dennis Coralluzzo telling me to lie to his partner Larry Sharpe back when I first worked with him. It's such bad business practice, showing another businessperson your questionable morality right up front. Maybe it was commonplace in wrestling, but that's not where my real-world degree was from. Dealing in precious stones was clearly different—you did everything possible to give the appearance of stability and unemotional decision making. Making people comfortable is the first step in earning their trust. Once earned, you do everything possible to grow the relationship and not fuck anyone over. That was a practice I'd see violated again and again in wrestling.

I didn't have any contact with WWE other than my call to JJ Dillon in talent relations when he practically threw Shane Douglas out the door and back into my arms. To me, they were the enemy. We wanted to do everything differently, and any association with them would be a negative. Everything about us was different. We were riding high.

Standing atop a cliff is exhilarating but scary. I'm cautious in business, not likely to ignore the risk and definitely averse to adding more to a shaky cart. But sometimes you can miss the road signs when all your news is good and life is a party.

# CHAPTER 10

# PARTYING

When you hear ECW Originals talk about the heyday of the company, chances are they're going to mention the Travelodge in South Philly. I began to have an issue with wrestler accommodations after shows, namely the fact that hotels began telling us never to return. I put everyone by the airport at first, but that lasted two shows. The following month we tried another hotel and that lasted one show. Then the Travelodge, or "the Loser-lodge" as I always referred to it, came into our lives.

The Travelodge was a sixteen-story round hotel just over the Walt Whitman Bridge, and after our first stay, I thought it prudent to have a frank discussion with management.

I told them, "I need twenty rooms on a fairly regular basis, but you're going to have to bend the rules a little for us. My guys are a little special." It was that easy—Travelodge became the destination for postshow debauchery for those so inclined, and there was a fair share of us who were. There were some guys that were straitlaced. You wouldn't catch Dreamer or Taz engaging in such behavior. Shane Douglas played it straight to us but was apparently dealing with a pill issue. We thought he was clean. Francine, Beulah, and Nancy were never in with the bad boys either.

When the Posse would party in a room, outside guests were not allowed, and I'm specifically talking about rats. If someone wanted to be in the company of a lady, they would bring her to a different room in the hotel and take care of business before coming into the Posse's inner sanctum without her. When we were together, we wanted to be able to speak freely and act without self-consciousness. Many times the party would spill into the hallway, with our guys meandering from room to room, drinking and smoking in the corridors. That kind of shit got us barred from the other hotels, but the Travelodge just seemed to roll with it, possibly due to their 14 percent occupancy. I always kept a room for myself on a floor where I didn't book any wrestlers. When it was time to go to bed and get those all-important two hours of sleep, I wanted it to happen in peace.

I can't imagine some random unsuspecting guest on a night we were there actually trying to get a night's sleep. Shit was going on all over the place. One weekend Cactus Jack brought his parents down from Long Island and put them up there with us. I wished he would've asked my advice first, but he didn't and they stayed there on a show night. The next morning, I answered a knock on my door to find Cactus standing there.

"Hey, Mick," I said, wondering if the normally straight-edged warrior was changing his lifestyle and had come looking for weed, but he hadn't.

"I'm sorry to bother you, Tod, but my parents are here and they're going to be heading down for breakfast, but there's an issue I was hoping you could handle before then."

I would've been happy to spring for their pancake bill, but the issue was a little more complex than that. It seemed Johnny Grunge had fallen asleep with his pants around his ankles in the hallway by the Foleys' door. Mick's parents would soon be stepping over that fallen heap of flesh to join their son for breakfast.

I accompanied Mick to his parents' floor and found three Spanish-speaking maids standing over Johnny.

"Meester, meester," they were saying as they poked at him with a feather duster. He was out cold. Turns out that a wasted Johnny got up to take a piss in the bathroom, opened the wrong door, tripped on the carpet, and landed in the hallway, pants down, ass up, passed out. Imagine that luck—two doors, a 50/50 chance.

"I got it from here," I told Mick and enlisted Teddy and some of the other boys to drag him back into his room. All was right with the world. Maybe I am a great crisis booker after all.

Drugs were a part of the lifestyle for many of us. I mentioned there were exceptions, the workers we didn't see once they left the ECW Arena. We might run into a few of them having a nightcap in the hotel bar, but we didn't see them for the extended activities upstairs.

In order of prevalence, weed was probably most popular. We smoked in the cars to the shows, outside before or during them, and back at the hotel after the shows. Pills, specifically Soma and Percocet, were all over the place. The Pitbulls would show up at the Arena with a briefcase with about five thousand pills in it. I don't know how they landed so many, but they'd open their gimmick and the guys would line up at the table. *Next!* It was like the ice cream truck had pulled into the park.

The Travelodge provided me with the single funniest and remarkable story from my ECW tenure. On one of our monthly stays after an ECW Arena show, my Posse was partying in one of the rooms when suddenly Hack jumped up like he'd been hit by a lightning bolt.

"Wait a minute," he said. "Is this room 735?"

It was and we told him so.

"Oh my gawd," he barked as he went to the corner of the room and began pulling up the carpet.

"What the hell are you doing?" I said. "Don't start wrecking the place."

Hack reached under the rug and pulled out a packet of coke. He was like Houdini, but drunker.

"Yes!" he screamed. "I left this here like six months ago. I totally forgot about it when we were staying in all those other rooms!" He was elated and we were popping like crazy, laughing our asses off. It was so random, but I'd never seen Hack happier. As we celebrated this magical moment, he stopped dead in his tracks, another light bulb going off.

"Wait a minute," he said. "Scorp, come give me a hand." He went out the door shirtless and barefoot with Scorpio in tow and raced down the hallway to a giant potted plant taller than him. Fonzie and I followed, and as we got there, Hack was squatting beside it. He told Scorp to grab the other side, and they both lifted it to reveal another bag of cocaine underneath. "Another one!"

It seemed a few months prior, Hack was heading out of the hotel and getting on a plane at Philadelphia Airport. He couldn't take the blow with him, so he hid it in a couple of places around the hotel and forgot about it until that night. It was there for months, and Hack was treating it like a religious miracle.

Considering how much Hack drank, he couldn't have worked those matches without a bump of coke to bring him back up. It's an instant change when that cocaine hits your system. It offsets the sluggish effects of the alcohol, and many of our guys used it to get them pumped for the ring. I was working all day at Carver Reed, running ECW, acting as president of both the Variety Club and the Pawnbrokers Association. Coke would keep me going when I was crashing. It was frighteningly effective.

Though cocaine was all around and many of the guys were heading down a darker road with opiates, pot still remained the most ubiquitous illegal substance in ECW. Younger readers might be flinching hearing cannabis was once illegal, given how decriminalization efforts are now sweeping the country. Harmless as it might be, there was a time you could legit go to jail for smoking a joint. Fucking Butchie never wanted it in the Arena, and one day before a show he started barking, "Who's smoking that shit?" He was getting hot about it and came looking for me.

"I'll handle it, Butchie," I said as I began searching the empty arena. I couldn't imagine losing our home base, so I needed to keep Butchie happy. I finally tracked down the offenders after climbing through the Mummers Parade floats in the back. Sabu, RVD, and Sandman were hiding behind a "Just Say No!" float, smoking their brains out.

"There you are!" I yelled for Butchie clear across the Arena.

I slipped behind the float, took the joint, and puffed.

"You can't smoke in here!" I took a few more puffs as I scolded them loudly to have enough respect to go outside and finish it. And we did.

I had a saying I used in interviews—"If you can pass a drug test, you can't work in ECW." Road Warrior Hawk loved that line and would quote it and howl. Hawk and a bunch of others from ECW ended up in early graves as a result of that lifestyle, so it's far less funny when I replay myself saying it now.

\* \* \*

ECW was a marriage killer, to be sure. Eventually, the married British EMT for whom we were running interference in the Arena left her husband and ended up with, you got it, 2 Cold Scorpio. Why marry within the topsy-turvy world of health care when you can partner with someone in a secure career like professional wrestling? It lasted a few months, until Scorpio got the call to head to WWE and become Flash Funk. He broke it off with her.

"I'm going to leave you in good hands," Scorpio told her before he left. At least that's what she thought he said. Like I told you, when Scorp spoke, no one really could be sure.

Those good hands belonged to me. I was between wives at the time, and I did enjoy the English accent, so why the hell not? She'd already split from her husband and I needed a driver, so we started seeing each other. My only hesitation was following Scorpio. It's well known in the business that he has a third leg. I prepared to disappoint the EMT in that arena but otherwise have a good time hanging with this cool chick. But after about six months, it was time to move on.

Shortly before the EMT, the Posse met the woman into submissive role-play who begat the "Tod is God" chant. She was sweet, cute, funny, and had a serious sexual fetish. She was into being dominated, and the Posse was more than happy to oblige. There wasn't any kind of physical violence or abuse; it was just that sexual role-play really turned her on. We nicknamed her "the Pony" after Raven asked one day about the "dog and pony show" he'd heard we had going the night before. She was actually a lot of fun. Hey, people are into different stuff—some like their martinis dirty, some like them dry, and she likes to be tied up, blindfolded, and given commands. To each their own.

One night in my hotel room, she asked to be tied to the leg of the table, naked and blindfolded. The Posse was in my room, so we first tended to her request, then sat around bullshitting and smoking. After fifteen or twenty minutes we forgot she was there—but that was what she'd asked for. Eventually, Fonzie, Hack, and Scorpio headed downstairs to the hotel bar and Paul called my room looking to come and smoke a doob. I invited him up, not really remembering there was a naked, silent submissive still tied to the table leg. In what can only be described as a moment fit for a Hanna-Barbera cartoon, Paul walked into the room, saw her, spun around bug-eyed, and flew out of the room at top duck-waddle speed. He flapped his flippers all the way down the hall and out of sight; it was the fastest I'd ever seen him move. I fell into hysterics.

My submissive guest made several repeat visits to the Trav-elodge, and I made sure she always made time for my entire Posse. I always went first, as it is truly good to be the king. Then she'd visit the rest of them, with Fonzie consistently going last. He never seemed to mind that positioning in our dog and pony show.

But Fonzie comes into more prominent play here by single-handedly killing the Pony. He had the utter audacity to fall in love with this girl, going so far as taking her home to meet his mother in Florida. Who am I to question from whence love comes? But we did always make Fonzie go last with her, and god knows what he had to deal with when it was his turn. Improbable at best, but I guess my guy saw through all that and fell for her anyway. Good for him. To this day, nearly thirty years later, Fonzie still refers to himself as "the Pony Killer," and the three of us still lovingly call him that.

Dog and pony show aside, my Posse wasn't really a rat crew. We spent our time getting high and making each other laugh. We talked wrestling all the time and enjoyed each other's company. Guys like Raven and Richards were more into the rat scene and getting attention from girls. We mostly hung with each other, with the exception of the occasional submissive tied to a table leg, of course.

All the partying brought about its share of casualties, but the biggest threat to ECW as a company had nothing to do with drugs or submissives. Our vessel was leaking fuel and spiraling out of control, and the yoke had been taken from my hands by someone I'd invited into the cockpit.

# CHAPTER 11

# STORM CLOUDS

**P**aul's personality issues, which I'd once chalked up as quirks, were beginning to have ramifications in the company. We'd worked together without incident for about a year, and I was able to ignore his occasional lies. They didn't seem to be about anything major, so I shrugged them off. They were random, like when I asked him about not getting a tape to SportsChannel like he was supposed to. He said they'd given him the wrong tracking number and he'd straighten it out. It ran right up to the deadline, but he overnighted a copy and got it there. He got it done and didn't even submit the bill for postage to me, so what could I really say? Maybe they did switch the tracking numbers, but I'd seen his tracking number gimmick a few times by then.

I became close to Paul's mother, and she told me a remarkable story that spotlighted the extent of her son's deceptiveness. She was reviewing Paul's math homework when he was in grade school and pointed out that he'd gotten one wrong.

"No, I didn't," he told her. "The math book is wrong. They made a mistake when they printed it." He was so casual and confident about it. She tried to reason with him, but he argued with her for two hours until finally she went to bed thinking, *Well, the book could be wrong. Sometimes books are misprinted.* He was that good.

He'd perfected it by the time I hired him. I referenced that math book story a bunch of times in ECW, and he popped every time I did. He was so proud.

Paul kept New Jack off a New York card one night by telling him the state athletic commission representative was coming down to the show looking for Jack after something he did to his daughter. I guess Jack believed it. Imagine how many girls you have to fuck with to believe that the New York State Athletic Commission rep was one of their dads.

New Jack and Paul got into an altercation one night in the dressing room, and Jack called Paul a "motherfucking liar." Paul got fired up.

"I'm a motherfucking liar? Name one thing I lied to you about!"

"You mean today?" Jack replied. We were all discovering Paul's on-and-off relationship with the truth. For the longest time, Paul never kayfabed me—I was the one he confided in. He was always telling me he hated this guy or that guy, without much explanation as to why. I finally realized he was extremely antisocial and couldn't get along with another human being, seemingly other than me. It spoke more to my tolerance than his affinity for me, sadly.

* * *

It wasn't hard to do the math on the MSG Network and Sunshine deals. Without advertising dollars to offset their cost, the TV payments were suicide, and a slow, painful one. It was like bleeding out over two months rather than stepping in front of a train. The hardest thing to reconcile was that I knew better. For a company with adequate size and scope, they were great deals—100 percent of ad revenue into your pocket. But wrestling in general was a tough sell in the first half of the '90s. The business was on the heels of a terrible low point, fresh with sex and steroid scandals. ECW was different, but how many executives in ad-buying companies knew that?

One show at the Florida Fairgrounds in Tampa highlighted the fact that we might've thought we were a little bigger than we actually were in the state. We pulled into the venue parking lot and saw about two thousand cars. We were psyched—how quickly we'd grown in Florida since running on the Sunshine Network. I clung to a sliver of hope that the Florida gamble was about to pay off. The Posse exchanged high fives as we drove around the lot looking for the entrance. We pulled over and asked a parking attendant.

"Where's the dressing room door?" one of us asked him.

"You with the band?"

Huh?

It was at that point someone looked over at the billboard and saw, Green Day...Tonight! Ah. Right.

"We're the wrestlers."

"Oh, you're in that shed down there." He pointed to a spot clear across the lot, where we parked, swallowed our pride, and did our show for about three hundred people. Alas, Florida was still not working out.

When it became apparent that Paul's millions of connections in New York were either not returning his calls or didn't exist, I started cold-calling companies and it began cutting into my bread-and-butter job. Desperation was setting in, and I was losing my day to tracking down executives and trying to sell them on our product. My Carver Reed employees would come into my office and tell me I had yet another diamond customer sitting on hold while I was calling Anheuser-Busch and telling them Bud Light was a great match for ECW.

Paul, on the other hand, seemed unaffected. That started pissing me off and confusing me at the same time. Why the hell wasn't he losing sleep over this TV deal? He was excited about our expansion, and he kept reminding me that the deal would pay for itself once the New York and Florida markets were built up. But that would take time, and time was money—big money. Like $6,000 a week money. I kept telling Paul the bank account was drying up, but he just kept talking about how huge we were becoming. He didn't understand the reality—winning the race is impossible if you run out of gas, and our tank was headed for "E."

I looked at the bank statements and calculated how much time we'd have left if we didn't secure advertisers. I thought presenting that to Paul with a hard date of execution would light a fire under his ass to break out of death row.

"You told me you could sell the New York show," I said for the umpteenth time.

"I'm going to. There's a guy who wants to sponsor the whole show. He's going to pay us a hundred grand a year to be the exclusive sponsor on MSG."

"Can I meet him?"

"Not yet."

I'd smack my head and try to shake the buzzing out of it. He'd tell me people get confused when they have to talk to more than one person, which was basically the "let me talk to the boys in the locker room" deal all over again, now with the advertisers. Time was running out.

"Fine," I said. "Then we pull the New York shows off MSG until the advertiser signs on."

"We can't. We'll lose everyone who is interested if we're off the air."

It was logical, but no less infuriating. I kept pouring money into this deal with the hope that it would someday pay off. But hope doesn't pay the bills.

I initially justified my deviation from the business plan by saying we'd be making ten times the investment in TV once the Florida and New York houses filled up and the advertisers came on. But just how long would that be? Time was not on our side. I'd been dedicated to my plan up to that point. We weren't overpaying talent, which is the first place wrestling companies go wrong. Our talent was realistic about the size of our company, and they didn't make outrageous demands. My most expensive wrestler was Terry Funk at $1,000 a match, which he reduced to $750 if we got him multiple shots, and I always did. Everyone else was making between $200 and $750 per shot.

Additionally, I allowed conventional logic to convince me that there were really New York investors Paul had lined up. Why else would he be so calm about the company's bank account draining? He obviously didn't want to be out of work; he must've been telling the truth. Maybe he'd had them hooked but they slipped off the line, turned off by our edgy product. Or maybe he'd said something to ruin the deal and was embarrassed to admit it. I didn't know, but I found a way for him to redeem himself.

I called in a favor through my uncle Mel Lewinter, an executive at Sony Music, and lined up a meeting with HBO in New York. If they bought the show, that would've certainly provided a lifeline. This seemed like our last shot. I'd already borrowed against my house and wasn't going further into debt. I was all in—I'd invested everything into what was now looking more like the *Titanic* than a wrestling company. Those personal sacrifices I made were the only reason anyone even *had* an ECW in which to work.

I asked Paul to prepare some tapes for the HBO meeting—our best stuff, the matches and promos that spotlighted our ingenuity. If there was a wrestling fan or two in that boardroom, I wanted them to immediately see how different we were. This was an emergency meeting, called at the last minute. HBO managed to squeeze us into their schedule as a favor, and I only had two days to prep. I started asking Paul for the tapes, and he told me he was working on it. The afternoon before the meeting I still had no tapes, no damn product to sell. I suppose I could've sat there and told them how wonderful we were, but having some video was really a must, since we're selling a goddamn TV show. But still no tapes.

"I'll have them overnighted directly to HBO," he assured me. "They'll be there before nine tomorrow morning, guaranteed."

Well, you never saw the show on HBO, so you already know how that went. They never got the tapes and the meeting was canceled. I was beyond embarrassed.

I couldn't believe Paul had dropped the ball like that. I was ready for HBO, with all the projections, the business plan going forward, and everything else about the company they'd want to see. I just needed Paul to do one thing—make the tapes. How could that not have been his top priority? I called him as soon as I got off the phone with HBO and screamed so loudly I actually had customers walk out of my store.

\* \* \*

The last thing I wanted to do was bring in an outside partner and reduce Paul's and my ownership stake in the company, but it seemed our last resort. I arranged for private investors to look at ECW for their portfolio. I managed to line up a couple of people—one requested a 20 percent stake in the company, and the second was a fan and just wanted to be a part of it, investing $100,000 for simply a return on his investment. The deal would slide me and Paul down to 41 percent and 39 percent, respectively, a 10 percent reduction for each of us, and our investor would be at 20 percent. I thought it was something we could live with in order to survive.

"I'm not giving up anything from my end," was Paul's reply.

"Paul, it's hundreds of thousands of dollars we're getting."

"I know. So you give the twenty percent from your end."

That would've effectively put me at 31 percent owner and Paul would've remained at 49 percent. That wasn't happening. I fought for splitting the shares, but he was unwavering. Our relationship changed forever on that day. It was the hardest thing to do, but I cut my 20 percent investor loose to go put his money elsewhere.

Paul had no objection to the guy offering $100,000 just for the return, as there was no percentage being relinquished on our part. We accepted his offer and agreed to a monthly repayment schedule. That investment money was helpful in paying some of our debts, but with TV amounting to a $24,000 monthly bill, not to mention thousands in back payments we owed Charlie and Ron, who produced our weekly TV show, it wouldn't last long.

I kept referring to our financial situation in terms of a countdown. I was really hoping something would happen, that advertisers would bite and at least alleviate the TV bill. The countdown started with a four-month clock—I'd calculated how long that $100,000 investment would last. Unless Paul produced his phantom advertisers or we started selling out Madison Square Garden, we'd be out of business in sixteen weeks.

Fifteen, Paul.

Fourteen, Paul.

That's how it was going. With each tick of that countdown, our relationship was deteriorating.

We got down to two weeks when Paul called and revealed a proposition he said he'd been working on for a while. Seemed there was an investor on the sidelines waiting to jump in, and like pulling a rabbit out of a hat, Paul unveiled Brian Travis. Well, he didn't really unveil anyone so much as talk about him. Paul said he was a club owner in New York who loved our product. Travis wanted to buy in and clear all debts, but in return he'd own the majority stake. Sounded more like we were being bought out.

I kept listening. There had to be something more.

"The only thing is, he wants me to run it and would like you to step away."

Bingo.

I'm not sure I let him even finish the sentence. "Shut... the fuck...up!" I yelled. "You're not talking to Ian Rotten here, asshole. I've run businesses for twenty years, you lying prick. You really thought I'd believe a guy who's never met me would buy a company only if Tod Gordon is gone?"

"That's what he wants! Don't blame *me*."

"Okay, then. I want to meet this Travis guy."

"I tried. He said he won't meet with you."

That was it. Insolvency was two weeks away, we'd secured no long-term advertisers, HBO didn't want to acquire a show it couldn't watch, Paul didn't want to accept the terms of the 20 percent investor, and I certainly wasn't signing my company over to the Invisible Man. I was done.

"It's yours," I said to Paul. "Do whatever you want with it."

I now realize it was unrealistic to think we had a shot at succeeding nationally. We were a niche product with a niche fan base, and that's the reason it got over—we weren't like the mainstream. To succeed on the scale we were striving for was unrealistic. Ted Turner couldn't run a national wrestling company; how could we have expected to? If I had it all back, I would have stuck to my initial business plan all along, saying no to deals that were outsized and keeping the local model. But it was becoming overwhelming. I couldn't work at that micro level, doing everything myself and still running Carver Reed. I needed Paul, and he was a genius. I've never denied that. We just should have built it slowly over time, with local TV, local shows, strong videotape sales internationally, and the gradual addition of shows.

I was angry when I gave up the company because I thought it was an unnecessary end to ECW. We had a bunch of chances to right the ship, but I just couldn't get my partner on board. I was mad at him and more so at myself.

Paul called me soon after I gave him the company when he realized one crucial thing—there really wasn't a company. There was no money, a bunch of debt from a couple of lawsuits and a ton of unpaid invoices, wrestlers looking for work, and a catalog of tapes. Very shortly after taking control of the purse strings, Paul

Heyman realized that I still owned the rights to the only thing of real value—ECW's intellectual property, including the library of tapes. Without getting that from me, Paul could never run clips of previous matches. He couldn't sell the videotapes, which was by far our strongest revenue stream in 1995. Paul said he needed me to sign over the rights to the video footage. I had him over a barrel, and he wasn't too proud to let me know it.

I had a decision to make—do I walk out on Paul and also the company and everyone in it? I had gotten fucked and wanted to pull the plug, but the thought of what it might do to those guys and girls making a living off ECW haunted me. I'd built them a place to come and live their dreams. I'd paid them what I could for their talents and given them a shot at taking what they'd learned at ECW and going elsewhere to make good money if they wanted to. I was proud of that. It's the best part of being a successful business owner—doing for others. They were all my kids. Even Paul's New York guys.

\* \* \*

I was in the hole to the tune of six figures when I relinquished financial control of the company to Paul. I was doing nothing further for ECW—Paul was in full control, and he could make it work or let it die. I knew the company would've died on the spot if Paul didn't get the video library. He asked me for it, and I said I wasn't signing anything over without getting something in return.

"How much?" Paul asked.

"Just the debt." I only wanted to recoup what I'd lost as a result of continuously putting up money to cover costs. Paul could pay me over time, years and years if that's what it took. If he agreed to it, I could live with turning over the footage and giving him a real chance to survive, and keeping all my friends employed. Paul said yes, and I was ready to do the deal. But I had to indemnify myself first.

I'm not a moron. I knew there was nothing in the bank, and Paul hadn't been taking a salary all this time, so there wasn't much in his bank account either. I also figured that Brian Travis was a figment of his imagination, so there was no way he'd be able to keep to the repayment schedule on which we'd agreed. I called Paul's mother. She and my mom still talked a fair amount, and they had a real friendship beyond their sons. I got on very well with the Heymans, so I explained the whole deal to his mother.

"I'm about to give control of the company to your son," I explained. "But there's just one issue—I signed a repayment deal with him that guarantees monthly reimbursements on my losses from ECW. I don't want to sign it unless that payment to me is guaranteed somehow."

"How much is it, Tod?"

I told her.

"I will send you that amount every month."

That was all I needed to hear. Mrs. Heyman was solid gold, and her word meant everything to me. I did the deal with Paul based on her word. She would send me the minimum amount, with Paul subsidizing anything above that if ECW had a good month. Of course, at the end of most months he'd tell me there was nothing there, that they'd gotten killed that month.

"No problem," I'd say. "I'll call your mother to cover it."

"No! Don't call my mother. I'll come up with it." We were like twelve-year-old kids arguing about a neighbor's broken window. There were times he was late with my check, and I didn't even bother to go to him. I would just call Mrs. Heyman.

"What?" she'd say. "I'm sorry." We'd hang up and I'd have a check in my mailbox two days later. She was better than Prudential.

It wasn't hard to surmise that Paul was probably using his father for the investment to keep the company going. Mind you, that wasn't offered when I was running around looking for investors and setting up meetings in New York like an asshole to try and sell a TV show without a tape. But now he could go to Dad and fulfill his lifelong dream of becoming Vince McMahon. Mr. Heyman was a successful attorney, and I figured Paul had a sizable credit line with him. Living at home into your forties has its privileges.

In addition to my video footage, Paul also needed me for ECW. There were business deals in place that I'd negotiated. Fumi Saito from Japan had a deal with me to buy each show for $5,000 for exclusive distribution in his country. He was great—he'd pay for four and five shows in advance, sending us checks for $20,000. Paul didn't want to rock that boat.

He also wanted to keep continuity with the boys, so he never told them he'd taken control. Of course, I told my Posse, but he didn't want anything to look different to the locker room; it might scare them off or something. He asked me to stay and help keep that veil of continuity, which I agreed to do. He still wanted to use me on TV, and I said that was fine too, provided those payments kept coming and the talent kept working.

It was a weird feeling, that transition from owner to figurehead, or ambassador. It happened in a matter of days, as the weekend was suddenly upon us and it was time to head to the next show. I went there without any decision-making authority for the first time in ECW, and it was there I saw the new name of the holding entity for the company. The paychecks no longer had ECW Inc. on them; they now said HHG Inc. That was a weird choice. I was surprised Paul chose something so different from the old ECW Inc., being that he wanted appearances to stay as consistent as possible for the talent. I figured the two H's were Heyman and Heyman. But G? Me?

I saw Raven looking over the check in the locker room that night. He laughed. "HHG, Tod? Like we don't know the G is for Gordon. Just call it Heyman and Gordon." And there it was, the continuity. Paul subtly let everyone who would be handed a check, wrestlers and contractors alike, think that I was still in authority.

Then the earth stopped spinning as I realized the really remarkable thing about the check—that there even *was* an HHG Inc. check so quickly. Paul had to open a bank account somewhere and order checks to be printed, which takes time even today. The check Raven was holding wasn't a temporary—HHG was printed on it, which meant the process had been started weeks ago. I'd only turned the company over to him a few days ago. If this were an Agatha Christie mystery, this is where the detective would gather everyone in the study and hold up the smoking gun.

Everything crystallized in a flash—HBO, Sunshine, MSG, Brian Travis. Paul needed the company to die in order to become the sole owner with his father's investment. That's why the senior Heyman was never offered to me as an option as we lay dying on the vine. For all I knew, those checks had been printed a year ago. Each one of those deals would have kept Paul from wresting full control of the company. If I'd succeeded in New York getting the HBO deal signed, then we would have kept on going with me in control at 51 percent. If we'd secured advertisers for MSG and Sunshine, we wouldn't have drained our bank account. Sure, we truly were coming up empty in our search for advertisers, but my repeated overtures to stop airing the shows and save $24,000 a month were always dismissed with Paul's guarantee that we were days away from selling commercials. Meanwhile, the SS *Gordon* kept taking on water and going under.

The Brian Travis scam was a final desperate straw to edge me out, saying this investor would buy into ECW only if Paul was in control and I was gone. Had I bitten, we would've been exactly where we were—Paul's father's money in the bank, Paul in control, me just working for ECW, and the phantom owner Travis functioning as the scapegoat for all unpopular decisions. I could see Paul in my mind—"I'm sorry Taz, but Mr. Travis wants Sabu to wear orange too. I'm as upset about it as you are."

It was played so perfectly. This was beyond cunning; this was Bond villain-level stuff. It was hard to live with for a long time. My mirror showed me someone I had a hard time greeting every day. I was outplayed, and I'd lost my baby in a game I didn't even know I was playing.

# CHAPTER 12

# ECW AMBASSADOR

We'd been talking about pay-per-view for years—from back when I had full ownership of ECW through my tenure there as an ambassador. I never thought the model was feasible, given the state of our bank account and the financial structure of pay-per-view provider deals. After your broadcast event, it can take months for the buys to be tabulated and any royalty paid. During that window, providers ask for commitment on your next date, should you be planning one. They book a host of shows, and you need to reserve your date well in advance. You also need the hefty down payment for that date, which was in the hundreds of thousands of dollars. You can see how the pay-per-view model is more doable for a big company that can float that kind of money as compared to a cash-strapped indie operation. You're going to be in the hole for hundreds of thousands of dollars until your events begin cycling regularly and yielding money.

There was never a time while I was holding the purse strings when I thought we should enter that market. We were already lurching too far ahead of ourselves by expanding into untested waters like New York and Florida, and pay-per-view would've killed us. However, at the start of 1997, Paul had full control and the fiscal responsibilities fell entirely on him; we were soon headed for our first pay-per-view. That is, until I began reading that wrestling writer Bruce Mitchell had gotten involved.

It was reported in the *Wrestling Lariat* newsletter that Mitchell did a hotline update where he bragged about doing his part to "clean up" ECW's violence, going so far as to suggest we should have "burned the tape" of the Eric Kulas/New Jack incident. Reports went so far as to suggest that Mitchell and Wade Keller contacted Request TV, the largest pay-per-view provider, about our violent product, giving the company second thoughts about carrying our show. This was the second time I'd wished Bruce Mitchell had chosen another line of work, after his first falsely reporting that I carried Ric Flair's bags.

Soon, the pay-per-view companies backed out of our date, and we had a planned pay-per-view in the shitter. It took several months and a letter-writing campaign organized by ECW superfan Tony Lewis to convince major carriers like Request TV and Viewers Choice to take a chance on ECW. Eventually they did, and on April 13, 1997, Barely Legal became ECW's first pay-per-view event.

Some months prior, I was approached by film director Barry Blaustein, who was filming a wrestling documentary for Ron Howard's Imagine Entertainment. One of the storylines in Blaustein's doc revolved around Terry Funk as the banged-up, aging veteran in the twilight of his career. Blaustein was tickled that Terry chose to ride out his last years in the ultraviolent ECW and asked if he could film some of our shows. I told him it was fine and passed him off to Paul, as I wasn't comfortable doing anything on camera for the film when I really didn't have control of the company. Blaustein and his crew would show up and cover the first pay-per-view, positioning it as a triumphant climax to Funk's involvement with the dedicated startup out of South Philly.

So much can be said about that historic evening. For openers, in what has become urban legend, it is absolutely true that the generators and power blew out less than sixty seconds after we went off the air, leaving the building in blackness. Had this happened mere minutes earlier, no pay-per-view company in the world would have ever touched ECW again. The picture of me, Paul, and the boys hugging in the dark arena is surreal. We were the Little Engine That Did, and our accomplishment was nothing short of a miracle—a testament to every single person who had anything to do with our getting there. That includes the boys you saw on camera, and everyone behind the scenes whose names you do not know.

Exhilaration aside, I would actually pinpoint this event as the beginning of the end. ECW lacked the deep pockets needed to float from pay-per-view to pay-per-view without yet getting paid. When the payments did come, they were based on buy rates, and we were far away from the kind of money that WWE and WCW were drawing with theirs.

With this new level of success came additional problems that, in retrospect, should have been anticipated. The wrestlers were now viewing themselves on a whole different level and wanted to be paid accordingly. Ironically enough, being on pay-per-view added cachet to the workers but further depleted the company's capital. Paul started giving raises and promising buy-rate bonuses that would further eat into the coffers.

The residual effects were soon evident. I noticed in the months leading up to the show there were fewer and fewer wrestlers huddling around the monitor to watch each other's matches. The locker room began a transformation to an every-man-for-himself mentality where their individual value was based on how much money they made. It was evident that my biggest fear—rushing into this market before we were ready—had manifested.

\* \* \*

Paul's and my relationship was not the brotherhood it once was, but we weren't at war with each other. We spoke a lot between shows, and he still ran ideas by me. The magic we created wasn't a fluke—it was born out of a rare symbiosis we had with each other. He eventually came to me with the ECW invasion of WWE angle. I told him I hated it.

"It's so wrong," I said. "It's against everything our fans stood for."

"We'd be *fighting* WWE, not joining it."

"Really, Paul? They're not going to think it's a real invasion. They're not stupid."

I thought this was a no-brainer. Paul was so bright and I couldn't believe he didn't get it, but it was his money now and he could do whatever he wanted. He wasn't hearing the common sense of not being associated with the mainstream, and I realized it was probably a deal made long ago. Jim Ross, the venerable commentator and WWE office member, later confirmed on his podcast that Vince McMahon had been paying Paul something like $50,000 to keep ECW afloat, eyeing that juicy ECW library. I suspected something was going on when I eventually saw WWE talent working in ECW. A guy with little personality like Al Snow would show up and Paul would try to find a gimmick that worked for him. He would get over with our fans and then go back to WWE with his new, winning gimmick. It was like a developmental territory before that was a thing.

Paul tried to explain the invasion angle as a promotional tool. "If we're on WWE TV, a million people who don't know us now will. *That's* how we're going to survive."

I was insistent that alienating our base was wrong no matter what. My role now was more advisory than anything else, so I dropped it. You didn't change Paul Heyman's mind about anything, especially if it was a deal inked with Vince from the get-go.

Sometime between 1995 and 1997, while working in this weird adviser/figurehead capacity, I began getting troubling calls from Fumi Saito about his ECW master tapes, as in he wasn't receiving them. I told Paul, and he said he'd sent them, which I communicated back to Saito. Then a few days later he called back, hotter this time.

"I'll look into it, Fumi. I'm sorry." I was in the shittiest position, having brokered this great deal for us, and now I had to take the rap for someone else's incompetence. I don't know if it was Paul doing the shipping or he'd delegated it, but it wasn't happening. I called Paul.

"Here's the tracking number," he said and started rattling off numbers. I cut him off. I'd seen the infamous tracking-number-minus-a-digit routine ten times before.

"Paul, you have to stop lying to me if we're going to keep doing things this way. I'm not one of the boys, and I'm not going to lie to Fumi."

"I will find out what happened and get him the tape. Trust me."

What choice did I have? I called Saito back and told him I'd spoken to Paul and he'd definitely get his tapes. He'd been a great source of revenue for years, sending us big checks for tapes in advance, and he didn't deserve this. I wasn't going to be the whipping boy for Paul, taking angry calls while he screwed contractors. Fumi Saito's next call went just like that, and I had no choice but to tell him it was no longer my company.

"Paul has control of the whole company now, and I can't control what he does," I said. I began telling that to all of our partners in various business ventures even before I told the boys. I wasn't going to start lying to people to cover. A few days later, I received a six-page letter from Saito. The first line read, *Your partner is a piece of shit*. The letter didn't get better from there.

I was tiring of handling issues I didn't create and didn't have the power to solve. That was middle-management bullshit. When the company was mine, I put out whatever fires I encountered. It was my responsibility. Now, it wasn't my company, nor my responsibility, nor my problem. I hung in there to protect my payments and keep the crew working. I wasn't worried about myself; I had Carver Reed.

Paul eventually tried that late-night promo shit with me, pushing my promo down the list after a show in some attempt to exercise authority. I saw how many workers he intended to film before me and I realized he was running that old gimmick to me now. It wasn't happening.

"Fuck you, Paul," I said as I grabbed my stuff. "I'm not Jason. I'll do it another day." I left before he could reply.

Most of the boys thought I was still in charge and would come to me with an issue that I could usually resolve without going to Paul. Over time, I saw more and more workers complaining about not getting their payoffs, and that was putting me in a tough spot. The locker room was becoming more divided and miserable. Some of the guys started coming up to me asking if I could get them work elsewhere, knowing I'd done it in the past with Public Enemy.

In late 1995, Teddy and Johnny came to me and said they wanted to go to WWE. I thought they would get over anywhere they went, but I suspected they'd be treated better in WCW and I could use my relationship with Kevin Sullivan to get them a better deal. Kevin was booking for WCW, and he was fond of using our people. I called him and said Vince had made Public Enemy an offer, but I thought they were better suited there. Sullivan said he'd check with WCW's Executive Vice President Eric Bischoff and get back to me. That offer from WWE was a good thing—once Eric heard that, he told Sullivan to double the amount for WCW. It was a super offer and I didn't want them to leave, but I loved those guys and wanted them to do as well as possible. They took the offer and worked in WCW for a couple of years before going to WWE and getting squashed by the tag team APA when Teddy and Johnny didn't want to lose by going through a table, which was their gimmick.

Though I was happy to see our guys move on to make real money, Paul was not. He saw leaving ECW as the ultimate act of betrayal. These workers took such risks, enduring inhumane punishment for ECW, and they were paid a few hundred bucks for it. When they were finally offered a $100,000 guarantee with upside potential, how could you not be happy for them? Their investment in us finally paid off for them. Whenever someone came to me about leaving, I told them to go, but to Paul if you left, you were dead to him.

Sandman and Fonzie came up to me in 1997 and said they were miserable without me at the helm and had had enough. They said they hated Paul and needed to get out of there, and asked me to call WCW. In doing so, they started a shitstorm I'm still asked about today.

\* \* \*

In short time, Sabu also got wind of Sandman and Fonzie's overture to me and asked me to help him get out too. I called Terry Taylor, who had worked for me in our early days and was now in a talent relations role for WCW. I told him about Sandman, Fonzie, and Sabu looking to leave ECW, and if they were interested, he could probably get them. He checked with Bischoff and, in a day or so, he called back saying they were only interested in Sabu at that time. I let Sabu know the good news, and then I broke the bad news to Fonzie and Hack. I told Sabu to call Terry Taylor.

A short time later, Paul pulled me aside.

"We have a mole," he said.

"A what?"

"Someone is trying to get our talent to sign with WCW. They're going to send everyone over there and kill ECW."

I suppose Terry Taylor called Paul and let him know about the inquiries made on behalf of Sabu, Sandman, and Fonzie. I was hoping Sabu cut a good deal with WCW, but it seemed Taylor called Paul before Sabu returned the call to Taylor.

Paul said that Sabu was not free to go. I couldn't believe it.

"Paul, this guy broke his neck for us. How can you begrudge him for wanting to get paid?"

He didn't care. I never saw Paul display genuine feelings for anyone, so I was appealing to something that simply wasn't there.

I'm sure you're thinking this is a free country and no man can stop another from taking a job where they want to. Here is a perfect illustration of the lengths to which Paul would go in controlling the talent. Paul went to Sabu and told him that he couldn't leave and violate the contract he'd signed with ECW, which was ridiculous as we never offered contracts to anyone. The talent were independent contractors, not employees. I actually couldn't legally bind a contractor to us.

I was furious and went to Sabu. "Sabu, you never signed a contract," I reminded him.

"Paulie said I signed one, so maybe I did. I don't remember." The guy was barely literate and had about a hundred concussions. Paul probably scribbled his name on a piece of toilet paper and held it up to show him.

"Fuck that," I said. "You tell Paul you're going."

Sabu wouldn't have a chance to do that. Paul jumped the line and spoke with Terry Taylor and told him that Sabu was under exclusive contract and ECW would sue WCW if they meddled with him again. I tried to call Taylor and smooth things over, but he said it wasn't worth the risk. WCW was going to pass on Sabu.

Now he's standing there telling me we have a mole.

"Paul, you have no mole. *I* called Terry Taylor for these guys because they're miserable here. The morale in the locker room is terrible, and we never had that here before. I'm just trying to help out my friends so they can have a career."

Paul's instincts kicked in, and he read the landscape like General Patton. He realized Sabu was one step from leaving, and Raven, Perry Saturn, and Stevie Richards had already jumped ship to WCW on their own. Even though they didn't take Hack or Fonzie, I told Paul they wanted to go too. A mole wasn't moving talent—his leadership was.

Then I told Paul that I was leaving too. I'd already given away the company, and now I was burning all the bridges I'd built in the business, like Fumi Saito. I gave Paul my final date, and he looked at me for a while, then had one final request.

"I'm losing the locker room, and I need to pull everyone together. You have to help me here." He had one big ask—would I agree to be the heel so he can fix the morale? "I have to get them back or else this thing will fall apart. You want that to happen?"

I didn't. But I also didn't yet know the full scope of what Paul was preparing to tell the locker room. If it was going to keep the talent working and not fighting with each other, I would deal with their knowing I had tried to get Sabu, Sandman, and Fonzie a job. None of them seemed to mind when I'd called for Public Enemy back in '95.

Paul went into his worker voice. "If you don't tell anyone about this, after a while you can come back as the greatest heel ever in the pro wrestling business. What's better than a heel owner?" He was very expansive on the idea, but I told him I knew he was full of shit. In truth, it was a really good idea. I never said he wasn't brilliant.

I told Paul to go tell them whatever he wanted, and he did. He went off and apparently called some of the New York crew to his house and before I knew it, the sheets started printing that ECW had "a mole" looking to destroy the company. Joey Styles did a story on the weekly 900 hotline saying, "Someone in the company is trying to bring ECW down!" The story was everywhere, and Paul used it to create an "us versus them" solidarity in the locker room. He'd told them a mole inside the company was planning on sending all the talent to WCW for an invasion angle that would leave ECW empty and bankrupt. Paul gallantly told the crew that this mole was looking to sink anyone who wasn't lucky enough to be stolen away, and fuck all our fans over. He used it to galvanize the locker room, and it worked.

Anyone truly in the know was aware that I could've sunk the company back in '95 when I walked away from running the operation and pulled my financing. I could've done it again by not relinquishing the video rights to Paul when he asked. I did that to keep everyone working, and some of those very people were showing up in newsletters with shitty quotes about me. Meltzer, Scherer, and all the writers were reaching out for comment.

"Are you the mole?" they were all asking. I told them I had no comment. There was no point in going into the whole story, and doing so would've violated what I'd told Paul he could do to restore order in his locker room. My contradicting him or revealing it was a plan I'd agreed to would be shitting on the company I built. I just couldn't do it. I still looked at the logo, the ECW Arena, and the talent and saw my creation. When your child grows up and moves out, they're still your kid.

\* \* \*

My decision to leave was precipitated by a host of things. More than a small part of me was feeling grossly taken advantage of by having to deal with good people like Fumi Saito and create diversions because of Paul's inability to keep his word. In the past two years I'd also been asked to stall wrestlers asking for their missing paychecks. I'd watched Paul do the whole dance before:

"My Halliburton is in the car."

"I didn't realize the check was unsigned when I sent it. I'll send another one right away."

"I ran out of checks. The new book is coming soon."

I wasn't doing that shit, and every time Paul asked me to, I said no.

Paul also started using me less and less on shows. I'd get there and he'd go over the show and say, "I have nothing for you, man." It wasn't my ECW anymore, so it wasn't hard to tell Paul I was done. I wasn't going to waste my time coming to shows anymore, and I certainly wasn't going to lie to everyone he was asking me to.

The mole thing, as stupid as it was, had gained so much traction in the wrestling media that people thought it was true. Paul had convinced some of the locker room I was trying to move a huge group of guys out in order to kill the company. Of all the ECW guys that ended up in WCW, Raven got in earlier on his own and then got Richards and Saturn in. I called WCW for Sandman, Fonzie, and Sabu—my friends. There was no master plan, no big invasion, no exodus from ECW. People have deduced all kinds of things over the years and read into the situation, but the facts remain the facts. I've heard members of Paul's New York crew say they would've killed me if they'd known I was talking with Terry Taylor. It's a bunch of horseshit. None of them were really surprised to hear I'd called for my friends. Jealous, maybe. But not surprised.

To his credit, Paul was very gracious on TV about my exit. They closed that week's show with Paul addressing the camera.

"It is with a heavy heart that earlier this week ECW accepted the resignation of Tod Gordon as commissioner of Extreme Championship Wrestling. Citing the pressures of raising four children and running a family business, Tod could no longer assume the responsibilities of being ECW's commissioner. We here at ECW wish Tod Gordon nothing but the best in all of his future endeavors and want to let him know that we intend to make him proud as we carry on *his vision* of ECW."

That was nice to hear, insincere as it might have been. It was a fitting eulogy for my time there, though I could picture Taz and Buh Buh spitting at their TV sets.

I recently saw Paul on a WWE interview show where he said he never took a dime from me. As true as that technically might've been, he failed to mention the 49 percent of my company that I handed him. As far as paydays go, find one damn worker at WWE that got that deal from Vince McMahon.

* * *

I kept in regular contact with Paul after I left ECW for good. I'm sure he hid that from the boys because I kept hearing how his New York crew wanted to kill me. It was necessary for him to keep up the ruse that I was the enemy who wanted their company bankrupted. I got it and I never did anything to shatter that illusion.

Some of the workers I was closest to in ECW would still reach out to me for advice, and I was happy to help. Sandman was called down to WCW headquarters in Atlanta in 1998 and offered a job there for a couple hundred grand a year. This is what our guys deserved—to be rewarded for the years of paying their dues on the road, taking chair shots and gigging their heads for two hundred bucks. As I said before, I always saw that as the natural evolution for our crew.

I also said before that I was alone in that view when it came to ECW's two partners.

"I hope you took it," I said to Hack when he called. But he didn't sign. He was in his rental car driving away from CNN Center.

"Nah," he said. "I told them I gotta think about it."

"Why?"

"My match in Japan with Onita."

"Your *what*?"

It seemed Paul, upon hearing about Hack's WCW meeting, told him he'd put together an exploding cage match against Onita in Japan and he'd lose that booking if he left for WCW. I was firm with Hack.

"Turn that fucking car around, *now*. There's a one percent chance that booking in Japan is even true. And even if it is, are you really putting *one match* ahead of a multiyear contract for hundreds of thousands of dollars?"

He turned the car around, went back upstairs, and signed a three-year deal.

Though I never stepped back into ECW, my life after that wasn't without wrestling. Far from it. I was contacted regarding the NWA's fiftieth-anniversary card to be held in October 1998 at the Hilton Hotel in Cherry Hill, New Jersey, an obvious wrestling hotbed. I was asked how much I'd want to be paid to return to wrestling and craft an angle that could see a blowoff at that big card. We agreed to a $3,000 payoff for a few appearances around South Jersey and a match at the NWA anniversary card. Plus, I wanted some of my ex-ECW guys to be used and paid for each of their appearances. They agreed and it was done.

There was one problem—they wanted us to be the heels in the angle. South Jersey is right near Philadelphia, and Cherry Hill is literally right over the Ben Franklin Bridge from Central Philly. This was ECW country. I'd have to find a way to make those crowds boo me and the ex-ECW wrestlers I'd bring in. They wanted us to be the invaders, stepping into the NWA shows and starting trouble, but what they didn't understand was that the crowd would turn and follow *us*. This was going to take some work, and I turned to my old booker Eddie Gilbert for help, posthumously.

The NWA had run Eddie Gilbert Memorial wrestling shows every year since he died in 1995, so I thought we could use Eddie's legacy as a device in getting heat. We could actually use Eddie's memory to carry the whole angle and involve the Gilbert family as well. I called Doug Gilbert and pitched the angle. He got it right away.

"Shit, man," he said. "There's gonna be some heat on you."

That was what I wanted to hear. I asked him to lend me one of Eddie's ring jackets and to ask his father, retired wrestler and referee Tommy Gilbert, if he'd come up to New Jersey for the blowoff match. They agreed to everything, and we were ready to start the months-long buildup.

The plan was to start crashing NWA shows in South Jersey. The ex-ECW guys would run in from the parking lot and lay out the popular NWA stars. I'd make appearances at the shows wearing Eddie's "Hot Stuff" jacket with my old pal Missy Hyatt—Eddie's ex-wife—on my arm. Then we'd get in the ring for the big blowoff steel cage War Games match at the anniversary card in Cherry Hill. It was to be a tag match with me tagging with Stevie Richards, Rocco Rock, and the Pitbulls against Coralluzzo, two of his NWA guys, and Doug and Tommy Gilbert. At the end, I'd be left in the ring alone with Coralluzzo and the Gilberts, and they'd beat the snot out of me and send my ass back to Philly.

Boy, did I underestimate my devoted ECW fans.

We did the run-in angle first, beating up the NWA guys at a local NWA show in Jersey, and the whole crowd popped and started chanting "E-C-W! E-C-W!" as we mauled their babyfaces. There we were, beating the shit out of the guys they were just cheering, and the whole audience turned and cheered *us*. That didn't go as planned, but I figured the next show when I came out wearing Eddie's jacket with Missy beside me would do it. I took the microphone and did my best to heel the crowd, but nothing was working. The more they cheered, the more pissed I got. I looked down into the crowd and saw that Georgiann Makropoulos, one of the sport's beloved newsletter writers, was in attendance that night. She wrote the *Wrestling Chatterbox*, which was a lightweight fanzine, but she was a sweet lady and wrestlers and fans alike loved her. I saw an opportunity and pointed down at her.

"Georgiann!" I began. "I noticed you stopped sending me your newsletter when I left ECW. How the fuck am I going to know when it's Sal Bellomo's birthday now?!" I thought the audience would turn on me now for messing with her brand of reporting. Nope. They popped. Damn it. Incidentally, she really did stop sending me her newsletter when I left.

I'd done everything possible to make me and my ECW guys the heels, but unless we were in a WWE ring, there was no way to make fans hate us. Coralluzzo started getting pissed that he wasn't getting the babyface reaction from the fans, so I offered to flip Stevie Richards. Stevie and his Daisy Dukes were getting the biggest pop in our group, so I had him turn on us and go with Dennis and the NWA guys. I thought that should bring the fans over to them, but it just didn't. Everyone was underestimating the power of the ECW brand. If nothing else, we'd set up an entertaining blowoff match for October 24 at the Hilton that was sure to draw a big crowd anyway, being the NWA's fiftieth-anniversary show.

When I arrived at the venue that day, I saw that Jim Cornette had come up to book the show. This was news to me, but I was indifferent. We'd already laid everything out, including how the match would go. That part isn't easy for me—I can craft angles, but specific matches weren't so easy. I'm a promoter, not a wrestler. But we'd set up a cool spot where they'd have me alone in the cage and practically kill me. That would make Dennis and his company the Super Babyfaces, and I was willing to put my well-being on the line for that to happen.

Enter Jim fucking Cornette. He'd gotten in Coralluzzo's ear and convinced him this was a setup, just like the NWA title tournament where we had Shane Douglas screw him in the end. Cornette didn't talk to me directly, but Coralluzzo told me what he'd said and, as a result, the match was off, and they were going to just do a straight match with a regular finish and be done with it.

I saw red. I'd spent months crafting this angle for him, with all roads leading to this show. Was Dennis so frigging weak that he'd throw all this work out the window just because Jim Cornette said to? I'd done everything I said I would for this angle, to the letter. It would make no sense not to follow the plan at that point. Cornette couldn't get past 1994. All he had in his head was, "Paul E...Paul E...Paul E..." He actually thought Heyman was behind this whole thing and that I was going to fuck them and get ECW over again. Had he actually spoken to me, we could've had a beer and a Sprite and shared our sentiments toward Paul. I'm sure we wouldn't have been that far apart. Instead, he worked Dennis over and got the goon to pour cold water on the hottest angle he'd ever been a part of—an angle I'd worked my ass off to bring to life for his company. Maybe Cornette wanted to book a finish where he tennis-rackets Coralluzzo when he finds him letting the air out of Tommy Gilbert's tires.

I found Doug Gilbert and gave him Eddie's jacket back.

"Thank you, brother, but we're not doing that match tonight." I gave him the coat and I left the show. I wasn't putting one more second into the deal when Cornette had swung into town for one damn night and upended the table with all my work atop it. I did take solace in reading the crowd had chanted "WE WANT TOD! WE WANT TOD!" when I wasn't in the ring that night.

I never spoke to Dennis Coralluzzo again before his death in 2001.

# CHAPTER 13

# WORKER DEATHS

**E**arlier I listed all the names of the workers that passed through ECW. It's a remarkable list, but equally as remarkable, though far sadder, is the list of workers in the ECW family that have met untimely deaths. I'd be remiss if I didn't take time to chronicle them here.

Our first loss was my first booker, Eddie Gilbert. Well, technically Eddie was my second booker after Larry Winters's one-show stint. Eddie was a good partner at that time, and he kept our TV product interesting during those Eastern years. He had more potential to be something outside wrestling than anyone I've worked with. He had a genuine fascination with the machinations of politics and politicians. He really hoped to do that after wrestling.

I detailed his change in personality before, and I have to emphasize that the drugs really did that to him, as they have for many others. Eddie died of a heart attack in Puerto Rico on February 18, 1995, at age thirty-three.

\* \* \*

Larry Winters—the first booker I hired, and the first booker I fired. He was there when I started Eastern and, as you know, he was one of the guys that came to me when Goodhart folded TWA. He and Artese asked me to start up something, and I did. You can kinda thank him for ECW.

Larry was always a good guy. He was bland but nice. There wasn't much further for him to go in wrestling—he was one of Goodhart's top guys, and he'd been a jobber in the AWA and NWA. He wasn't going to fit into the long-term ECW plans and was gone before 1994.

Larry passed away from a heart attack on January 27, 2015. He was fifty-eight.

* * *

Ted Petty, aka Rocco Rock, was such a great guy. Years after our time together in ECW, I'd started booking him in 2002 for 3PW (Pro-Pain Pro Wrestling) while I was there. I booked Teddy for a show in Philly on the same day he had an earlier shot in New Jersey. He said he'd go on early and would be in Philly in plenty of time for our show. Then Teddy's girlfriend called me while she was driving and said he didn't look right and was gasping for air. She said she thought he was having a heart attack and was taking him to the hospital.

Heart attack? Teddy was in the best shape of anyone I knew. He didn't do drugs that I knew of, except maybe for steroids. If he did anything more, he did a good job kayfabing it. He shouldn't have been gasping for air while sitting in a car.

Then she called back a short time later while I was working the show at the Arena.

"Tod," she started. "Teddy died." It had been a heart attack.

It felt like I'd been shot in the chest. I was shocked by the news, but I had an added dilemma, as I was in the middle of a live show—should I tell the workers and risk sucking the air out of the room for the rest of the night? I decided to tell no one and just walked around like a zombie all night. I made an excuse about

Teddy having a flat tire and said he wouldn't be there. I sat with my head in my hands all night, devastated.

That was September 21, 2002, when Teddy left us at age forty-nine.

* * *

I loved Johnny Grunge. I said it earlier and I'm repeating it. We were boys and hung together often. He didn't travel with the Posse, but I'll call him an honorary member. He was a weekend warrior for us and drove a truck for his father-in-law during the week. He'd call me from the road while I was at work and we'd shoot the shit. He was lovable and harmless, an absolute carnival sideshow if you just stood to the side and watched him operate.

Whereas Teddy's death was a surprise, I can't exactly say his partner Johnny's was. He was a ticking time bomb, and everyone knew he was going to die if he didn't make changes. He'd walk around the locker room asking if anyone had pills, then pour handfuls of whatever he was given into his mouth. I don't think he even knew what they were; they were all different colors. It was like he was gobbling down handfuls of Skittles.

I'd watched Johnny balloon up and get unhealthily fat in the months before his death. The last few times I saw him we were doing ECW Reunion shows in the fall of 2005. We stopped at a rest stop on the turnpike, and Pitbull Gary and I watched Johnny perform the most amazing display of glutinous ingenuity. He was standing in front of the car eating a burger, apple pie, and a large soda. He put his foot up on the front bumper and rested the drink on his stomach like a shelf so he could double-fist the burger and apple pie, alternating bites. He must've stopped traffic as people drove by. I couldn't believe it.

We did a show in a theater in Cleveland that night, and Johnny was supposed to make a run-in save on Pitbull Gary, setting them up for the next night in Pittsburgh. As two heels were beating on Gary, which was Johnny's cue to run to the ring, nothing happened. I was backstage as Shane and others started yelling, "Where's Johnny?"

I remembered him telling me he was hungry a while ago, and despite the unlikelihood of finding him, I headed to the concession stands. There he was, counting out change for the clerk. "Seventy-five cents, seventy-six cents..." I grabbed him.

"You're late for the save!"

"Oh, shit!" He started for the ring but then turned and shoved his hot dog and popcorn into my hands. "Hold this." Then he was gone, hauling his expanding ass down through the fans and to the ring. I started running down to ringside holding his frigging hot dog and box of popcorn. After he made the save, albeit a very, very late one, we left ringside only to realize Johnny hadn't made it out of the ring. He was so big at that point that he couldn't roll out under the bottom rope. He got himself stuck between the mat and the rope and was flailing like a netted sea turtle. I sent Gary back out to free him. It was pathetic. I thought, *This guy is in such bad shape he's going to die in the ring at one of these shows.*

A few months after the Reunion shows, Johnny's wife called and told me he'd died in his sleep. I wasn't exactly shocked, though I was no less heartbroken. Johnny would always say, "I'm not here for a long time, I'm here for a *good* time." That good time ran out on February 16, 2006, at age thirty-nine.

\* \* \*

Balls Mahoney and Axl Rotten go together in my mind. Not only did they form the tag team called the Hardcore Chair Swingin' Freaks, but they were identical in style, and when they discovered drugs, they were doing that shit with each other, shooting each other up.

Balls was a nice guy and never problematic to work with. He was always smiling, always in a good mood. One thing he did that rubbed the boys the wrong way sometimes was complain about injuries. Generally speaking, everyone is hurting in a pro wrestling locker room and no one particularly cares about your issue. Balls would walk in and go on about having dropped this or that on his ankle or banging his head on a cabinet door. On one such occasion, I remember Perry Saturn grumbling "Cunt" under his breath when Balls left the room.

Balls and Axl were also both aligned in their unawareness of the importance of personal space. Balls would lean down with his mug inches from mine and start spitting rapid-fire about how I absolutely had to watch his tapes of himself working in Smoky Mountain Wrestling.

"Me and Candido, Tod. We had great matches. You think I'm just a brawler, but you'd see I can really wrestle if you watch them." I'd lean away and ask for two or three feet. I could tell you what he had for lunch that day.

Axl was more of a leaner. After a show, he'd be good and whacked and throw his arm around me and practically lay his head on my shoulder. "Brother, brother, brother," he'd slur. "We did it, man. We really created something." The last thing I wanted at the end of a show night was a three-hundred-pound mound of sweat laying on me, but what can you do.

The focus of their matches was how they could make themselves bleed more. I don't know if that ever drew money—they weren't working main events. But they were pretty good at coming up with new ways to mangle themselves. They'd come up to Paul and say, "Hey, what if we wrapped the barbed wire around a baseball bat and used that?"

"Sure," Paul would say, then look across to me and make his *What the fuck?* face.

That heroin shit is rough. Opiates are the undisputed champion, and it's nearly impossible to unseat them when you decide to challenge them. In a tragically fitting way, Axl and Balls left us just two months apart, February 4, 2016, and April 12, 2016, respectively. Both men were forty-four years old.

\* \* \*

The most intense Dudley brother was probably Big Dick. He mostly sneered and growled during the crazy promos that featured various numbers of the inbred clan displaying tics and outbursts. Big Dick was unflappable, able to stay in character the entire time and block out the madness around him. We fed those guys some crazy lines, and on occasion one of them would crack up. But never Dick.

He was agile for a big guy too, doing moonsaults off the top rope at six foot seven and over three hundred pounds. He even did it with a cast on his leg, which was an outgrowth of his having had a legit surgery. He kept the crutches and cast for a long time afterward as they became part of his gimmick.

Our interactions were limited to sharing the occasional doobie and his incessant impression of a wrestler named Nova. Dick happened to be present when Nova came up and introduced himself to me on his first night.

"Hi, Mr. Gordon," he said, offering his hand excitedly. "My name's Nova. I worked for you tonight." As soon as he walked away, Dick put on a soft, kiss-ass voice and repeated his greeting. He did it for months whenever we passed each other.

Big Dick went limp for good on May 16, 2002, of kidney failure at the incredibly young age of thirty-four.

\* \* \*

I had a love/hate relationship with New Jack. He didn't know that—he thought we had a love/love relationship. There were times I couldn't stand him, but I kept in contact with him until the end. He just didn't get it sometimes. He'd show up at Carver Reed at eight in the morning, shirtless and high, asking me if he could have a few bucks to get breakfast. I'd have five or six employees out on the floor opening up, and New Jack would be loud and just in the way. It's not how I wanted to start my day, walking into my office with New Jack putting his feet up on my desk and lighting a cigar.

He'd hit me up here and there for a hundred bucks and tell me he'd be back Tuesday to repay me. I'd see him Tuesday, but he would usually hit me for another hundred to seal the "big deal" he had going down. I'd tell him when he repaid the first loan, he could have another.

I got a phone call from him long after ECW that disappointed me greatly. He called and matter-of-factly told me he had video of me snorting coke and Fox News wanted to pay him a "lot of money" for it. He didn't want to turn it over, of course, but he'd fallen on tough times and could use the money. Naturally, if I gave him $500 he'd be able to turn down their offer of thousands. Boy, was I lucky to be getting such a deal.

This was the stupidest work I'd ever seen. I was there for him all the time in ECW, whenever he was in danger of getting in trouble, fired, or just needed bail money, and *this* is what I get in return? Fuck that. I was more annoyed that he thought I was stupid enough to think Fox News would give a shit what Tod Gordon was doing in a hotel room in 1996. It was the worst stickup New Jack had ever committed in his life. I told him to give them the tape. My singular pet peeve is having my intelligence insulted. This pissed me off.

A few days later he called back. "Tawd," he said, somber. "I'm sorry, man. I was stupid."

"You *are* stupid, man. Not only was it fucked up, but what a lame-ass play." We were all right after that.

I got the call from Mike Johnson when Jack died. He partied hard, more so as years went on, but I was still surprised. Jack was one of those guys that seemed indestructible, and it was a bitter pill accepting he'd just dropped from a heart attack at age fifty-eight. As is so often the case, lifestyle catches up to these guys in the form of some other malady, and I suspect that the years of coke and pills did Jack in. He died on May 14, 2021.

* * *

Mike Awesome was brought in by Sabu in December 1993. Sabu was our TV champ at the time, and he flew in Mike on his own dime so we could see him. Sabu was more generous than he could afford most times. I'd often remind him to pay for his shit *first*, then do for others. He was the most generous guy I knew, but he also needed a business manager more than anyone I knew.

Mike Awesome was a jacked monster, standing six foot six and weighing three hundred pounds. He worked on and off for us when he was in between commitments to other federations and international bookings. Mike got over for us after a spot where he practically folded JT Smith in half on the guardrail. JT wasn't hurt, but he sold it like crazy and it made Awesome into the monster he looked like.

I had very little interaction with Mike, but he was a part of the stew that made us unique. He hung himself on February 17, 2007, at age forty-two.

* * *

The Pitbulls, Gary and Anthony, were definitely an extended part of our group. They weren't traveling with the Posse, but when we got to buildings, they'd head right over to us and sit. Everyone knew these bad motherfuckers were de facto enforcers for us. I never asked them to be, but when they got word someone might be messing with my guys, they were on it.

Anthony had a scary intensity to him. I don't think it was a put-on—he could just look at you with those bug eyes stuck in that big, fat, bald head and you'd tremble. One night we were at a strip bar and a dancer sat down beside him for a cocktail. I was sitting and talking with Gary when we both took a pause and watched Anthony lean in with that murderous intensity and ask her to join him at his place after her shift. With his bugged psycho eyes, he said, "I won't try nothin', I just want you to join me for company and conversation." She was speechless as this hulking mouth breather asked her for some "company and conversation." That's what came out of his mouth, but the visual looked like he was considering what her spleen would taste like. She bailed and Gary and I ribbed him about it, saying how scary he looked, but he honestly had no idea.

"What? What?" I'd hear that shocked phrase from him a few more times, like when I brought my second wife to a show and, upon meeting her, he looked down at her chest and said, "Are they real?"

Gary shoved him. "Dude, what the fuck? You can't say that to the boss's wife!"

"What? What?"

He truly thought nothing of asking the weirdest shit, like when he told Francine, who'd been managing the Pitbulls, that part of her managerial duties was blowing him.

"You're the manager, and that's how the business works," he told her when she laughed in his face. He was totally serious. That small detail about a manager's responsibilities had escaped me despite all I'd learned about the business. I wonder if he would've told Sir Oliver Humperdink that same thing if I'd had him managing the Pitbulls.

Anthony was shooting Nubain when it became a thing to abuse. Nubain is an opiate used as a pain medication to supplement anesthesia. It found its way to our locker room among the heavier users, and Anthony was one of the guys that embraced it.

There was a time when it looked like he might be able to turn things around. Gary told me Animal of WWE's Legion of Doom had called them and wanted a Pitbulls versus LOD angle. Gary told me Anthony was excited about the prospect of the run and getting in shape for it.

But it wouldn't happen. Anthony's end was particularly horrific. On September 25, 2003, both he and his girlfriend overdosed on fentanyl, and their two babies crawled around their dead bodies for two days before they were found. He was thirty-six.

\* \* \*

Only one wrestler was considerate enough to tell me in advance they'd be missing our upcoming show because they planned to be on a drug binge—Hawk of the Legion of Doom. I got that call on a Wednesday, a full three days before our Saturday shot he'd be missing.

"I want to let you know I'm going into lockdown this weekend, so I can't do the show," he said. "But I'll do two for the price of one next month."

"Lockdown? Like, jail?"

"No. Me and some guys are going to lock the doors and party for a few days. Won't be coming out till Monday."

Well, at least he told me. What could I say? I'd just replace him and cash in my rain check the following month. He made good on the deal, working two dates for one payday.

Hawk was another guy who never gave me a problem. A few years after he worked for us, his substance issues became so well known that WWE turned them into an on-screen angle. Though I knew Hawk partied, it never affected his work in ECW. Well, unless you count calling out of work to get high for a few days.

In ECW, he was never in a condition unfit for performing. I first booked him in 1993, and he worked a handful of dates into 1994 without issue. But that was the last time I worked with him, and I know his problems became pretty consuming down the road and eventually took their toll. Less than a month after Pitbull

Anthony's overdose, one of his prospective opponents in the Pitbulls versus LOD feud, Hawk, died of a heart attack on October 19, 2003, at the age of forty-six.

\* \* \*

Bam Bam Bigelow had headlined WWE's WrestleMania XI against football legend Lawrence Taylor in 1995. He was a local talent, living in nearby South Jersey, so we were able to book him without expensive travel. He debuted for us less than a year after that WrestleMania and was such an easy talent to deal with we'd bring him back in 1996, and by mid-1997 he was a regular on our roster. Bam Bam was a sight at six foot four, four hundred pounds, with flames tattooed across his shaved head. He was one of those guys you wouldn't shoot with a gun for fear of making him angry. If he sat at the end of the bar, he'd probably clear the place out.

Despite appearances, Bam Bam was a sweet, quiet, hard-working guy. He just *looked* like a maniac. In addition to having a great look, he was remarkably agile. He could do a standing drop-kick, which, at his size, was incredible. The thing that kept him out of the top rung of the business was his inability to work the mic. If he'd been a talker, he could've been top of the card in every federation for a long time.

Working Bam Bam's style at his size was already beginning to take its toll. He was only in his mid-thirties when he came to work for us but was already having difficulty. You couldn't tell by watching him in the ring, but outside you could see him struggle. He was suffering from a bad back and wanted a reduced road schedule, so ECW was a perfect fit for him. We ran weekends and mostly at local venues, so he had weekdays off and didn't have to cram himself into an airline seat when he did work. He was a dream for us—a big name, great talent, easy to work with, and reliable. He never missed a show.

I never saw evidence of drug abuse while he worked for us. I know he got mixed up with pain pills as he tried to treat his back, which is the nightmare scenario for so many athletes. Bam Bam drifted away from the business and ultimately landed in Florida, where he died of an overdose in 2007. He was forty-five.

\* \* \*

Bobby Duncum Jr. could have been a hell of a star. He started working for ECW in my final year of 1997, and I had few interactions with him except for one night in Allentown when he and Shane Douglas burst into the bathroom while I was taking a piss. Shane was on his way back from the ring when he apparently beat up a fan.

"Okay," I said, trying to finish up. "Why are you in the toilet with me?"

"Cops are after me," Shane said, still dripping with sweat from the match he'd just had. He turned to Duncum, who was right behind him. "Light me up," he said.

"Huh?" Duncum replied.

Shane offered his face. "A good one, Bobby. I gotta lump up fast." Bobby paused a second, but the sound of an approaching mob was at the bathroom door. He hauled off and punched Shane in the cheekbone. Shane asked for another and Bobby obliged, knocking him to his knees. Shane stood and half his face had immediately swelled. Just then the cops burst in the room. I threw myself against a urinal.

"Um, excuse me fellas," I said. "Pissing here."

"We're here for him," an officer said, gesturing to Shane and ignoring my attempted diversion. Douglas showed his face to the cops and said he'd been viciously attacked by a fan and had to defend himself.

"I hope you're gonna lock him up before he hurts another wrestler," he said. The cops conferred briefly and headed back out to find the violent offender. If nothing else, I knew I could count on Bobby Duncum Jr. to fuck up my face if requested. He got KO'd for good by a hot dose of fentanyl on January 24, 2000, at age thirty-four.

* * *

Nancy Sullivan's death was obviously the one that came from furthest out in left field and was absolutely the most devastating. We were so sorry to see Nancy go when she left us to work in WCW and rejoin her husband Kevin Sullivan, who was booking there at the time. The Posse got together and said our individual "I love yous," and she was on her way.

Once in WCW, she was booked into this stupid on-camera love triangle storyline where she started seeing Chris Benoit behind Kevin's back. As life sometimes imitates art, she did begin seeing Benoit off camera as well, ultimately leading to her and Kevin's divorce in 1997. I have no idea why Kevin would've put her in an angle like that. I can't even understand having one's wife or girlfriend in this business in *any* capacity. Working in pro wrestling with your wife is a surefire relationship killer, only slightly ahead of working in pro wrestling *without* your wife. You'd have to be a moron to do it.

I found out like everyone else did about the infamous murder-suicide where Benoit killed Nancy, their son Daniel, and then himself—in the news. It was an absolute kick to the gut. It was awful. I remember Hack crying that night. Nancy was his manager in ECW, and he loved her and respected her. We all did—she was our sister and our mother, all at once. When we got too raucous in the van, she'd put us all in our place with a simple, "Guys, come on now."

I can't believe I still read comments from fans being critical of WWE's decision to take Benoit off their DVDs and blur his name.

Even sheet writers have asked when it'll be okay to put him back on the taped shows. My answer?

When hell freezes over.

Oh, I'm sorry...is Nancy back alive? I didn't think so. Believe me, the world will be just fine never seeing Benoit again. For fans who think he deserves a place in wrestling history, you should do yourself and the world a favor by taking a minute to remember Nancy and Daniel instead. Take that same amount of time you're spending thinking about Benoit and think about the two innocent souls he destroyed. Who gives a shit who he pinned in Philadelphia?

The most haunting thing about the entire tragic event is that I wonder if it could've been prevented had Nancy stayed with us. When Kevin left for WCW, he didn't take her. She worked with us even through his booking there when he took Sherri, Eddie Guerrero, and whoever else was here. I always found it odd he didn't initially bring her to WCW with him. But what if she'd stayed here for good, away from WCW, away from Chris Benoit?

The world lost an absolute angel on June 25, 2007, when Nancy and her son Daniel passed, and Chris Benoit offed his miserable self.

\* \* \*

I first used the pint-sized powerhouse Chris Candido in Eastern back in 1993. We formed a tag team called the Suicide Blondes, featuring Candido, Chris Michaels, and Johnny Hotbody, who was, of course, brunette. I pitched that to Eddie, who thought it was as hilarious as I did, and Hotbody joined the Blondes. Chris would soon leave for WWE but return to us in 1996, where it was obvious he'd grown in all ways, though I don't feel he did anything particularly memorable in his final year in ECW. Chris was talented but small and didn't have the charisma needed to overcome that pitfall.

Chris died on April 28, 2005, of acute pneumonia.

\* \* \*

Rick Rude was another early departure. He was a pretty serious guy and not really the kind of worker I jelled with outside the ring, but I think we got along so well because (a) I always had cigarettes on me for him to bum, and (b) I was down to do some coke with him when the opportunity presented itself. Rick looked great in the ring—the guy probably had 1 percent body fat. He was also great on the microphone and a legit tough guy from that scrappy crew of Minnesotans in wrestling.

I was shocked to hear about Rude's death, because he was so young and always in impressive shape. He died at age forty from heart failure on April 20, 1999. When you consider his age and condition, you have to wonder what chemicals contributed to that fatal diagnosis.

\* \* \*

Louie Spicolli was brought in by Sabu, and I knew from his first weekend in the company we were going to have trouble. Before the night's end, Louie would end up passed out, facedown in his mashed potatoes at the diner.

Louie worked with Dreamer for a bit. Tommy must've taken a liking to him because he'd put him over during their program, but Spicolli could never find footing here and was gone within a year.

The mashed potatoes escapade proved not to be an isolated incident. Louie overdosed on February 15, 1998, at twenty-seven years old.

# CHAPTER 14

# INDIES

Getting back to the chronology of my story, I'd been out of ECW since late 1997 when I got a call in 2002 from Brian Heffron, the Blue Meanie. It seemed he and his new girlfriend, porn star Jasmin St. Claire, were starting a promotion called 3PW and wanted my help. I'll repeat the most noteworthy part of that—*Meanie and his girlfriend, porn star Jasmin St. Claire*. A head-scratcher, for sure. Anyway, they'd booked Sandman, New Jack, and Sabu for a three-way main event and were nervous that the unruly trio might burn down ECW Arena. They wanted me to come in and book the finish so none of those guys made a problem before the match, and also referee it so none of them made a problem *during* the match. I took the gig for a quick grand; they were my friends, so it was barely a night's work.

This offer came right on the heels of another wrestling opportunity going belly-up. A year prior, Sandman had been approached by a guy named John Collins to help run a federation called Main Event Championship Wrestling, or MECW. The letters were likely not coincidence, since they approached Hack to be their main guy. He told Collins the job was beyond his scope but he should call me if he wanted someone who could run a promotion in the Philly area. I took the call and agreed to put together

236

a mega TV taping for their first show. I'd be booking a dressing room filled with many workers I'd never met, like Barry Windham and Marcus Bagwell.

I thought MECW had potential because there seemed to be some real money behind it. I was paid a few thousand, as was Hack, and I know all the boys were happy with the payoffs. Collins was running the show, but the financing was from a guy named Gary, up in Canada. The first show went well and they seemed pleased—so much so that Collins was soon out of the picture and Gary offered me a million dollars a year to take the reins and run MECW entirely. I considered leaving Carver Reed behind and doing it—I thought this could be like ECW but with an actual budget. The promise of that excited me.

Ultimately, it was not to be. That first show became MECW's last, when small legal entanglements like money-laundering arrests tripped up some people behind the venture. They were gone, the federation was gone, and the million bucks a year never materialized. The MECW name was later used on the independents, but in no way did it resemble the well-financed operation from 2001. I was glad I hadn't walked out on Carver Reed and when Meanie eventually called about 3PW, I agreed to come down and book their main event finish. It was one night—piece of cake.

This was my first time meeting Jasmin, star of the critically acclaimed *World's Biggest Gangbang 2*, and she was very formal yet cordial. She addressed me as "Mr. Gordon," and the night was a breeze. Meanie and Jasmin were thrilled everything went off without a hitch, and the locker room seemed to respect me. The show drew well, and all the boys were well behaved with me there, so they asked me to come back every month as a regular thing. I'd book the shows, appear on camera a little, and basically hang out with my friends for a thousand bucks a pop. Not a bad deal.

While there was some good talent there, the standout was Matt Stryker. I saw something in him from the jump and tried to give him cool stuff to do. He was great at impressions, so I had him do that gimmick where he became every wrestler he could imitate, up until he no-showed me for what he perceived was a better opportunity, as he put it. Turned out it was just a tryout—not even a paying gig. In exchange for screwing me, I had him job to April Hunter the following month. He had a nice commitment from me and a steady gig working in front of fans. I was like a dad to those kids, and I had to mete out punishment when needed. He was doing a cool Macho Man takeoff with Talia, aka Velvet Sky, as his Miss Elizabeth, but I stripped him of it when he no-showed.

I brought ECW referee John Finnegan into the company as well. He was the best referee I'd ever worked with and I wanted him in the ring with our guys as much as possible. I also started bringing my guys like Scorpio and Pitbull Gary onto the shows. It was easy booking since they only ran once a month and always in Philly. You couldn't drag angles out forever. Each show was a blowoff, like the old days before ECW got TV.

The more outrageous my ideas were, the more Jasmin and Meanie liked them. In time, I had Talia in a dog collar and leash, acting as a sex slave I gifted to Jasmin in the ring. A favorite creation of mine was my sugar daddy role with Jasmin, Missy Hyatt, and Gorgeous George. I remember referee Finnegan repeatedly shaking his head in disapproval at me. When I walked up to him at center ring and glared at him as part of my heel persona, he muttered, "Straight to hell, Gordon." I had to turn away to keep from laughing. That became Finnegan's stock comment upon seeing me for years afterward. I got a text from him the other day on my birthday that closed, *You're still going to hell.*

I had no expectations of 3PW ever becoming what ECW was, but I was having great fun booking it. One thing that became far less fun the longer I was there was Jasmin herself. She was bankrolling the company, but I could stand her less and less as months went on. She was repugnant. She'd slide up to me, point

to a wrestler, and say, "See him? Go tell him I want to fuck him."
Right—like I was her fucking pimp.

She had me bring in Missy Hyatt just so Jasmin could put
herself over her. Jasmin cared about one person: the one wearing
her dress. That was it. She did it to vend her own pictures and
videotapes to fans. I'd had enough and phoned her to quit. The
conversation went like this:

"Please stay," she said.

"You don't understand. This is becoming another job to me,
and I'm not looking for another job."

"I'll give you fifteen hundred per show."

"You're not getting it, Jasmin—it's not about the money."

"Two thousand."

"What time is the show?"

*Is this how the boys used to work me?* I wondered as I got a 100
percent raise in ten seconds. I'd really called to quit. Then she
really offered me $2,000.

We rolled on for a couple of months that way. Then Jasmin
texted Meanie and said she was in the hospital with a burst
appendix and couldn't come to that month's show but not to
worry, a guy would be driving down with a sack of money for
payouts. I was skeptical—I'd never not paid someone who worked
for me, and I wasn't about to break that record. Sure enough, some
guy did bring the money to me at the ECW Arena and all was well.
But I wasn't comfortable with the near miss, and when Jasmin
stopped calling me to discuss booking talent for the next show, I
told Meanie the operation wasn't long for this world. I didn't even
know if he and Jasmin were together anymore, or exactly what
"together" meant in the first place since she walked around the
venue lining up guys to fuck after the shows.

Not surprisingly, Jasmin no-showed the next card as well.
She hadn't put much effort into following up the burst appendix
excuse with anything more believable, as she texted Meanie that

she had been arrested for making prank phone calls. I didn't know one could be incarcerated for that, but jails across the country must've been bursting with twelve-year-old boys.

"Brian, I'm not fucking these guys over tonight," I said to Meanie. "I'm going to the arena and leaving the lineup sheet on the table, and you do with it what you want. She's using you." Meanie was in a tough spot, and he ran the show with payoffs generated by the door. But I was done with Jasmin and her company. She slinked away from 3PW, and Meanie tried to keep it going, but without Jasmin's cash there was nothing to keep it afloat.

It was probably my raise that broke them.

\* \* \*

A few years outside the wrestling business did me well, from a mental health standpoint. Then in 2006, Pitbull Gary and I began working on an MMA project we planned to house in the ECW Arena. We adopted the name Xtreme Fight Club (XFC) and began planning the layout of a training facility, complete with all necessary gym equipment and mats. The plan was to outfit a school for wrestling, MMA, and boxing and run live events for each throughout the year. I was able to secure our old venue for a song, and Fucking Butchie was ready to jump in and help with our planned modifications to the space.

"You don't need no contractor," he said. "I'll do everything."

It was a sweet gesture—Butchie was always willing to help me out, but I also needed the construction to be done perfectly and everything to be level. I had a feeling unleashing Butchie on the project might see a few bench press machines standing on a definite slant.

"Butchie, you'll be getting a bajillion dollars in rent from me. I might even make an offer on the building so we don't have to bother with rent. You'll come out fine. Just let me get someone else to do the work."

"Well, I got a cousin who can come in and do it."

Of course he did—he's Fucking Butchie. He'll offer to help until he's blocking the road completely.

Gary was planning on financing the costly project himself via his girlfriend's pending divorce settlement. Her ex-husband was apparently loaded to the tune of tens of millions of dollars, and Gary's girl had the paperwork in place for a sizable chunk of that money when the divorce was finalized. Gary and I had most of it already earmarked for making XFC a reality. Once that check came in, we could start.

While planning for XFC, Gary told me he'd gotten a call from a couple of friends who were running a small indie wrestling promotion in Philly and needed a rub. They wanted me and some of the ECW crew to come out and do a spot for the group, called Pro Wrestling Unplugged (PWU). It was run by Trent Acid and his tag partner Johnny Kashmere, and they worked small local venues.

Gary told me Sandman was going to do it with him, so I agreed to the shot. I showed up at this garage where the show was being held and I was treated like a king. They had two traffic cones in front for my car, while Gary and Sandman parked two blocks down the street. They even had a bottle of Grey Goose waiting for me inside because they knew I liked vodka. It made for a comfortable night.

They asked me pretty quickly if I'd book for them. They had their own group of wrestlers, consisting of a handful of students and a few regulars. That was actually the part I liked most about it; it reminded me of ECW in that way, whereas in Jasmin's 3PW I'd have to assemble a show consisting of disparate talent every month. Here, I knew who I was using and we could build angles that way.

Some of those PWU kids were so talented. They were swinging from ropes across the arena. The standout there was Devon Moore. It was a no-brainer to marry him with Scorpio in a feud that lasted six months. We got pretty innovative, and I came up with some good stuff. Having full autonomy made booking fun again.

As quickly as I'd been asked to book, I was also asked if I could secure ECW Arena for PWU. Guess that's one of the benefits of getting Tod Gordon involved with your federation, beyond the standard South Philly credibility. I got them in, and in no time we were drawing five hundred people to the Arena, which was an accomplishment considering Ring of Honor (ROH) and Combat Zone Wrestling were also running wrestling locally as well.

I soon got a call from John Zandig, who ran CZW, asking me why I was bothering getting "those kids" into the Arena. He said the venue was his now for CZW. True, CZW was running shows there, but they also had shots in Delaware and Jersey to spread out the product. I told Zandig I was working with PWU now, and if I'm involved with any federation, then I'm running in the fucking house that I built. He didn't push it, and down the road we actually did an angle for them where we invaded CZW, with Sandman entering the Arena by chainsawing through the bottom of the ring.

On camera for PWU, I was only managing Johnny Kashmere, but in the back I was doing everything. The one ECW name I brought in regularly was Scorpio, who worked the monthly shows. Pitbull Gary was one of the teachers at the PWU school running out of the back of the Arena, so he was a regular too. During class, Gary would run the kids into the ground doing his "circle of pain" exercise, where they stood around him and had to mirror whatever he was doing in the center of the circle. While he handled the physical part of class, I took trainees into the back and taught them how to cut the almighty promo. I've said it a few times already but it bears repeating: If you can't talk, it doesn't matter what you can do in the ring. Your wrestling career will be limited in the age of TV and video. I would have the kids cut a babyface

242

promo, then have them switch it up and do the same promo as a heel. We did interview after interview, for hours. I wouldn't let them leave the place until they were convincing.

Trent Acid, Kashmere's young tag partner, was becoming a handful. He was a fan favorite and a talented worker, but his drug habit was overtaking him and he wasn't even thirty years old. One night he ran out back and was jumping up and down on someone's car. I charged out of the locker room after him, and I think if I had gotten to him before the boys grabbed me, I would have choked him to death. I knew he had a habit, and it had made him a total asshole. The night he fell asleep in the ring was the final straw—if he packed up and disappeared it would have been fine with me.

His partner Kashmere then began to brighten my days with his panic attacks. He started missing shows and was very up front with me about it, but I'd built an entire angle with him as the centerpiece. I tried to just make changes to the shows until he told me I shouldn't really count on him to be a part of it anymore. It was a mess.

Other guys were becoming disrespectful by showing up late and waltzing in like they were the goddamn Rock. The tag team S.A.T., short for Spanish Announce Team, were like that. They were talented guys, but they started wandering in whenever they wanted, like anyone outside our building knew who the hell they were.

A couple of guys that *were* known outside our building was Insane Clown Posse, the rap duo with infamous wicked-clown makeup and a dedicated following of crazy fans who called themselves Juggalos. In addition to having a cult following in music, Violent J and Shaggy 2 Dope were also wrestlers. I was able to bring them in and work a four-month angle with a blowoff cage match where I was handcuffed to Shaggy.

The angle was intense and we had to separate our PWU fans from the Juggalos in the arena, like the bleachers at an Army versus Navy game. We had an evenly divided audience, with one side cheering while the other side was booing. When ICP would lose their advantage and start getting pounded, the audience would reverse. It was working well.

Everything was going according to plan until Violent J came up to me with a change.

"We gotta turn babyface," he said. J was concerned about being heels for so long that it might cut into record sales. I had to go back and rewrite everything I'd laid out. If I was going to flip them quickly, I'd need to bring in an unlikable force to push fans over to ICP's side. I called Raven. It was the perfect solution and got over with the fans. My crisis booking saved the day yet again.

PWU was a fun run, but I'd had enough. The time came for my exit, so I scripted my finale, culminating in my in-ring retirement. It was great to exercise my creativity and do things that had never been done, like a card where fans really chose the combatants. It ran its course and that was the end of PWU. It was barely a blip on the wrestling radar. Sadly, Trent Acid overdosed in 2010 at age twenty-nine.

While PWU might've been gone, I at least had our hybrid extreme combat federation XFC to focus on. Right? Not so much. It seems with great wealth comes access to great attorneys, and when Gary's girlfriend had her day in divorce court, she got shit from her ex. We couldn't build out the Arena as we'd planned without a multimillion-dollar investment, so XFC went belly-up also.

I decided that was as far as I wanted to go in pro wrestling and, with the exception of a few appearances, that was my retirement. I was fine refocusing solely on Carver Reed and letting my legacy in the sport stand where it was.

Legacy? Did I have one? The world moves fast, and it's easy to become yesterday's news. One morning I opened up PhillyBurbs. com, a local news site, and saw that yesterday's news was *that* day's news.

The headline read, "ECW Pioneer Leaves the Wrestling Business." The article was written by Eric Gargiulo, a young man who did some announcing for me in ECW and later in PWU. I didn't know what to expect, so I read.

"It is questionable as to whether the way you watch pro wrestling today would be possible without Tod Gordon."

Hey, first sentence, not too damn bad. I read on.

"Tod Gordon was the unsung hero of ECW and a true innovator and pioneer in professional wrestling. Sure, Paul Heyman was the creative genius behind ECW. However, someone had to roll the dice and give Heyman a chance. Tod Gordon rolled the dice and changed the industry forever."

This kid got it. I barely remembered him, but he spent the next twelve paragraphs recounting the times I'd had a positive effect on him while working together. He cited the times I'd asked for his opinion while booking for PWU. He complimented my business acumen as well as my creativity. It was flattering, and I started to wonder why I hadn't hired him to book for ECW back in 1993. The scene in the Marriott lobby would've been quite different.

"Hey Ric," Sullivan would've said upon seeing Flair. "This is Tod Gordon of ECW. He just hired Eric Gargiulo to book."

"Never heard of him," Flair would've said. "Enjoy your salmon."

The article continued:

"I would watch the way Tod would interact with the talent. This was a different generation of wrestlers as opposed to the crew we shared a locker room with over ten years ago. Veterans like Taz, the Dudleys, Sabu, Rob Van Dam, Shane Douglas, and Raven were replaced by young, cocky, and sometimes naïve kids who had a different understanding of pro wrestling than their predecessors. Tod was able to adapt and command great respect without shouting or embarrassing anyone to make a point. Everything came back to wrestling, and nothing happened on the shows that didn't benefit the company. How could anyone argue with that?"

It was a nice tribute, and if Eric felt that way, then other workers likely did as well. It comforted me and confirmed I'd walked away at the right time, my reputation intact.

One day while cleaning my office, I pulled out a book called *World Wrestling Insanity Presents: Shoot First...Ask Questions Later* that I'd stuffed in a drawer. I leafed through it and saw some telling passages.

"Unfortunately," one such paragraph began, "because WWE owns everything ECW now, they get to write, or rewrite, history. And that's why the whole Tod Gordon saga becomes kind of confusing, I guess, because he's barely mentioned. It's a shame, too; people may drink 'Paul Heyman's Kool-Aid,' but Tod Gordon bought Paul E the mixing bowl and helped create the recipe." The author, James Guttman, got it too. Maybe the truth would prevail. Maybe a legacy had been carved during my ECW years, if nothing else.

My wrestling ventures after ECW didn't even come close to providing the personal or professional satisfaction that Extreme had. I think all of our former workers felt that void too, but you have to move on and can't cling to the past. Though that doesn't mean some won't try.

# CHAPTER 15

# ECW AFTERLIFE

In 2005, WWE relaunched the ECW product after buying the trademarks and video library from Paul Heyman's bankrupt HHG. No one in the world thought the new in-ring product was anything near the ECW they remembered; some of the workers in the ring looked familiar, but that was where the similarities began and ended. No one reached out to me in any capacity, and thank God for that. I would not have been able to sit idly by and watch the mangling of ECW's legacy. I would've become a problem, and my guess is that Paul and those in power in Connecticut knew that. Besides, what good is Tod Gordon without my ability to actually run that company? My on-screen contribution to ECW was negligible and certainly not a major driver of its success.

I only watched the WWE's version of ECW for the first few weeks and almost didn't make it past week one. Truthfully, I almost didn't make it past the first ten minutes when they sent a zombie out to the ring. I was really surprised Paul was attaching himself to what they were doing, but he was appointed head writer. I suppose that glued his mouth shut, and he found some justification for what was being aired under the banner bearing the brand we'd created. For WWE it was just another brand extension, for which they used some former ECW talent. They mixed them with workers from their mainstream roster who shouldn't have had anything to do with my three letters, and *wouldn't* have if not for being absorbed by WWE.

Then I realized what WWE was doing—by tarnishing the ECW product enough, fans might stop chanting "E-C-W!" at WWE shows. That must be a real blow, having an arena full of your fans start chanting another company's name when something cool happens in the ring. It looked like Vince McMahon was trying to kill the product, thinking that, eventually, if anyone heard "ECW," they'd think of *this* shit and not the hellacious glory of years past. They'd kill the ECW brand, and the chant along with it.

Incidentally, that chant is one of the things I'm most proud of. In both WWE and WCW, and every independent in between, whenever a table was pulled out from under the ring or someone was bleeding excessively, fans chanted "E-C-W! E-C-W!" Whenever someone used a chair as a springboard, they chanted it. I've been told by multiple sources that Vince's blood would boil when it happened. Our company was out of business, but fans didn't forget it, and the WWE-produced DVD called *The Rise and Fall of ECW* outperformed most of the other DVDs WWE was producing. Vince wanted to burn ECW to the ground and, since he owned it, he could.

After ECW, every federation tried to make their three letters have some significance beyond just a symbol on the marquee. They never understood that you can't manufacture that, nor can you train audiences to do it by rote. WCW tried rather pathetically to do that by using a furry mascot named Wild Cat Willie who ran around the audience during TV tapings trying to drum up a chant using his initials, "W-C-W!" To call it an embarrassing failure is being kind. No one ever had to prompt an ECW crowd chant—it came from the heart.

I was never contacted by WWE for anything regarding the ECW relaunch, documentary DVD, or their WWE-produced ECW pay-per-view. However, I did get a call from Paul asking me to be a part of his DVD, *Ladies and Gentlemen, My Name Is Paul Heyman.*

"I can get you a grand for an interview," he said. "It'll be for the section about ECW." Paul knew I would still put over our partnership and not bury him on his home turf. I'd remained tight-lipped about our problems for all those years, and he knew I wasn't about to say anything out of line. *Why not do the DVD? I* figured. I sit and talk about ECW with plenty of people for free, so the grand is gravy.

When WWE ran at the Wells Fargo Center that year, I headed down to the arena, where they'd set up an interview room in the basement. On camera they asked about the company as well as mine and Paul's partnership, and I gave my answers, not necessarily political but certainly reserved. I sugarcoated my responses about my issues with Paul, saying he stretched the truth here and there, might've been creative as to why a payment wasn't made. It was a little bit of a jab, but I was still taking care of him.

Paul, I would eventually see, did not exercise such restraint in his interview segments. When I finally saw the DVD, I was floored to see Paul bury me, continuing this mole cover story and saying he fired me, comically enough. I didn't think he'd still perpetuate the tale that I was in some way trying to hurt the company behind his back. I wasn't stupid enough to think he would have admitted to knowing about those two calls I placed to WCW on behalf of my friends, but I thought he just wouldn't mention it at all. Right there, I realized he still hadn't smarted up any of the guys, hadn't told them we'd worked them with that mole story to keep the company running smoothly under him. I'd bitten my tongue and stayed quiet for years at that point, and I did so for more than a decade after that. It wasn't easy.

But I never spoke to Paul again.

\* \* \*

WWE wasn't the only group trying to book the past. Also in 2005, Shane Douglas attempted to revive the ghosts of ECW with his Hardcore Homecoming reunion shows in Cleveland, Western Pennsylvania, and Philly. The Cleveland show I referenced earlier featured Johnny Grunge losing his battle with the bottom rope and having to be saved. The trip was most memorable because my daughters were both in college nearby and we converged in Cleveland, then drove to Pittsburgh together. It was great getting a big hotel room and spending time together, until we got down to the convention and they disappeared. I finally found them working the photo booth for Hack, who's known them since they were little kids. One took the money and the other snapped the Polaroids. He probably paid them in beer.

Shane organized the shows with a partner, but beyond booking the venues and talent, he was pretty clueless. Workers walked up to him with all kinds of ideas, to which he'd say, "Okay, sounds good." The shows were treated as if seeing ECW guys in a ring again would be enough for the fans. That might work in Cleveland and Pittsburgh, but Philly was going to need a little more effort than that. The ECW Arena had been hosting CZW, PSU, and ROH, so local fans were getting their share of innovative young workers trying to raise the bar and reinvent the sport again.

I didn't hear from Shane again until his 2012 launch of yet another ECW-influenced federation he was calling Extreme Reunion. He asked me to be part of it as I had for Hardcore Homecoming, but also asked if I'd come on board and help him promote the first show in Philly at the National Guard Armory. I realized he must've been having a hard time selling it and decided he needed the Todster at the last minute. He sold it to me as the first step in a new revolution for the ECW guys, which would soon be taken all over the world after it exploded here. That sounded great and I like Shane a lot, so I wished him well but said I wasn't going to be promoting with him. I agreed to do the Philly shot and that would be it. How on earth would this be in any way different from the derivative ECW shows sprouting up all over the place with our old roster? I didn't think it would be.

The plan for the night was to have me come out during the main event match between Scorpio and Shane and double-cross Scorp, thus engineering Shane's win. That was supposed to get the big babyface pop for Shane and send everyone home smiling. That projection couldn't have been more off if I told you the two living Beatles were singing the national anthem that night.

Our smart fans knew Shane was behind the show, so the night began with the entire crowd chanting, "Thank-you-Shane! Thank-you-Shane!" But the quality of this show was one of the worst our fans had probably ever seen, so by the end of his match wherein I helped him get the win, the chant "Fuck-you-Shane! Fuck-you-Shane!" filled the armory. This was supposed to be the monumental and symbolic start to Shane's new venture, and instead it was a prophetic foreshadowing of its doom. Sure enough, shows were soon being canceled, and the company suffered an eight-month hiatus in 2013. You just can't come back from shit like that, and trying to do so was just a long, painful death.

* * *

I started appearing at wrestling conventions in the past few years, and that's given me a chance to see some of my old friends up close and personal after many years. A few months ago, I saw Rob Van Dam for the first time in probably twenty-five years. He gave me a big hug and called over to his wife.

"Katie," he said, "come here and meet Tod Gordon from ECW."

I shook her hand and was relieved RVD had remembered me, my name, and where we'd worked.

He went on with his introduction to Katie. "Tod was an original too."

Was he kidding?

He continued. "I think he was there almost as long as I was." He wasn't kidding.

"Rob," I said, "I kinda started the company. I signed your damn checks." How could I forget with his stupid-ass long last name?

A wrestler's faulty memory isn't on display exclusively at conventions, but it's a great place to find five or six of them in one day. I also hear guys on TV and podcasts who have such a faulty recollection of events I witnessed, events I was a *part of*, that it makes me wonder what else has been misreported to the public.

When I run into Buh Buh or Dreamer, I get a polite handshake, maybe a quick hug, then they're on their way. When I saw Taz at a WWE show in Philly shortly after he started there, he was warmer than I expected. We hugged and he said, "If it wasn't for you, brotha, none of us would be superstars." I appreciated it, but wondered where the phone call saying as much had been for the past twelve years. Maybe he was sincere, or maybe it was a performance for the others present in the room. He hasn't come to Thanksgiving, so I haven't asked him.

For all the press our mole ruse got, no fan has ever come up to me at a convention and uttered a negative word. They've only given me respect and thanks for the product we gave them, a few fans even going so far as to say ECW saved their lives. I know you might be rolling your eyes as you read that, but trust me—I've met them.

"I was suicidal but when I found ECW, I needed to stay alive until Tuesday night to see what you guys were going to do next." That's a quote, verbatim. It takes your breath away when a fifty-year-old guy is standing in front of you saying he credits the last twenty-five years of his life to something you did. I love our fans, and I still mark out when they come up to me and want to talk ECW. It's the best.

Second best might be when a wrestler outside ECW comes up and reveals what a big fan they were. A few years ago, Sandman and I were doing a show at a minor league baseball stadium in Buffalo where "Mouth of the South" Jimmy Hart was organizing the promos. He was an iconic manager in almost all federations *but* ECW. He greeted us with, "We watched all the time. We loved the shit you guys were doing." He then said he had no promo instructions for us based on all he'd seen in ECW, then turned us loose on the mic. That's the ultimate respect.

One night during a celebrity bartender fundraising event for the Variety Club, Philadelphia Flyer Chris Therien was there with a bunch of his teammates. He came over and said, "We just want to let you know we all fucking *love* ECW!" The rest of the Flyers smiled and waved to us, and I realized I'd found one locker room with fewer teeth than ours.

I was plagued by a horrifying migraine that night, made worse by the excessive heat and humidity at the riverfront affair. Raven was standing next to me when I complained that I'd left my migraine prescription medication at home. He jumped into Dr. Scotty mode and asked what I took.

"Fioricet," I said.

He reached into his pocket. "I have these. They're the same."

"What are they?"

"Percocet. Same thing."

I told him I'd never heard of Percocet.

"It's the same. Fiori*cet*...Perco*cet*...both in the *cet* class."

He asked how many Fioricets I took, and I told him two, so he dropped three Percs into my hand.

"You have to take more of these," he said. "They're basically like aspirin."

"You sure?"

"Of course I'm sure. Let me get you a screwdriver to wash them down with."

That sounded like a plan, and before I could thank Dr. Scotty, I was washing the meds down with the vodka and OJ, planning to continue my charity event free of pain. If I'd only known how right I'd be.

The literal next thing I remember was standing next to Cecily Tynan, the beautiful weather anchor from Philly Action News, and posing for a publicity photo.

"Sir," she said, trying to get me out of my standing stupor. "Would you mind taking your hand off my ass?" I was standing there posing for the photo with her left cheek in my palm. That snapped me out of the Perc haze pretty quickly. In retrospect, I guess I owe her a big apology. And a bigger, "Thank you." In truth, I can't remember anything after Scotty gave me that shit.

Raven went on to get tossed out of the event, but not for gimmicking his boss. It seemed Raven had been giving free drinks to anything in a skirt during his shift as celebrity bartender (including one Scottish guy, which was rather odd), and the establishment was less than amused.

ECW had served me well, and my venture into the indie scene served its purpose too, however temporary. Years had passed since my time in and around the ring, and I was okay with that. It was clear that a sunset stood before me, ending a chapter in my life that had brought me immeasurable joy and comfort in my darkest times. Holding on in the face of death is selfish and unnatural in the bigger picture, though no less hard.

I only wish I were talking about wrestling.

# CHAPTER 16

# LESLIE

I was extremely blessed to have a sister who was so much more than just that. Beyond just jokesters and partners in crime, Leslie and I were best friends as kids and remained so through our entire adult life. Every day started with a phone call to or from her, just sifting through the minutiae of life. She was always my go-to when I needed an ear. People are sometimes lucky to have that one person who knows you on a level no one else ever approaches. For me, it was Leslie.

She had a PhD and flew around the world coaching large companies' CEOs to grow their businesses. She was a powerhouse; everyone respected her opinions and suggestions. Somehow, in the midst of all that, she was a mother and even managed to write and stage a musical called *Jobs* about the outsourcing craze of the early 2000s. It ran at a local theater here in Philly and I proudly attended. It seemed there was nothing Leslie couldn't do.

As her younger brother, I was also in the enviable position to benefit from her wisdom on a daily basis. As I mentioned earlier, we had the same sense of humor into our adulthood, and we served as godparents to each other's kids.

I didn't only lean on Leslie with mundane life decisions—I also turned to her in working through the pros and cons of going into the wrestling business. She offered a clarity I sometimes lacked and, more than anything else, she was so very supportive. I kept going to her as ECW grew and I had difficult decisions to make. She was always there for me, despite her traveling the world over; no one was ever as supportive, or less judgmental.

One day in December 2018, after my morning phone conversation with Leslie and an otherwise normal day, I received a call saying she was being rushed to the hospital after beginning to speak unintelligibly. It was troublesome, to be sure, but she didn't have any medical conditions of which we knew. It was mysterious and scary.

That night she was rushed into surgery when they found a brain tumor called a glioblastoma. They removed as much as they could and she was soon on the mend, gaining strength and making me laugh again, albeit with her gallows humor. Once she was out of the hospital, I'd call her in the mornings like usual.

"Hey, Les. What are you doing?"

"Dying. You?"

I'd tell her to shut the hell up and we'd bullshit about whatever was happening in our respective lives. From that point on, I was there after work every day, and all day on Saturday and Sunday. It went on like that for a while, but then she took a downturn. Doctors presented us with an option for another operation, which they said might add a few months to her life. They left it up to us—Leslie's condition was too bad to allow her to decide for herself. I conferred with her two adult children, Emily and Jason, and gave them my vote—thumbs down. Of course, it would be hard to stand idly by and just let her ride off, but sometimes that's what love is. Her children couldn't give that directive, and I understood. They hung on to the chance that she'd be given some extra time. Delaying a goodbye you are not prepared to make is an enticing prospect, so I didn't offer any opposition.

Leslie underwent the next operation and Emily uprooted her whole family, moving from California to Pennsylvania and into Leslie's house to care for her full time. My sister never came out the other side after that second operation. One day while in physical therapy, she turned to me as she struggled to cut out paper shapes with a pair of kids' scissors. She just shook her head—*Can you believe this?* "I'm glad I have a PhD," she said.

On November 12, 2019, Leslie was taken from our lives forever. As I write this, it's more than two and a half years later and not a day goes by without my looking at the phone, ready to dial her. A situation of any importance now feels more confounding without her guidance. A funny story that would have had us in stitches now gets little more than a smirk. Part of me is gone; I'm forever changed.

A month after Leslie's passing, I lost my mother at age ninety-four. We'd arranged for full-time help a few years prior so she could remain as comfortable as possible. She always recognized us when we visited, but our conversations would go off the rails. She'd ask me how Carver Reed was.

"Fine, Mom. Just came from the store."

"No, not the store...the man."

"Carver Reed?"

"Yeah. How is he? We had lunch last week."

Mind you, he'd been dead for about ninety years at that point.

Three months after my mother's death and four months after Leslie's, the pandemic began. I sat in quarantine as the months rolled on, shocked and dumbfounded by the year I'd just lived. It brought me back to one of mine and Leslie's favorite one-liners:

"But besides that, Mrs. Kennedy, how did you like the parade?"

# CHAPTER 17

# BIRTH

**A**ny pain I carry over things I've loved and lost is softened when I look at what I've gained. I'm blessed with the most loving kids in the world. My two girls, now in their thirties, are so different but no less wonderful. Ally, my oldest, was drawn to California for film and television work in which she found some success. Fittingly enough, one of the shows she auditioned for was the Netflix series GLOW, based on the campy women's wrestling federation of the '80s. Of my two girls, Ally is the wild child, so naturally she rolls up to the audition flush with bravado. They asked her what she knew about wrestling.

"Oh, I've been in the ring," she told them. "My dad was ECW commissioner Tod Gordon."

They sent her into a wrestling ring on-site, and within thirty seconds they realized that Ally's time "in the ring" was likely standing in it while dad worked. The Commissioner Gordon name drop meant nothing to the casting people either, and Alexandra's chances at becoming a Gorgeous Lady of Wrestling fizzled.

Rebecca stayed with me at Carver Reed from the day she graduated Penn State and has been my right-hand woman in the business. She was the practical, studious one, always toeing the line and making thoughtful decisions. Both of my girls are me, each reflecting a different part of my split personality. Maybe that's why we share such a strong bond.

My son Charlie is a big guy and probably would have made a great wrestler himself, but thank God he didn't have any interest in pursuing it. As a young man he was content to do more productive things than chasing the vagabond wrestling lifestyle, like sitting around and playing video games for hours.

Charlie's lack of interest in wrestling as a career didn't obstruct his love for the spectacle of the sport. He watched it all the time, and I brought him to a few events. When he was little, I arranged a backstage tour at a WWE show here in Philly. He got to meet everyone on the card, from the Undertaker to Shane McMahon. That was all he wanted; we didn't even stay for the show.

WCW's *Bash at the Beach 99* remains his favorite wrestling memory to this day. The event coincided with his birthday, and we watched the pay-per-view event at home. There was a junkyard battle royal that featured some of our ex-workers in exactly the setting you'd imagine. Guys were climbing on junked cars and knocking each other into piles of debris. Public Enemy picked up a detached car hood to use as a weapon, and if you were watching you might have wondered why it had "Happy Birthday Charlie" spray-painted on it.

Now you know. Johnny and Teddy were my boys.

Charlie joined me and Rebecca at Carver Reed for a while, but the COVID-19 epidemic shook everything up. Charlie locked down and Rebecca found out she was pregnant. She wanted to come back to the store, but I forced her to stay at home and not take a chance getting this mysterious virus while carrying her first child. In late 2020, my first grandchild, Max, was brought into the world. I was beyond ecstatic, but like so many other families, our time together was hampered by the masks. I couldn't even kiss the little guy for months. But we're back to some semblance of normal now, and I see him all the time. The other day he ran to me as always, but when he plopped onto my chest, he said, "Pop Pop." I think he chose the perfect name for me, considering I spent thirty years trying to do that to crowds.

I can't get enough of him.

* * *

My wife Adrienne came into Carver Reed for a gold chain four-teen years ago and, in many ways, never left. She made the mistake of laughing at one of my jokes and unwittingly opened herself up to my trying to woo her. Feeling myself exquisitely funny and overall adorable, I asked her out, and we've literally been together ever since, dating for seven years and married for the past eight. When you meet someone who touches your soul, and hopefully you theirs, life is good.

Thank God I found someone with the same sarcastic sense of humor as mine. Someone of a different mindset might be turned off. I'm a jokester at heart, and I'd imagine that could be annoying at best, misconstrued as mean at worst. Adrienne gets it.

* * *

I have an eye on retirement for the first time in my life after having worked at Carver W. Reed since the summer of 1970 when I was in high school. That's fifty-two years as of this writing, and I think I've honored my commitment.

I read somewhere that explorers are undisciplined and there-fore need settlers to take over once the new land is claimed. That's the ECW story in a nutshell. We were all pirates, full of that carefree energy and a desire to break new ground. We didn't care much for the rule book, and no one who has ever innovated does, by the way. I honestly don't know how ECW could've been what it was and survived the long haul. We would've needed some help from the establishment, I think. That sentiment doesn't jibe with the rebel spirit, but if we weren't going to crash and burn, we would've had to conform a bit.

We needed someone with long tentacles that could've tapped into media and advertising and gotten real muscle behind us. We were like a nimble wildcat that the field mice couldn't help but notice, but in a short time we'd wandered blindly into the elephant flatlands.

Despite differences with Paul and the messiness with which my dream come true ended, I can't help but get a little nostalgic. Today, I look back and see a band of rebels who'd become fractured and divided, with half of them now tragically dead. But my reminiscences are not sad. If I close my eyes, I can still feel the pride I had in my bar federation that grew up and roared loud enough to get the world's attention. That excitement was addictive. I can hear Paul's voice, his laughter in my ear as we sat on the phone for hours, best friends steering the most magnificent vessel on the seas. New Jack's loud-ass voice is somewhere around me too, driving me and everyone else crazy. I can so easily and vividly land right back on that ship when I think back.

I'm honored you spent this time with me. If I did my job, then you spent that time experiencing the journey through my eyes. Maybe my enemies weren't yours exactly, or your perspective on events differed from mine, but my take is the only one I'm qualified to give you. My errors and flaws were on full display here too. Anyone who says they don't have them is full of it. My goal here was not to shit on anyone per se, but if I had heat with someone, I had to print it.

There's also been a lot of creative storytelling out there as to how ECW ran, my role in it, and how and why I left. I stayed quiet for a long time and let the existing narrative live on. I don't enjoy conflict, nor do I care to stand in a crowded room and try to shout over all the voices to put myself over. I simply decided to give a full recounting of the truth as it relates to my experiences in ECW.

Everyone I've written about has their own take on things too. But you paid for mine. So you got it.

Today is the only reality I have. As for yesterday, this book is a great document of what that was. And the best part of a book is you can close it.

I'm happy, blessed in so many ways, and ready to close a lot of books at this time. Things are good, brother. I just have to remind myself to take it a day at a time, and not to worry.

And why should I worry?

Dory's here.

# ACKNOWLEDGMENTS

## TOD

This book would not have been possible without the following:

Our agent Colleen Oefelein and editor Jacob Hoye for their steadfast attention to this work. It was as important to them as it was to me.

My beautiful wife Adrienne, the love of my life, who now at fifteen years and counting has proven true the adage "the third time's the charm." I thank her for putting up with me devoting so much time to this book and staying with me after having read it.

My three children, Alexandra, Rebecca, and Charles, for always having my back and a lifetime of unequivocal love and devotion.

My lifelong best friend and sister Leslie, who, before passing in 2019, encouraged me to write this book and let people know what I overcame and what I accomplished.

Mike Johnson and Dave Scherer for their assistance with research and details, and also George Tahinos for his great photos.

My writer, Sean, who took on an impossible task of letting me just tell random stories to him over Zoom for literally sixty-plus hours, and somehow managed to put them into an accurate and legible timeline. It was a Herculean task, and I'm grateful for the amazing job he did.

And finally, to every fan of ECW and any other fed I ran, for appreciating the fact that I only put on shows I would have wanted to see as a fan. No one wants to be forced to watch a wrestling show because it's the only option, and ECW came along as the unstoppable "other option" for the wrestling fan.

Together, you and I changed history.

## SEAN

Thank you, Tod, for entrusting me with your life and legacy. Our sessions were as much memoir constructing as they were writing sessions on *The Sid Caesar Show*. In the process, I gained both a great book and a friend.

Thank you, Colleen Oefelein and staff at MacGregor & Luedeke Literary. An agent who cares for your work is essential to the process. On that same team stands our editor Jacob Hoye at Permuted Press. Thank you all for suiting up and delivering this baby.

Art is easier to produce with a stellar creative team and a supportive home, and I'm fortunate to have both in my wife, Nicole, a partner in all ways for the past twenty-plus years. Our finest collaborations resulted in Mia and Lana, who, thankfully, enjoy not knowing what to answer when asked what their dad does.

Wrestlers and fans of Kayfabe Commentaries alike have validated what I've done in that sphere of the sports entertainment world. Largely due to them, I'm afforded the opportunity to continue bringing you entertaining and enlightening stories.

For better or worse.

# ABOUT THE AUTHORS

At age thirty-seven, **Tod Gordon** had a midlife crisis and, instead of buying a sports car, founded ECW. The federation was quickly seen as the third wrestling organization, a younger and hipper alternative to WWE and WCW. ECW and its revolutionary effect on the business have been the subject of books and documentary DVDs for nearly three decades. Tod is also the owner of Carver W. Reed, the Philadelphia jewelry and pawn institution founded in 1860. He has also served as president of both the global charity the Variety Club as well as the Pennsylvania Pawnbrokers Association. Tod lives in Philadelphia with his wife Adrienne. This is his first book.

**Sean Oliver** is the author of six books, including three Amazon bestselling wrestling books as well as three novels in the supernatural thriller genre. He has also written for the screen and is a 2021 Writer's Digest Writing Competition winner in the script category for a TV pilot called *Trixie*. Sean is also an actor and voice artist with over a hundred major motion picture and TV credits.

He's directed national television commercials, co-owns the wrestling production company Kayfabe Commentaries, and co-hosts the *Kliq This* podcast with Hall of Famer Kevin Nash. He is also a teacher in New Jersey, where he lives with his wife and two daughters.